Jean

Don't Walk in My Shoes

PublishAmerica
Baltimore

© 2010 by Jeannie L. Rhodes.

All rights reserved. No part of this book may be reproduced, stored in a retrieval system or transmitted in any form or by any means without the prior written permission of the publishers, except by a reviewer who may quote brief passages in a review to be printed in a newspaper, magazine or journal.

First printing

All characters in this book are fictitious, and any resemblance to real persons, living or dead, is coincidental.

PublishAmerica has allowed this work to remain exactly as the author intended, verbatim, without editorial input.

ISBN: 978-1-61546-084-7 (softcover)
ISBN: 978-1-4489-9496-0 (hardcover)
PUBLISHED BY PUBLISHAMERICA, LLLP
www.publishamerica.com
Baltimore

Printed in the United States of America

Katie,
Sorry you couldn't
be here. Enjoy reading.

Love,
Jeannie

Dorothy Allen

Contents

INTRODUCTION 9

Chapter 1
THROUGH THE EYES OF A FOUR-YEAR-OLD 13

Chapter Two
THANK GOD FOR MY AUNTS AND UNCLES 17

Chapter Three
A DRASTIC CHANGE 25

Chapter Four
AN ALMOST DEADLY MISTAKE 35

Chapter Five
BACK WITH MABLE AND MY DAD 47

Chapter Six
UNKNOWN TERRITORY 60

Chapter Seven
THE WALK THAT CHANGED MY LIFE 67

Chapter Eight
NOT-SO WEDDED BLISS 83

Chapter Nine
LIFE IN A QUANDARY 90

Chapter Ten
LIVING UP NORTH 102

Chapter Eleven
MY FOURTH AND FIFTH CHILDREN 114

Chapter Twelve
MY LAST CHILD 128

Chapter Thirteen
OUR PROPERTY ON LIVERGOOD STREET 149

Chapter Fourteen
THE GOOD LIFE ON ENGLAND STREET 169

Chapter Fifteen
WHO AM I? 199
Chapter Sixteen
MY FINAL CHAPTER 209

Acknowledgments

I, first, want to thank my husband, Rick, for his continuing support of my work during this last year. You have been a Godsend to me. You lifted me up during the times when the going got tough. When I decided to write this book, you were amazed that I had such a long term goal to become an author. You believed in me from the very beginning. I love you dearly, forever and always.

I would also like to thank Linda Hutton for her guidance and encouragement. She was instrumental in inspiring me to do a better job of writing. Her creative writing expertise helped me be more aware of my writing mistakes. When I told Linda my mother's life story, she agreed that it was well worth writing. In addition to working with Linda, I found a new friend that I will always be blessed to have met.

A special thanks to Brenda Rigg who expertly answered an entire array of computer questions I posed to her almost daily. Brenda continued to be patient with me as she clarified the answers to my questions in layman terms that I could understand. She definitely made my writing an easier process.

Also, I would like to thank all my friends and family members who supported me and cheered me on during the completion of my book, Don't Walk in My Shoes. Your inspiration meant so much to me. I feel blessed to have all of you in my life.

Lastly, I want to thank Publish America for publishing my book. Each person who contacted me was always kind, enthusiastic, and helpful as they guided me through the publishing process. Thank you all for making this undertaking a great experience.

INTRODUCTION

My life's story begins when I was four years old. The year is nineteen thirty four. My memory of the beginning of my life started at this point. I remember very little, and most of what I do remember seems like a dream that keeps recurring. My trauma appears to never end.

My mother died at this time. Now, it all seems so surreal to me. One moment she was having a new baby, and ten days later, she was gone. She was only forty years old. The memory of her funeral continued to be hazy to me for many years.

My father gave me and my brothers away several times in our lives. First, I was sent to live with my Aunt Lou and Uncle Joey. Then, I was sent to live with Aunt Gilda and Uncle Orr. I was passed between them for two years. In the end of that time, I was sent back to live at my dad's house. He had remarried only a month after my mother had passed away. His new wife, Mable, did not want me to stay with them.

Mable was an evil woman who abused me both mentally and physically. I just knew that she was the devil herself. She tortured me for ten years in many different ways. She didn't allow me to go to school. She locked me into the closet repeatedly. She whipped me until I had welts on my body. She jabbed a knife into my skull. And many times, she called me names and told me that she hated me. I prayed to God constantly. I asked him to take me out of this hell that I was forced to live in. Then, the worst thing happened!

At the age of twelve, my wicked step-mother set me up to die. I was literally set on fire. This was a horrifying experience that caused me to have a near death experience. I was on death's doorstep. The angels beckoned me to come home. However, it wasn't my time, yet. I had a mission here on earth that needed to be completed. God had a bigger plan for me to accomplish. But, for now, I needed to heal.

I spent a year and a-half in the hospital burn unit. Then, I was sent back to where the devil resided. Although I wasn't completely healed, the hospital had done all that they could do for me. I was still unable to walk, and my right arm had not been used in a year and a-half. The rehabilitations were all up to me. I slowly regained the use of my legs and arm.

After I recovered, more torture prevailed. Over and over again, I suffered during the next two years. My only salvation came when I found out that my wicked step-mother had cancer. Soon, she was going to die. Unfortunately, she remained vicious to me until the very day that she passed away.

After Mable's death, I felt that the weight of the world had been lifted off of my shoulders. However, this feeling was short lived. I started having recurring nightmares that this evil woman was coming back to get me. For years, the nightmares continued. Finally, I pleaded with God. I told him that I forgave the evil woman for what she had done to me. Only then, did the nightmares stop.

After Mable's funeral, my dad quickly went to the courthouse and signed the papers to give all of his kids away. No one wanted me. I was too old. I was placed in a nursing home. My life consisted of just work, work, and more work. At sixteen, I rebelled and unsuccessfully ran away. The court was going to send me to a girl's prison.

I was saved by the local Sherriff. He gave me room and board for my housekeeping services. But, my luck didn't last long. I fell down the basement stairs and broke my arm in two places. I was no longer of use to them. I wasn't wanted, again. My depression and desperation led me to St. Vincent's Hospital where my only friends lived.

My friends were the nuns that worked in the hospital. After I was burned, I stayed at their hospital for six months. I got to know them pretty well. With their help and God's help, I was given a real job at the hospital. And, the nuns allowed me to live with them. I was thrilled! I was making a real wage and had my own bedroom! I was in heaven!

At seventeen, I met and married the man of my dreams. He was a handsome charmer who showed me the first kindness since my mom died. He mesmerized me. After a short dating period, he convinced me to marry him.

After only a few years of marriage, I realized that my dream man was an alcoholic who abused me both physically and mentally. His drinking tore us apart. Also, he was a dreamer who wanted the easy way out. He was a poor provider that allowed his family to almost starve to death. I felt alone and left out in the cold most of the time.

We moved from place to place and had four kids in four years. Life was a constant struggle. However, I didn't give up. I had the philosophy, "You made your bed, now you lay in it!" I fought depression, poverty, and the uncertainty of life itself. This all felt too familiar.

Even though I had a fourth grade education, I looked for a job. I had many different ones. I cleaned houses, washed dishes in a restaurant, ironed, and made enough money to get by. Finally, I got a real job making good money. I worked in a sewing factory for nine years. My confidence continued to build.

With a regular income, I was able to save money and buy my first home. I raised my six kids here. They had a stable home. This was my goal for them. I never had that. I had accomplished my dream.

As the kids grew up and left home, my financial pressure eased up. Life got easier. It was time to move forward. We were able to purchase a bigger and better home. My husband retired. We were free to have fun, again. We enjoyed walking, bike riding, making quilts and crafts, and occasionally took a trip to Las Vegas. We were reaping the rewards of our work. Unfortunately, our easy time only lasted a few years when my husband got sick.

He was diagnosed with lung cancer. He made a decision to forgo the radiation treatments. He managed to live five more years and died at the age of seventy one. We had been married for fifty years. I was hurt and angry. And, I felt lost. Now, what was I going to do without him?

A new stage of my life began. I had to figure out who I was. After a few years of soul searching, I bought a smaller house in a quiet neighborhood. Then, I reconnected with old friends and started going to church. I filled my life with helping others. Now, I felt needed again.

When I was seventy seven, my daughter decided to write a book about my life. I willingly agreed to work with her and tell my life's story. This was a difficult process for me. I wanted to keep my past buried. It was all too painful to me. But, now I was ready to let go. Many times, I cried my way through the difficult events that shaped my life. I still didn't understand why things happened the way they did. However, I learned that talking about these problems helped me in many ways. It was a much needed process. In order to move forward, I had to heal. By verbalizing the anguish and difficulties in my life, it helped me to purge myself of them. Also, it helped to reduce the monsters that I had made inside my head. But mostly, I needed to let go.

I hope by telling my life's story it inspires others to let go and move forward. Also, I encourage everyone to have faith in God. Many times, God was the only one whom I could turn to in my times of need. I believe in Him with all my heart. His power propelled me forward. His strength gave me a shoulder to lean on when I faltered. And, His love was always present, and it will be for you, too!

Chapter One
THROUGH THE EYES OF A FOUR-YEAR-OLD

My name is Dottie Mae Tillman. The year is 1934. I am four years old. I am small for my age, and kind of skinny. My clothes often are too large for me which makes me appear even smaller. I have almost black hair poker straight hair. And, my eyes are so brown they look black. The color of my skin betrays the fact that I am a descendant of the Cherokee Indians. I am a proud serious child.

Today, I am riding my bicycle down the sidewalk in the front of my house on Franklin Street. I look back and see my mom and dad sitting on the front steps of our porch. They are having a quiet conversation as they watch me whiz past them. I feel the wind blowing my hair away from my face. It feels good. Right this minute, I feel very content being a typical four year old. However, very soon, my world is going to change. The contentment I feel at this moment will be gone. I unfortunately will not experience it again for many years to come.

My forty year old mom is pregnant with her fourth child. Mom is usually a little chubby in size. But right now, her stomach if quite large due to her pregnancy. Her almost black hair softly frames her face. I think she is beautiful. Soon, she will be leaving for the hospital to have this new baby. I don't feel threatened by another child coming into our house, because I know my mom loves me very much.

Our house is already full of kids. There are five of us. Claire, Marta, and Chick are my dad's children from a previous marriage. My two half-sisters and my half-brother are all older than me. Chick is what we call retarded. He needs constant care. Claire is typically like a big sister should be. I look up to her for guidance. Marta is always kind and gentle. Also, I have a little brother named Timmy. He is the youngest child and only two years old. Although there are so many of us in this small house, we get along well and enjoy each other's company.

My mom was married one time before she met my dad. She had a daughter, Lena Ally Dons. Lena lived with us for a short time until she was sent to live with her cousin. Lena's father was killed while he was in the war. My mom acquired money from his insurance policy. My dad looked on this as an opportunity to buy a house that he had his eye on. So, he married my mom. Her money bought the house we now live in on Franklin Street.

Grandpa Fore, my mom's dad, always thought my dad married my mom for her money. Grandpa knew he had no say in the matter. Yet, he worried about my mom's future with this man. Grandpa was livid when my mom actually married my dad. He knew the truth. He called my dad a gold digger.

The day finally arrived for my mom to deliver the new baby. She and my dad left for the hospital. Soon, we were told we had a new baby brother. He was born January 10th, 1935. They named him after my mom's dad, Briton Fore. The baby's full name was Tomas Briton Fore. I decided to call him Tommy. We all waited anxiously for the arrival of our new little brother. Finally, mom and dad came home from the hospital. The new baby wasn't with them.

I didn't know at this time that my mom had been sick. She was still very sick. She was confined to her bed. She was so weak that she couldn't rise up out of the bed on her own. Consequently, she wasn't able to take care of Tommy. Now, I understood why Tommy didn't get to come home. My Aunt Lou had come to the hospital and took Tommy home to live with her. Mom wasn't getting well. She went back to the hospital. ten days after Tommy's birth, my mom passed away. The date was January 20th, 1935.

I was too young to really understand what was happening, but I felt the loss. Our house was full of activity as my father prepared for the funeral. Rows of chairs were placed in the living room for friend and family members who wanted to attend the funeral service. It was common practice for funerals to be held in the deceased family's home. I silently watched as everyone scurried about rearranging the furniture. The idea of a funeral felt so surreal to me. The area in the front of the chairs was left open for the arrival of my mother's casket.

The next time I saw my mom, she was in the casket in our living room. The casket was left open for the viewing and visitation. I asked my dad to lift me up so that I could see her. I felt an overwhelming desire to see her face. Then, we all sat down in the chairs behind the casket. The funeral service began.

When the service was over, my dad told me to take Timmy by the hand and walk a block and a-half down the street to a friend's house. The house belonged to Mrs. Bunks. As I stood there on the sidewalk with Timmy's hand in mine, I watched as they carried the casket out of the house. They put it in the hearse. I felt so sad that it hurt all the way through my chest into my heart. They shut the door on the hearse and drove away.

Everyone was leaving. I wanted to go with them. I felt as if I was left out. No one said a word to me. They all ignored me and Timmy as if we were invisible. Even at four years old, I knew this wasn't right! I felt that I should have been allowed to go with them! This was my mom! My four year old mind could barely comprehend the magnitude of feelings that I was experiencing. I was truly in a state of shock!

After everyone left, Timmy and I walked to Mrs. Bunk's house and waited for my dad. Mrs. Bunks was a very nice lady who occasionally took care of us. I liked her, but right now, I just wanted to go home. I had no choice but to bide my time until my dad came back to get us. So, I sat in a chair and held Timmy in my lap. I wanted to protect him from the hurt. He was so small. He had just recently learned to walk. I always protected him. Right now, it helped me to have him close to me. We stayed right there in that chair until my dad arrived.

My dad picked us up and took us to my Aunt Lou and Uncle Joey's house. Uncle Joey was my grandfather's brother. My dad really didn't explain anything to me; he just took us there and dropped us off. Tommy was already there living with them. We all settled in for the night awaiting our fate.

My dad made a decision to rid himself of all his kids. Timmy and I stayed with Aunt Lou and Uncle Joey. Claire and Marta went into two separate foster homes. And, Chick was sent to a special home in Lincoln, Illinois. I was young, but I understood what was taking place. My family was breaking up. I didn't get to see Claire, Marta, and Chick after the day of my mom's funeral. I missed them. They were all a vital part of my life. Now, I am not sure where my future lies.

Chapter Two
THANK GOD FOR MY AUNTS AND UNCLES

Aunt Lou and Uncle Joey's house was located next to the building where people got their driver's license. It was located in Taylorville, Illinois. The house was very small. It contained only three rooms. The kitchen was located in the basement of the house. Timmy and I slept in one of the two bedrooms upstairs. We didn't care that the small house was crowded. We just appreciated the fact that Aunt Lou and Uncle Joey loved us enough to take us into their home when no one else wanted us.

My brother Tommy had been living with Aunt Lou and Uncle Joey since the day he was born. They raised him as if he was their own child. Tommy would never know his real mom and dad. Aunt Lou said that she had adopted him. She supposedly paid the doctor at the hospital fifty dollars as payment for his adoption. Tommy's name was changed to Tomas Briton Fore. He called Aunt Lou and Uncle Joey, "mom and dad."

Aunt Lou kind of looked like a witch. She was old. Her hair was long, grey, and pulled back into a bun at the back of her head. She was tall and rather thin. She actually told me that she was a witch. She convinced me that this was true. She gathered up chicken feathers and burned them in the coal stove. Then, she told me that this would make it rain. I don't remember if it indeed rained, but I believed that she could make it happen.

Every morning Aunt Lou took her medicine. She poured it from a bottle into a tablespoon and drank it down. She explained that this medicine helped to get her heart started in the mornings. I later found out that the medicine was actually whiskey.

Although Aunt Lou was a little weird, she taught me many things. She taught me how to cook. We made beans, cornbread, and delicious dumplings. We took eggs and rolled them into flour and dropped them into the beans. Also, Aunt Lou taught me to be a lady and carry myself with dignity. She had a particular way of commanding my attention.

I knew when Aunt Lou meant business. One day I was playing outside. I watched the boys climb the tree in the back yard. I wanted to climb it, too. So, I proceeded to climb the tree. The boys started laughing at me. They told me they could see my pantaloons. This was my underwear that went from my waist all the way to the tops of my knees. My pantaloons were handmade out of flour sacks. The flour sacks were the only material we used to make clothes. Aunt Lou heard the boys laughing and came out of the house.

"Dottie Mae, you get out of that tree. You are showing your bloomers. Young ladies don't do that!" Aunt Lou yelled up to me in an angry tone.

I immediately climbed down from the tree and sat down sheepishly with my head down. I was ashamed. But, Aunt Lou wasn't done with me, yet.

"Pull your dress down," she insisted.

I pulled my dress down over my knees. I knew that a lady never showed her knees. A proper girl's knees must be covered at all times. Aunt Lou had taught me well.

We loved our aunt and uncle, and had a lot of respect for them. They were fine people. I looked up to Uncle Joey. He was my Grandpa Fore's brother. Uncle Joey was the strong silent type. He was stern, yet gentle. He had always been a hard working man. As for now, he is a retired carpenter. His work still stands today. He helped build the Taylorville High School in his younger days.

Uncle Joey was a true Christian and believed in the Bible with all his heart. He lived in accordance with the Ten Commandments and was passionate about the Holy Scriptures. He instilled the works of the Lord in me. Often, he sat by the big oak tree in the front yard reading his Bible out loud. Timmy, Tommy, and I attended church with Uncle Joey and

Aunt Lou every Sunday. This helped to further instill my trust in the Lord. Timmy and I enjoyed the sermons and the family outing every Sunday.

We regularly attended the Pentecostal Church nearest to our house. Many times, we had to jump a wide ditch that was filled with water to get to the church. I was too small to get all the way across to the other side. I always managed to get my feet wet. No one seemed to mind. We all proceeded to go into the church.

The church service was given by Gus Bellows. He was a young married preacher who had several kids of his own. After church, we sat at the Reverend Bellows' table to eat. After the main meal, we had some kind of pie. The adults drank their coffee while all of us kids played together. Often we played with a tambourine. We were making our own music. Or at least, we thought we were playing music. Most of the time, it was just noise. I really loved to come to the Bellow's house. It was fun. I never wanted it to end. Eventually, Reverend Bellows bought a larger concrete building in Hewittville, a suburb of Taylorville, to have more space to worship. We attended those services, too.

Gus Bellow's brother, Chancy, was a preacher, too. They both actively preached on Sundays. Chancy baptized me in the Flat Branch Creek. I was awed by this cleansing experience. It was special. I was inspired to live my life in a good Christian manner. Gus and Chancy gave me guidance, but Aunt Lou and Uncle Joey were my mentors.

I really loved living with my aunt and uncle, but I had a few problems. Timmy and I were hungry all the time. There was never much food in the house. Uncle Joey and Aunt Lou didn't have much money. They lived off of their meager monthly Social Security checks. I knew they did whatever they could to provide food for us. However, it never seemed to be enough.

Once, Timmy and I sat under the front porch and ate prunes. Aunt Lou gave them to us for a snack. We ate the outer part of the prune. Then, we used two bricks to crack open the prune seeds. We didn't want to waste any of it. We ate the center of the seeds, too. They were very bitter, but we ate them anyway. It seemed that we could never get enough food.

Grandpa Fore move in with us, too. He was really old. His build was tall and slim. Aunt Lou told me Grandpa had some German heritage. His facial features were chiseled and strong looking. He was my mom's father. His room was in an area of the house that looked like a garage that had been converted into living space. It was totally separate from the rest of the house. We had to go outside to enter Grandpa's room.

The little house we lived in was so small that we were cramped for living space. So, Aunt Lou and Uncle Joey made a decision to move to a bigger house in the country. The house was big enough that we could spread out a little more. Uncle Joe, Aunt Lou, Tommy, Timmy, and I lived in the front of the house. And, Grandpa Fore had a room of his own in the back of the house.

My new house was way back in the sticks and quite primitive. It looked like an old house you might see in the hills of Kentucky. The house was so old that it didn't have any paint on it. The wood on the outside of the house was real dry, withered, and grey in color. In addition to that, the house had no electricity. We used kerosene lamps for indoor lighting. Also, the drinking water was retrieved from an underground well in the front of the house. There was a large ditch near the well that always seemed to be full of water. The well had a metal pump with a handle. After pumping the handle several times, the water came up from the well and poured out of the pump's spout.

Many times, I pulled my wagon to the end of the lane to get drinking water. I pumped enough to fill a five gallon can. Then, I put the lid on the can and pulled the wagon back to the house. Collecting the water was one of my daily chores.

I met my friend Eve while I was living with Aunt Lou. We were neighbors. Eve's family lived near us. They had a bunch of kids. I often talked with Eve and developed a friendship with her. I didn't realize it at this time, but Eve was going to remain my friend for a long time.

Timmy and I continued to live together until times got tough for Aunt Lou and Uncle Joey. Three kids and Grandpa Fore were too much of a financial strain for their meager income. The pressure began to mount up. They struggled for a year. Many times, it was almost impossible to keep food on the table. They just couldn't afford three kids. A decision had to be made. This wasn't easy for them. They loved us all. Tommy was their own child in their minds. And, Grandpa had nowhere else to go. They had to keep him. So, they made a decision to let me and Timmy go.

I did not want to leave Uncle Joey and Aunt Lou, but I understood their dilemma. We had lived with them for a year. When the time came, Aunt Lou and Uncle Joey explained that Timmy and I were going to move in with my mom's brother, Uncle Orr. He was married to Aunt Gilda. I was OK with this decision. I knew my aunt and uncle were doing what was best for me and Timmy. I didn't hold anything against them. They were doing what they had to do. I felt lucky to have enjoyed their company for a whole year. I learned so much from them in such a short time.

Aunt Lou and Uncle Joey walked me and Timmy down the road to Aunt Gilda and Uncle Orr's house. They lived only a short distance from our house. Their house was similar to the one we had just left. It was a small shack in the midst of the timber with all kinds of trees surrounding it. To my delight, Uncle Orr had ducks, chickens, and a large garden. I thought to myself, *I am going to like this place.*

Uncle Orr and Aunt Gilda had never had children of their own. So, Timmy and I had plenty of room to roam. Timmy was three years old, and I was five years old at this time. In a very short time, Timmy was taken back to Aunt Lou's house. I don't know what cause Uncle Orr to take Timmy back. Now, I was an only child for the first time in my life. I figured I could get used to this!

I really did miss my two brothers, but I seemed to adjust. I knew they weren't very far away from me. But, it turned out; I really never got to see my brother's after they took Timmy back. I tried not to think of this. It made me sad. So, I filled up my time with other activities.

I liked my Uncle Orr. He was a tall distinguished looking man. I thought that he was rather handsome. He had a big garden that he worked in every day. I helped him whenever I could. I wasn't sure exactly what to do, but I tried. Uncle Orville was patient with me. He showed me how to hold and handle the vegetables carefully so I wouldn't bruise them. I also learned by watching my uncle work. I enjoyed being near him. He seemed to like me too. Most of the time, he displayed great patience with me. However, I did get him mad at me one time.

I always played with Uncle Orr's baby ducks. I put them in a large wash tub that held rain water. I sat and watched them swim in the water. One of the baby ducks just didn't want to swim. So, I kept pushing it down into the water time and time again. I thought I was teaching the duck to swim. Unfortunately, the duck drowned. I killed it!

Uncle Orr saw what I had done. He was furious with me. He put me over his knee and spanked my bottom!

"That chicken cost me money," he told me. I was shocked. I didn't know I had drowned a chicken. I thought it was a duck. I thought ducks should be able to swim. I felt bad about the whole incident. I started to cry.

I cried because Uncle Orr was mad at me, and I cried because he spanked me. Mostly, I cried because my butt hurt. I learned this lesson the hard way. I was never going to mistake a chicken for a duck again.

That night I had to stand on a box to wash the dishes. Uncle Orr had paddled me so hard that I didn't want to sit on my butt. Doing the dishes was one of my daily chores. We all shared the household duties. It was an unspoken law in this house.

Uncle Orr had never laid a hand on me before that day. Usually, he just raised his voice a little, and everyone listened. The minute he raised his voice, we all knew that someone had definitely done something wrong. Uncle Orr meant business.

One of my daily chores was to get milk from Aunt Lou's cow. The first time I did this, it turned into a real adventure. Aunt Lou's house was about two country blocks away from Aunt Gilda's house. Usually, I walked down the road and picked up a bucket of milk and carried it home. Today it was later than usual. Aunt Lou knew that it would be dark soon. So, she pointed out a path through the timber, and told me to use it as a short cut to get back home. I had never gone that way before.

"Just follow the path and it will take you right back home. That is the fastest way to get there," Aunt Lou explained.

It was already getting dark by this time. My sense of direction wasn't very good. After all, I was just five years old, and I was carrying a heavy five gallon bucket of milk. Somehow the path split into two parts. I was confused. I didn't know which path to take. Unfortunately, I took the wrong path. I was lost and I got really scared. The fear gripped me like a vise around my chest. I did the only thing that I knew to do. I started screaming bloody murder. I was hoping that someone would hear me and come to my rescue. Sure enough, Uncle Orr heard me screaming and came running through the timber to find me.

When he reached me, he said, "What's wrong? What's wrong?"

"I saw a snake!" I told him without hesitation. Uncle Orr calmed me down and patiently guided me back to the house. I really didn't see a snake, but I didn't tell him that. I just made that story up because I didn't want Uncle Orr to know I was scared because I was lost. And, I felt guilty because I screamed so loud that I frightened him.

Aunt Gilda and Uncle Orr were staunch about their religious practices. They were Seventh Day Advents, and they lived in strict compliance with the laws of the church. We all went to their church in Decatur, Illinois. Saturday was considered their day of Sabbath. So, we went to church every Saturday. No one was allowed to work on that day. Even our food was prepared the day before.

Uncle Orr had a little truck that we rode to church in. I rode in the back of the truck, because it only had a front seat. Uncle Orr put a seat in the bed of the truck for me to set on. When it rained, I had to stick my head through the back window to keep my head dry. Of course, my back side got wet. But, I didn't care. I just loved going to church. It was a pure joy for me. We never missed a service. This practice also helped me to establish a wonderful relationship with God that I carried with me throughout my life.

Uncle Orr and Aunt Gilda had rigid rules in their household. They taught me how to behave properly at the dinner table. Everyone kept their one hand in their laps while we ate. The only words spoken at the dinner table involved, "Please pass me the, whatever." Conversation was not allowed during our meal time. They said that it interfered with chewing your food properly. Good manners were adhered to on a regular basis.

Aunt Gilda was a motherly looking woman. She was short and fat. Her hair was red. She kept it pulled back away from her face. She treated me as if I was her own child. She taught me how to be a little lady. But mostly, she taught me how to show respect to myself and others.

I idolized Uncle Orr. He never laid a hand on me unless I was totally wrong. He was a good decent person, and I loved him very much. He treated me better than my own father. Most of the time, he had the patience of a saint. He read the Bible to me on a regular basis. This was a part of his daily routine. I felt truly blessed to be a part of his world.

For one full year, I was blessed with a wonderful family atmosphere. I felt loved by both my aunt and my uncle. I liked their easy regimented lifestyle. Then, suddenly my world turned upside down.

Aunt Gilda became unexpectedly pregnant with her first child. She and my Uncle Orr were going to move back to Portland, Oregon where they had lived before. They told me I would have to go live with my dad, because legally they didn't have the jurisdiction over me. There was no way they could take me out of the State that I currently lived in. I understood their dilemma. I didn't get mad at them. They were kind people, and I knew they would never do anything to deliberately hurt me. But still, I was sad and disappointed. I wanted to stay with them forever. I knew that I couldn't, and I had to accept this fact. I had to go live with my dad. I had no idea what my future might hold or the hell that I would experience living at my dad's house.

Chapter Three
A DRASTIC CHANGE

Timmy and I were taken to my dad's house the very next day. He lived on Vandervere Street in Taylorville, Illinois. He co-existed with two other families in a very small house. My dad, his pregnant wife Mable, and five of her children lived in three rooms of the house. Mable's second oldest son Carl, and his wife Lucy, lived in the two rooms next to my dad's. And, a third family lived in the back two rooms of the house. Their last name was Conavich. They were a poor Polish family who could not speak English very well. With all these people in such a small house, there was no room for me and Timmy.

I was a very small child, so my space was going to be in the inside the bedroom closet. The closet was the only space available. My dad placed an army cot inside the closet for me to sleep on. I guessed I was lucky that I was small enough to fit in there.

My dad remarried one month after my mother died. My new stepmother's name was Mable. Her maiden name was Maloney. She had been married once before to a man with the last name of Rich. He was the father to Mable's five children. Consequently, my dad got a package deal when he married Mable.

Mable's kids were all older than me. Hinny, the oldest son, had already left home. I rarely saw him. The second oldest son, Carl, was married to Lucy. They lived in our house. And, Kathleen, Dickey, Rena, and Beth Ann lived with us, too. Mable was going to have her seventh child in a short while.

Needless to say, Mable was not happy about taking in two step-children. She did not want to be bothered with kids from a previous marriage. She had plenty of her own kids to deal with, and didn't want me near her. She treated me with indifference most of the time, and ignored me as if I were not there. When she chose to talk to me, she was mean and short tempered. It seemed to me that she enjoyed being hateful. No one in the house appeared to be happy. Carl definitely wasn't happy.

Soon after Timmy and I moved in, a fight broke out between Carl and my dad. Carl had seen Timmy eating food out of the garbage can. Timmy was always hungry. He had not been getting enough to eat so he found food wherever he could. When Carl saw Timmy eating out of the garbage can, he was livid. He went into a rage. He aimed his rage towards my dad. He blamed my dad for not taking better care of his kids. Carl and dad yelled at each other for a few minutes. Then, a fist fight broke out. Carl hit my dad square in the nose. Blood came streaming down from it. My dad went directly to the phone and called the police. The police came to the house and arrested Carl.

My dad was beside himself. He didn't know what to do. He needed time to think. He grabbed his fishing rod, me and Timmy, and went fishing. Wow! What a surprise! I had never been anywhere with my dad in years. Timmy and I were both excited. We were going fishing.

I think my dad was feeling a great amount of guilt. Carl was right. My dad had not taken good care of his kids. He had given us away to whomever would take us in. My dad sat quietly fishing. I was sure he was mulling over the past in his mind.

I didn't fish much. Mostly, I played in the crawdad holes. I filled each hole with mud. Timmy played with me while my dad fished. I totally enjoyed this time with just me, Timmy, and dad. I treasured this peacefulness. I knew we would have to go back home soon. I also knew the tension in our house would be unbearable. But, right now, I was living in the moment. Sooner than I wanted, we went back to the mad house.

My dad had made a decision while he fished. He was going to take Timmy back to Aunt Lou and Uncle Joey's house. I didn't want Timmy to go. However, I knew Tommy would be there with him, so I accepted that he wouldn't be lonely. Although I would miss him terrible, I knew he would be much better off living in a home with people that cared for him. Aunt Lou would take good care of him. As for myself, I was all alone in a place where no one wanted me. Mable went out of her way to show her hatred towards me.

I was living with constant tension. I felt like I had to walk on eggshells just to keep out of Mable's way. I had no choice but to live here. I had nowhere else to go. So, I tried several strategies to go unnoticed.

At first, I stayed out of Mable's way. I figured if I stayed out of her way, she wouldn't be so hateful towards me. Unfortunately, that maneuver didn't work very well due to the fact that we lived in such a small house. Mable seemed to have so much animosity towards me. She searched me out and created undue stress. Second, I really worked hard at doing whatever Mable told me to do. I cleaned house, washed and dried the dishes, scrubbed floors, and did numerous other household chores. However, I couldn't seem to please Mable no matter what I did or how hard I tried. But, I didn't give up. I kept trying to please her.

Mable's attention soon turned towards the birth of her new baby. She conceived the first baby of the New Year! She had a boy. He was born January 1st, 1936. Mable named him after my dad. She named him, Ray Tiller Jr. Everyone seemed to be extremely happy about his birth. Ray Jr., my dad, and Mable's picture were put in the local paper. In the picture, my dad was leaning over Mable and looking at the new baby with a big smile on his face. He was really proud! This was a special occasion. After the excitement settled down they brought Ray Jr. home to our small house. It was clear that we needed to get a bigger house.

Shortly after Ray Jr. was born, we moved to another house, and I started school. I was in the first grade. I went to the Hewittville School. The school was a two story red brick building with a large playground. I didn't stay at this school very long before we moved, again. This time we moved to Elm Street, and I went to North School. Within a short time, we moved again. I now went to Memorial School. After that, we moved so many times that I couldn't count them. In four or five years, I had attended every school in the Taylorville area. I never got used to any of them, because I wasn't there long enough.

I really liked going to school. It was fun. I enjoyed the kids and the teachers. I even liked learning new things. I especially enjoyed the special projects that we did in class. Unfortunately, I was not allowed to go to school very often. Mable knew I enjoyed going to school. She seemed intent upon making me suffer in any way that she could. Consequently, she started keeping me home from school to clean the house.

Once when Mable did let me go to school, I came home with a blue banner that I had made in class. I was really proud of it. I made it out of cardboard. Our class was going to go for a ride on the Blue Banner train the next day. I was really excited about the trip. But, Mable got angry with me.

"You are not going to ride that train. It cost money and we don't have any," she told me.

The next day, Mable deliberately kept me home from school. I was disappointed and hurt. I was being punished, and I didn't understand why.

Another disappointment came when we had a picnic planned at school. I was happy that we were going to play outside and have a picnic. However, I did not get to go to school that day. Mable kept me home. It hurt me so much to miss out on the fun. I didn't understand why Mable kept taking the joyful experiences away from me. She made every day a constant struggle. Unfortunately, this way of life got worse as time went by.

Many times, Mable would only allow me to go to school once a week. It was like a game she played. She made me do chores every morning. The chores included doing dishes, cleaning house, and getting coal from the coal shed out in the back of the house. When all of these chores were finished, Mable might let me go to school. She insisted that I work up until time she decided to set me free.

"Now get out of here! Go to school!" she said.

I responded quickly and ran out the door. I ran all the way to school. I was usually late when I walked into the classroom. I hated to be late. It embarrassed me to walk into the classroom when everyone else was already seated. I knew this just wasn't right. However, it was out of my control. I couldn't do anything to change this pattern.

The school started to take notice of the fact that I was only at school one day a week. The principal sent the school nurse to our house to see if there was a problem. When Mable heard the knock at the door, she peeked out the window to see who was there. Quickly, she sent me to the other room while she answered the door. She barely cracked the door open.

"I came to see why Dottie isn't coming to school," the nurse said.

Mable was harsh. She didn't care what anyone thought.

"As long as she lives under my roof, she is going to do as I say and nobody else!" Then, she slammed the door in the nurse's face. Mable was so mean: the nurse turned and walked away. After the nurse left, Mable took her rage out on me. My penance was to do the laundry, scrub the floors, and clean whatever Mable decided needed to be done in the house that day. She made me work continuously all day long. And, of course, I didn't get to go to school that day.

My fourth grade teacher felt sorry for me, because I didn't have any appropriate clothes to wear to school. I had so few clothes. I wore whatever I had available. My teacher felt sorry for me and bought me a new dress. When I arrived at school one day, my teacher took me into the coat room and helped me to put on the new dress she had bought. I wore the dress all day, and I felt really special. This was such a blessing to me. When school let out, I changed back into my old dress and went home. This change in clothes became a pattern every day I was allowed to come to school.

Mable didn't care how I dressed, and she wouldn't allow me to have friends. She watched me like a hawk. One day, a girl at school asked me to stop by her house on my way home. I liked this girl. She was a nice girl. Her name was Cathy, and her dad was a local attorney. I thought she was rich. When I went to her house, she went through her closet and picked me out some beautiful clothes to take home. I was elated! I was so proud to have these new clothes. However, when I walked into the house with the new clothes, Mable grabbed them and threw them into our wood burning stove. I watched as the clothes totally burned up. I was just sick about this. It hurt me so badly. This episode left me sad and hopelessly depressed.

Mable was mean and hateful to me both mentally and physically. I felt that she hated me because I was her step child. She validated that feeling repeatedly. She often called me a gypsy. She made it sound like it was a dirty word.

She looked down her nose at me and said, "You are nothing but a gypsy! I hate to even look at you!"

I didn't understand why Mable took delight in hurting me. I knew there was nothing I could do about the way I looked. I tried to ignore her cruelty. I had no choice. I was stuck with her.

I was very small for my age. My clothes were always too big for me. My dresses hung on me like a sack. Everyone called me little Dottie. I was small because I didn't get enough food? I was always hungry. Mable attributed to my lack of food.

Mable never allowed me the same food as the rest of her children. At the dinner table, it was apparent. When I reached for a pork chop, Mable poked a fork into my hand to stop me from getting myself a piece of meat.

"You don't need that! " Mable yelled.

I didn't get any meat. The same thing happened with other foods, too. Mable denied me a reasonable meal. Again and again, I left the table hungry. Therefore, I never gained much weight. I was skinny. Most of the time, I was totally stressed out.

I was constantly battered and badgered by Mable. She didn't act so mean with the rest of the kids; just me. And, she didn't need a reason to aim her anger at me.

"I hate you! I don't know why your dad brought you here!" She often told me.

Her bad attitude towards me caused me to feel sad most of the time. She reinforced the fact that no one wanted me. No one loved me. I knew I had to accept my fate. I thought these circumstances were one of those things that happen in life. I had to accept that. I had no way out.

While I was young, Mable used tactics to display her anger in a subtle way. She often slapped me or pulled my hair. Many times, I didn't know why she hit me. She also seemed intent to hurt my feeling whenever she could.

She once told me, "When your mother was on her death bed, your dad was sitting in a movie theater with me!"

I didn't know if I could believe her or not. I didn't trust her. I tried not to think about her awful comments. I knew she was being spiteful because she hated me.

As I got older, the punishment became more severe. At times, she beat me until I had welts on my body. I wasn't able to clean anything good enough to please her. Out of the blue, she hit me. I found myself ducking when she came near me, because I expected a slap to the face or head. I tried harder to do the job right to avoid her wrath.

Mable made me scrub the floor on my hands and knees. While I did this, she watched me. She taught me how to clean the hard way. She taught me what not to do. If Mable wasn't satisfied with what I had done up to a particular point, she poured the entire contents of the bucket of water all over the floor and insisted I clean up the mess. Consequently, I figured at this point I must do a better job of cleaning unless I wanted to do the job twice. But, no matter how hard I worked, I couldn't do anything to suit Mable. I felt like I was doomed to suffer through more torture.

The evil behavior worsened over time. At nine years old, Mable told me to clean the bedroom. She told me to move all of the furniture and clean behind it to get the room cleaned the right way. I was still a small child and had very little physical strength. The furniture was big and much too heavy for me to move by myself. However, I tried and I tried. I was unsuccessful. I found this task to be impossible for me to accomplish. Mable was in the kitchen peeling potatoes. She came into the bedroom with the paring knife in her hand. She came in to check on me to see that I was cleaning the room exactly the way she told me to do it. When Mable seen the furniture had not been moved, she went into a rage. She was out of control. She brought the paring knife down onto the top my head. Blood gushed from the wound and ran down into my face. It scared me to see so much blood! My head felt like it was on fire. Mable hurried to the kitchen, got a handful of sugar, and put it into the wound. I figured she used this to stop the bleeding. In minutes, the bleeding stopped.

When my dad came home, he saw the gash on my head and asked Mable how I got hurt. She lied to him. She told my dad I hit my head on a nail. She always lied to my dad to cover up the cruelty she inflicted on me. My dad never questioned her words. He must have believed her, because the incident was no longer an issue. He was oblivious to what went on in his own household.

I yearned to tell my dad what Mable had done to me. However, I was not allowed to talk to him one on one. Mable repeatedly threatened me with retribution it I attempted even a small conversation with my dad. She didn't want him to know about her evil behavior towards me. Since I was afraid of her wrath; I kept it all to myself. And, most of the time, my dad was not available. He was gone away from the house. He was not there to protect me from harm or distress.

I believe that my dad was afraid of Mable, too. She displayed anger towards him in viscous way. When she was angry with him, she slept with a butcher's knife under her pillow. I heard her threaten him with it several times.

"I will cut your throat if you don't do as I say!" she threatened him. Obviously, she was a jealous woman. And, I had no doubt that she would use that knife on him if he didn't obey her rules. She was an evil woman. My dad seemed to ignore that fact.

My dad never seemed to pay close attention to what was going on in his own house. He didn't pay any mind to his kids. In his generation, the women took care of the kids. He had enough on his hands just getting and keeping a job. He also made his own fish bait and sold it for extra money. He knew how to get by without having a regular job. He was a bit of an entrepreneur. And, I believe he was a little lazy. Most of the time, he was away from the house and family.

Jobs were scarce in the nineteen thirties and forties. Most guys worked for an organization called the WPA. This stood for Works Progress Administration. Their building was located on Vine Street. My dad worked for the WPA whenever he could. I jokingly called the WPA; we play around, because the jobs were not steady ones. In today's generation, the organization would be considered a temp agency. The WPA found their employees low paying jobs that gave them just enough money to eek by on. One of the jobs my dad was given was digging ditches. It was back breaking work, but this job didn't last long. Most of the jobs were short term, low pay, but it was income. With little money coming in, it was constant struggle to put food on our table.

The state provided food for poor families like ours. An organization funded by the State helped our family by giving us food orders. Rinker's was a large warehouse that stored large quantities of food. Every week trucks delivered food to this warehouse. The food was then distributed to poor families like ours. Large groups of people waited at the warehouse when the trucks came in. Food stamps were used to purchase the food. I was one of the people waiting at Rinker's. It was my job to pick up the food for our family.

At eight years old, I pulled my wagon down to Rinker's to get fresh vegetables and fruit. Rinker's was located about three blocks from our house. It seemed like quite a distance to me. The wagon was heavy, especially when it was loaded with food. It was hard for me to pull it back home. Ray Jr. tried to help me push or pull it, but he was just too little to do much good. I usually ended up putting him on the back of the wagon. He was so sweet. I didn't want him to hurt himself. He always tried to help me. I appreciated his help and his company. I don't remember a time that my dad ever came to get our food.

If dad wasn't at work, he was fishing. He was an avid fisherman. His claim to fame was a special kind of catfish bait that he made himself. He called it, stink bait. The name was apt, because it did indeed stink. Other fisherman came from all over town to buy his bait.

The catfish bait had a special receipt and an extensive procedure for making it. The receipt called for dog food, fermented cheese, blood, and oatmeal. The cheese was bought in Pana, Illinois at a cheese factory. The cheese was packaged in a can. The can had to set until the cheese fermented. The can actually rumbled when the cheese was ripe and ready to be made into bait. Boy, did it stink! My dad got the blood at the local slaughter house. And, the oatmeal and dog food was used as fillers. These two ingredients also helped to keep all the ingredients stuck together so it could later be rolled into a ball for bait.

Dad put on rubber gloves to knead his mixture together. He mixed it in the basement of the house. I usually helped him. Believe me, it smelled really badly down there. The smell was so repulsive that dad gagged and sometimes vomited while he was mixing the bait. When that happened, he knew the bait was really going to catch some catfish. After the bait was thoroughly mixed, dad scooped it into small jars that held it until it was sold. The stink bait sold out fast. Dad always sold every single jar he made. After a customer opened the jar, he rolled the bait into a small ball and placed it on his fishing hook. Within minutes, he caught himself a catfish! The catfish loved this bait.

I loved and respected my dad. I always put him high on a pedestal in my mind's eye. I always did whatever he asked me to do without question. I had no expectations. Even when he didn't hold up for me, I never got mad at him or had any bad thoughts towards him. I just accepted him exactly as he was. Because he was my father, it was my duty to respect him.

Physically, my dad looked like an American Indian. His hair was dark brown and as straight as an arrow. His eyes were very dark brown. His skin was dark, so he tanned very well in the summer time. He had high cheekbones, a large crooked nose, and very large ears. He was tall and always on the slender side.

My dad's zest for life showed in the way he wore his hat. When he got ready to go somewhere, he put his hat on and cocked it to one side. He was ready for action. I believe that he thought that he was quite the ladies man. He usually had a big spiel for any woman who came into contact with him. He never seemed to lack for female company.

Dad had many activities that he loved to do. First, he loved to dance. Any opportunity he had to go dancing, he grabbed it! Second, he hunted and trapped animals with his friend Daniel Boone. Actually, Daniel's last name was Leeds. We just called him Daniel Boone. He and my dad set their traps regularly, skinned the animals, and sold their hides for money. But most of all, my dad loved to fish. Fishing was his passion. He was gone most of the time doing just that. He was oblivious to anything or anyone else in his life.

Chapter Four
AN ALMOST DEADLY MISTAKE

When I was twelve years old, I made a terrible mistake that almost cost me my life. Mable sent me in the bedroom to clean the bedsprings. The bed springs looked like open coils wired to an outer frame. I knew this tedious job would take a while to accomplish. I was told to use gasoline to thoroughly clean the bed springs. The reason we used gasoline was to kill the bed bugs. The gasoline was put in a large pitcher with a big handle. It was heavy. My job was to pour the gasoline on the bed springs to kill the bedbugs. Mable gave me three matches. She instructed me to pour gasoline on the entire bed springs. Then, she told me to light a match and touch it to the springs. The matches were the old farmer's matches with wooded sticks. I always did exactly what I was told to do without question. However, before I finished, I was interrupted by Carl's wife Lucy.

Mable and my dad were leaving to go to the grocery store to get some bread and lunch meat for our meal. It was about noon on July 22nd, 1943. It was a very hot day. Lucy came by to visit us and to babysit while Mable and my dad were gone. Lucy came into the bedroom and asked me what I was doing? I told her Mable instructed me to clean the bed springs. Lucy realized I was busy, so she went into the living room and sat down with a book she had brought with her to read. Before Mable left, she came back into the bedroom and again told me to pour the gasoline on the bedsprings and light a match to it. She wanted to make sure I followed her instructions to the letter.

After Mable left, I continued to follow her instructions. I cleaned the springs real good with the gasoline. Then, I lit the match. As soon as the match was lit, the whole picture of gasoline in my hand caught on fire! It sounded like an explosion. Whoosh! My hand was on fire and the flames were moving up my arm! The flesh was instantly burning! I tried to drop the pitcher. But, it seemed to be stuck to my hand. I tried harder and somehow managed to drop it. The flames scared me so bad I started running. The back door was open, so I ran outside in a midst of flames. I circled the house and ran back into the house through the open front door. Fiery flames fell from me as I ran through the house. The house itself was on fire. Lucy was horrified as she watched this scene unfold. Thank God, she was clear headed enough to take action! Lucy saw a large ring of fire that surrounded me. However, it didn't appear that the flames were touching my body. Lucy hurriedly stripped my clothes off in a flash. She grabbed a bed sheet, threw it around me, and took me out of the burning house. We ran to our closest neighbor's house to escape the flames. By this time, I was in total shock.

I stood on the neighbors porch wrapped in the sheet. I waited for the ambulance that had just been called. My mind was in another world. I wasn't really cognizant of my surroundings. By this time, my fire ravished flesh had stuck to the sheet. I barely remember getting into the ambulance. But I do remember my dad getting into the ambulance with me.

"Oh, my God! Oh, my God!" my dad kept saying over and over. I could hear the anguish in his voice. Minutes later, I arrived at St. Vincent's Hospital. The nurse immediately administered a shot of morphine to control my pain. That was the last thing I remembered before I blacked out. I was unconscious. I don't know how long I stayed in that state of mind.

The next thing I remembered seemed like a dream. I was sitting on a cloud above my bed. I looked down and seen my body lying very still on the bed. I looked like I was asleep. As I looked at myself, I thought, *that can't be me? This can't be real?* Then I looked up and saw seven angels' hovering on a cloud above me. They appeared to be surrounded with beautiful, glowing, iridescent lights. The lights reminded me of pictures

I had seen of the Northern Lights. I could see every color of the rainbow. One of the angels' kept calling me.

"Come on Dottie, come on!" One of the angels spoke as she reached out to me. Her arms were outstretched like she wanted me to take her hand. I wanted to go with her! However, when I reached for her, she seemed to back away just out of my reach. I tried harder and harder to reach her. The same thing happened. Then suddenly, I woke up!

When I woke up, my dad was sitting on a chair beside my bed. Chancy Bellows, our family preacher was kneeling on the other side of the bed. He was praying fervently. He had earlier been painting in one of the wings in the hospital. He still wore his paint clothes and held his old stripped paint hat in his hand. My dad had asked him to come and pray for me. My doctor, Dr. Monahan, was at the foot of my bed. As I looked at them, it gave me an eerie feeling. I realized at that moment, they all thought I was going to die, and this was their last ditch effort to save me. My dad, Chancy Bellows, and Dr. Montague has put me in God's hands. God had brought me back! Unexpectedly, I woke up. Everyone was surprised!

When my dad saw I was awake, he asked me, "Would you like some ice cream?"

"Yes, I would," I told him. So he called the nurse and ordered me some ice cream.

"We thought that you were going to die," he told me. I was really surprised by that statement. Because, it never occurred to me that I wouldn't survive. I just somehow knew that I would be OK. I didn't realize, at this time, how terribly my body was burned.

The first realization of the extent of my burns happened shortly after I woke up. A thin layer of skin on my elbow had grown and attached itself to my torso. The doctor had to cut it away from my body. I didn't feel any pain, and the procedure was done rather quickly. The constant morphine shots kept my pain at bay. After the skin was cut away, my arm was placed on a donut shaped pillow. The pillow cradled my elbow and kept it away from my body. This was a small complication compared to my many other burns.

Bandages covered many other areas of my body. My chest, stomach, left arm, and the inner parts of my thighs were the areas that were burned the worst. One of my breasts was completely burned away. Also, the burns were so deep on my chest area that my heart was visible. The skin was gone. I could actually see my heart beat. Dr. Montague told me my burns were the worst type. He called them third degree burns.

Some of the burned areas had become infected. The smell emitting from me was horrid. The nurses placed candles in a circle around my bed to absorb and mask the odor. I guessed that this was the only method they used to control the smell.

Every time the doctor or nurses came into my room it scared me. I didn't know what they were going to do to me. But, I knew for sure my pain level was going to be worsened by their visits. I felt like a guinea pig as they examined me. No one seemed to know what to do with me. I quickly learned to speak up to them.

"Don't touch me unless you tell me what you are going to do to me!" I said. I could deal with whatever they did to me as long as I knew what to expect. So, in turn, they explained every step of the process that was going to be done to me each time they came into my room. As long as I knew what the procedure was, I would work with them even though I knew it would increase my pain.

Every day the nurses came into my room to change the bandages. As I sat on the side of the bed with my feet dangling over the edge; they used tweezers to pull the old bandages away from my body. The pain was intense. I could barely stand it. As the nurses did this daily routine, they asked me to recite The Lord's Prayer. I did just as they told me. I knew this helped me to take my focus off of the pain. The nurses were nuns and I trusted them not to hurt me anymore than was absolutely necessary. I patiently watched them carefully pull the bandages off. Blood squirted out of my side each time the bandages were removed. It spurted out in a steady stream. Quite often the pain caused me to black out. One day while this procedure was being performed, I actually passed out and fell off of the bed. The nurses picked me up and placed me down on the bed while they finished rewrapping the bandages. I knew they tried to be gentle, but it was impossible to save me from the pain.

The nuns at St. Vincent's Hospital were my best friends. Every Sunday they put me in a wheelchair and took me upstairs to the Chapel for services. I looked forward to worshipping with them. They were closer to me than my own family. My favorite sister was Sister Peyton. She was my closest friend. She was kind and compassionate. Often, she came into my hospital room to just sit and talk with me and share some time together. I had no other visitors other than Sister Peyton. I appreciated that she took the time to comfort me with her presence. She made me feel special.

For six months I endured endless procedures, but I was not healing. The doctors and nurses were at a loss. They didn't know what to do next. They used up every method available to them to heal me. I was not healing. In desperation, a decision was made that I was not aware of. I have been in this hospital since July 22nd. It is now October 7th. Today is my birthday.

I was told that I was going to have a birthday party. All my life, no one had ever mentioned my birthday. I knew what date it was, but it had never been celebrated before this time. I was so excited! Today I was going to have my very first ever birthday party. I am now thirteen years old.

My dad's friend, Joe Shifter, came to the hospital to see me. He always acted like a father towards me. He told me he was going to take me home for my birthday party. Joe was a local funeral director in Taylorville. He brought his hearse to the hospital to take me home to celebrate my birthday.

Joe and my dad loaded me into the hearse, and we were off to my house for the party. I had to be carried into the house, because I had not walked in the last six months. When we got inside, I was taken into the bedroom and propped up in my bed. The house was full of people ready to celebrate my special day!

All my brothers and sisters were there when I arrived. Everyone was waiting for me to come home. Also, many of my neighbors came to see me and brought me gifts. Wow! What a great day I was having. I was elated to see so many toys and gifts. And, they were all for me. I was so happy!

I started opening the gifts. One gift was a turquoise bracelet with a matching ring. My favorite gift was a doll. It was the prettiest doll I had ever seen. The doll wore a bonnet and a white dress with shoes to match. This was my first doll. I was delighted. This was the best day I had ever had! The time went fast, and soon, I had to return to my hospital room.

Joe took me back to the hospital in the hearse. When I got there, to my surprise, the gifts were already in my room. My doll was propped up on my bed. It looked like she was waiting for me. I really enjoyed the fact that the toys were there and they were all mine. In the past, I never had toys to play with. Although I wasn't able to get out of bed to play with my new toys; it felt good having them close to me. I felt very content.

I fell asleep with wonderful thoughts in my mind. But, I was awakened around midnight by Joe Shafer, my dad, and Dr. Montague. Joe started talking to me when he realized I was fully awake.

"Well, Sissy, you are going to take a ride with me and your dad. We are going to take you to a new hospital. It is a research hospital in Chicago, he explained"

"Can I take my doll?" I asked. That was the only question I had.

"Oh no, you can't take anything with you," he answered.

It made me sad to think I couldn't take any of my toys with me. I pouted for a while. I should have been able to take some of my toys with me. This wasn't fair. But, I had no choice but to accept this unhappy turn of events.

I later found out that my dad could no longer afford my care at St. Vincent's Hospital. He had to make a decision to move me for several reasons. First, the new hospital would not cost him any money. It was a teaching hospital, so it was free. Second, my burns were so severe that I needed more than what this current hospital could give me. The fact was; I was not healing. Very little progress had been made in healing my burns.

The hospital I was being taken to was a research hospital. It was located on a Naval Base in Chicago. The hospital accepted me as a patient. Everyone knew I needed a lot more time to heal. This hospital had more high tech methods of treating burn victims. This was the next step in my intricate care. My dad paid Joe fifty dollars to take me to this new hospital.

I didn't really understand what was ahead of me, but I was ready for the new adventure. Joe and my dad loaded me up in the hearse, and we were on our way to Chicago. After riding for a while, we all began to get hungry. Joe stopped at a restaurant to get some coffee to help him stay awake. He asked me what I wanted to eat. The only food I wanted was a pickle and a cup of hot chocolate. I thought that was pretty funny, but it was the two foods I had been craving the most. Joe and my dad went into the restaurant and brought me exactly what I had asked for. Then, we continued on our journey.

On the way to the hospital, we had a flat tire on the hearse. We were going over a railroad crossing when the tire blew out. The loud noise startled everyone in the hearse. As Joe got out of the hearse to fix the tire, I asked him to please open the curtains so I could see what he was doing. The hearse had purple curtains that were always drawn shut. It was dark outside. I wanted to see the street lights. Joe opened the curtains for me. Soon, the tire was fixed, and we were on our way. The flat tire delayed us a bit. By the time we got to the hospital, it was morning.

When we arrived at the hospital, I was introduced to Dr. Kramer. He was going to be my new doctor. I will never forget the first thing he did to me. He immediately reached over and pulled on my bandages. This caused me a great deal of pain. I yelped. I thought to myself, *this doctor must be crazy! He is deliberately inflicting pain on me!*

"Oh that hurts doesn't it?" he asked. "The bandages are stuck." But then, he added, "We are going to fix that problem right now."

Well, I was sure happy to hear that statement. I was ready to proceed with anything that would help me get healed. I was hopeful at this point.

By now, the morphine I was given before I left St. Vincent's Hospital had worn off. Dr. Dr. Kramer quickly told me I was already addicted to the morphine. I had been taking it regularly for six months. He told me it was time for me to be weaned off of this particular pain medicine. This process was necessary in order for me to get healed. I wasn't sure exactly what he was talking about, but I figured he would do whatever was in my best interests. I trusted him right away.

I was then taken to an area with a large swimming pool. The pool was filled with green water. The nurses carefully put me in the pool. One nurse held my head, and the other nurse held my feet. My body was immersed into the tumultuous water. The water was swirling and seemed to be whipping me back and forth. The whole pool had a roaring sound. I wondered what would happen to me if they were to let my head go. I wasn't very trusting of them at this point. It was scared. Within minutes, the troubled water turned red from my own blood pouring out of my body. I was bleeding as the water loosened the bandages away from my wounds. I remembered Dr. Kramer had told me the bandages must come off in order for me to heal completely. And, the nurse explained to me exactly what they were going to do step by step. They genuinely tried to ease my anxiety.

After the bandages came off, the nurses took me out of the pool and placed me on an upright table with wheels. My feet dangled off the table. The nurses had a bowl of a substance that looked like yellow gelatin. It was a solid, yet pliable. It looked sticky. The nurses used their hands to literally toss this yellow stuff onto the areas of my body that were burned. When it made contact with my body, it melted and ran down both the front and back of my body. It felt good. It instantly soothed my burns. When the nurses finished the treatment, I was taken to my hospital room.

In my room, I was placed under a fixture that looked like a cradle to me. I had no clothes on, and my nakedness bothered me. I felt terribly exposed to anyone who came into my room. At first, I was alone in the two bed room. On the second day, a woman was put in the bed next to me. She had also suffered a bad burn. She didn't stay with me very long. After that, I had the whole room to myself for a whole year.

Dr. Kramer patiently talked with me about my awful burns on the outside of my body. He also explained why I had not been burned on the inside of my body. When I saw the flames engulfing me and the ring of fire around me, I started running. But, the best thing I did, unconsciously, was to hold my breath as I ran. The doctor said I did the right thing at the right time. Because I held my breath as I ran, I didn't breathe the fire into my lungs. Also, I didn't swallow during that time either. Those two things saved me from burning the inside of my body. He told me if I had swallowed, I would have surely died. In addition to that, he said my burns were a result of the fumes from the gasoline rather than the actual flames of the fire. For once, I had done the right thing. God helped me to do the right thing. I knew God was watching over me then and now.

Although the nurses explained step by step the treatments that were being done to me, I still wasn't sure about this cage that was placed over me. It was made of wire. There were three bright lights inside the structure. The caged spanned from my neck area to the lower part of my thighs. I curiously asked the nurse why the lights were necessary.

"The lights will keep you warm and draw the fire out of your body so you can further heal," she explained.

I understood her reply. But, it was uncomfortable staying in a fixed position for days at a time. I felt trapped. I could only lie on my back. I couldn't roll over on my side to sleep. My sleep was restless in this position. I started to get frustrated, but that didn't help. This cage remained over me for about two weeks.

The fact that I couldn't wear any clothes bothered me. Everyone who walked into my room wanted to look at my burns. Numerous doctors came in to look at me while I was under the cage and during my healing process. The doctors all wore uniforms. I was embarrassed by their inspection. None of the doctors talked directly to me. They simply conferred with each other. They acted as if I were not there at all. It hurt me to be ignored by so many people.

After the cage was taken away, many surgeries followed. I had to have numerous skin grafts. So many, in fact, that I couldn't count them. My right arm was grafted first. This graft failed to take the first time. It had to be done again. This time the graft worked. Because my right arm was burned so badly, it took a multitude of grafts to cover it completely. In the end, the skin on that arm felt very rigid. The doctors slowly built the skin in layers upon layers. When the grafts were finally finished, the skin on my right arm was thick and hard. It reminded me of patchwork on a quilt. My chest was grafted next. Again, it took many skin grafts to completely cover this area. And, the process continued until all the burned areas were covered with skin.

The skin grafts were taken from many areas of my body. Square patches of skin were cut from my stomach, legs, back, and any other areas of my body where good skin could be harvested. This was an ongoing process. Eventually, my body started to get weak from the blood loss.

After a time, the doctors realized my liver was not building the blood fast enough. Dr. Kramer told me my blood was drying up as fast as my body could make it. Because of that, I had to have numerous blood transfusions. Over a period of time, I was given sixty-five to seventy units of blood. The hospital asked their staff members to donate blood especially for me. I felt very lucky that so many people gave their blood so I could get better and go home.

My diet was changed to accommodate my healing process. The doctor recommended that I eat liver every other day. The liver seemed to be almost raw when the nurse gave it to me. I hated it! But, I ate it anyway. I wanted to get better. When the doctors realized the liver wasn't helping me. They stopped giving it to me. I also was told to eat a cup of peanuts every day. The peanut oil helped my skin stay moist. I liked peanuts, but I got tired of eating them. I came up with a new idea.

"Could I have chocolate covered peanuts?" I asked the nurse. They were my favorite treat. The nurse agreed and brought them to me right away. That was great. I was happy the nurse worked so well with me.

Many of my prayers were answered during this time. I prayed a lot. Dr. Kramer commented that I had a lot of faith in God, and that, God would heal me. He constantly encouraged me to keep praying. Dr. Kramer believed my continuing faith in God was the reason I was surviving the constant trauma my mind and body was going through. Again, in my mind, I never had a doubt that I wouldn't survive. I always had faith in God and determination that drove me without question. I knew I would get continually get better.

My main problem was loneliness. My only contacts were doctors and nurses. No one came to visit me the whole year I was in the hospital. I felt like I had been forgotten. None of my family members made the trip to Chicago to see me. I really would have liked to see a preacher. But, it didn't happen. Loneliness became a part of my life.

One day I received a special gift. A child down the hall from me sent a coloring book and some crayons to my room. I hardly ever left my room, so I was surprised anyone knew I was there. I was so happy that someone thought of me. My right arm was immobile, so I used my left hand to color. It was hard because I was right handed. I tried and tried until I managed to write my name and color with the left hand. It was difficult, but it gave me something to strive towards. I was eternally grateful for the gift.

Time marched on, and I started to feel better. I began to heal enough that I could set in a wheelchair. Now, I was mobile. I had been so lonely in my room for such a long time. Now, I needed to explore. Curiosity got the best of me. I kept hearing some commotion outside of the hospital. It sounded like a military drill.

"Hip, one, two, three. Hip, one, two, three," I heard someone shouting.

I wanted to see who was out there. I rolled myself over to the window to look out. It looked really cold outside. There were a few inches of snow on the ground. I saw a group of military men marching together. Their uniforms looked like they were in the Navy. I wanted to get a closer look. I wheeled myself out into the hallway.

"You've got legs. So, why don't you get out of this wheelchair and walk?" I told myself out loud. I thought I could walk even though I had been bedridden for almost a year and a-half.

I lifted myself out of the chair. I immediately fell to the floor. I was shocked! I laid there for a minute not knowing what to do next. I was mad at myself because I couldn't walk on my own. The nurse came at once and picked me up. She put me back into the wheelchair. Then, she scolded me.

"Don't try to get out of this chair again without assistance, "she said.

Although this experience seemed like a failure, I didn't let it get me down. I was happy to be in the wheelchair. At least, I was mobile. I could now get out of my hospital bed and visit with other people. I was definitely getting better.

The hospital had done all they could do for me. All of my skin grafts were completed, and I was healing very well. I still had large scabs all over my body, but they were getting better all the time. My mental state of mind was also improving. It felt good to move about and socialize. I was feeling very good. It was now time for me to go home.

I was apprehensive about going home. I felt safe here at this hospital. I didn't know what to expect when I got home. One thing I knew for sure, I did not want to deal with my evil stepmother.

Chapter Five
BACK WITH MABLE AND MY DAD

The hospital had done all they could do for me. They were sending me home. Even though I still had quite a lot of healing and physical therapy to do; I was on my own. The rest of the healing process was up to me. I was finally released from the Chicago hospital. It had been a long year. And, in a way, I kind of hated to leave. Everyone at this hospital had treated me so well during my stay. But now, my time here was over.

Going back home wasn't something I was looking forward to. I was very apprehensive about the mess I was going back to live in. I knew I wasn't going to be happy there. During the last year and a-half, I had built up a great deal of animosity towards Mable. I just knew that she had set me up to die. That thought made me seethe with anger every time I thought of it. She was the reason I caught on fire. When I looked at the multitude of scars on my body, I cringed. And, I would be looking at them the rest of my life! Along with that, I still had to deal with Mable's hatred towards me. It depressed me to think about the past, and my future didn't look very bright, either.

Joe Shifter and my dad came to Chicago and pick me up in the hearse. They were taking me home. In most cases, this would have been an exciting event. It wasn't for me. Both Joe and my dad tried to make me feel comfortable as I rode back home, but I withdrew into myself. I was quiet all the way home. I knew nothing had changed since I had left. The ride home was a long one. I felt my body getting tenser and tenser the closer we got to Taylorville. My anxiety level continued to grow.

When we finally got to the house, I was carried in and placed on the living room couch. I was still unable to walk, so I was very dependent upon others to help me. The living room was to be where I would be staying for a while. The couch made out into a bed at night. And, a chair was placed beside the couch for me to sit on. I managed to pull myself off of the couch onto the chair. That was the extent of my capabilities. I didn't like being dependent upon anyone, so I knew that I would have to work hard to walk again. I also had to start moving my right arm. It still hadn't been used much for a year and a-half. So, I needed to start working it daily to get it moving again.

I was really worried about how Mable would treat me. Luckily, she seemed to back off and leave me alone. Most of the time, she treated me with indifference. This was a blessing. I was grateful for the reprieve. However, I was still going to be careful in her presence. My fear of her wrath lay right under the surface of my mind. I surmised that my Dad must have had a long talk with her, because she wasn't treating me as mean as she had before.

Fiona, my youngest half-sister, was my best support. She was only three years old. She encouraged me to walk every day.

"Come on, Dottie, take my hand," Fiona encouraged.

I took her outstretched hand and tried to walk. At first, my legs didn't seem to want to move. My progress was slow. We could only walk around the couch once before I tired. Fiona constantly encouraged me to go further. I appreciated her unrelenting encouragement. Eventually, I was able to walk on my own.

My physical therapy was extensive. My right arm took a long time before I could move it well. The tough skin on it was so rigid that it was hard to stretch my arm completely out. The ligaments were drawn too tight making my arm stay in a fixed bent position. Therefore, my right arm was about four inches shorter than the left one. The doctor had given me a ball to squeeze. He recommended I work with the ball every day until my arm got stronger. My first stirrings of feelings in that arm felt like a tingling sensation in my fingers. I knew this was a good sign. Over time, the arm responded well. I never had any doubt that I wouldn't be able to use it again. I had faith in God that it would soon be functional. Eventually, I began to use that arm for everything. My struggle with doing everything left handed was over. Now, I had conquered one obstacle. I was ready for the next hurdle.

My burns were not completely healed, so I needed to do water therapy every day. The areas where I had multiple skin grafts had scabs on them. The scabs were all over my body. The largest one was on my chest area. It was so hard and big it felt like I was wearing a shield of armor. The scab was so thick that it was heavy and cumbersome. After the water was warmed, and put in the tub, I lowered myself into it. I continuously splashed the water up onto my chest. The water therapy was part of the healing process. The water softened the scabs so they didn't itch and pull so much. After soaking in the water for a while, I always felt better. However, I felt uncomfortable doing this because Mable had to help me with this task.

The tub I did my daily soak in was the metal type that hung on a hook on the outside of the house. The tub had to be brought into the kitchen and placed in the middle of the floor. It was quite a job to get it inside, heat the bath water, and fill the tub. Mable was forced to prepare the tub for my daily soak. I could tell she resented doing this for me. I felt tense during the whole process; and Mable didn't try easing my tension. She merely ordered me to get in and out of the tub. But, most of the time, Mable ignored me and didn't talk directly to me during the entire bath. I guessed that my dad must have told her to take care of me. She complied. This was the very first time Mable had ever done anything for me directly.

After a few weeks went by of doing the daily baths, a wonderful thing happened. The large scab on my chest loosened and slipped off of my body. What a relief. Talk about a weight being lifted off of me! I was actually excited about this new development. I was finally healing. However, Mable had a different viewpoint. She acted like the discarded scab was a dirty thing.

"Take that thing to the back yard and bury it!" Mable ordered my dad. He did just as she asked. Soon after that incident, all of my scabs on my body healed and disappeared.

Physically, I was making incredible progress. I was walking well. And, my right arm was back in working order. I was getting stronger and stronger. It felt good to be self-sufficient again. I now had a little more freedom and more responsibility in the house.

I was able to bath Ray Jr. and Fiona and take care of their daily needs. I felt as if they were my own kids. They were a part of me. I never minded taking care of them. Occasionally, we were all allowed to go see a movie at the Ritz Theater. Seeing a movie was our only form of entertainment.

I don't remember being a kid and doing the types of things that kids usually do: accept one time. My half-sister Rena was a year older than me. I was fourteen years old and she was fifteen. Mable sent Rena and me to my aunt's house to get something for my dad. On our way there, we stopped at the local hangout for teenagers. The meeting place was called The Spot. The local teenagers hang out here and drank soda pop. Of course, there was the usual flirting going on between the boys and the girls. Rena joined in with the crowd, but I was too shy to say anything to anyone. I just sat there and enjoyed watching everyone. I was having fun and laughing when my dad unexpectedly walked in the door. He had been looking for us. He was furious. He grabbed Rena and I by the shoulders and dragged us both outside.

"Don't you ever bring my daughter in here again? You can come in here because I can't say anything about that," he said, "but, you better never bring Dottie back in here."

I was shocked at my dad's behavior. Most of the time, he didn't even act like I existed. I didn't understand why he was so angry. I knew Rena and I hadn't done anything wrong.

After that day, Rena seemed to be gone most of the time. She went looking for a job and found one right away. She was hired as a waitress at King's Café. Rena wanted to be independent. Also, she wanted to get away from home so she could be her own boss. She was worldlier than me. I knew she would find a way to be free of Mable and my dad.

Mable continued to treat me with indifference. She waited until I was completely healed before she started being her old mean self again. I expected that her mean attitude towards me would eventually come back. It surely did. I was always on guard around her. As I became stronger, Mable's attitude towards me worsened.

My work load slowly increased. Mable kept me home from school repeatedly to work in the house. One of the jobs I was required to do was ironing shirts. Mable took in shirts from paying customers. The shirts had to be washed, starched, and ironed to perfection. The shirts came in on a weekly basis. They were washed and rinsed using on old wringer type washer. The washer had to be manually filled with water to wash the shirts. Then, the washer had to be drained and filled with water to rinse the shirts. After the shirts were washed and rinsed, starch was put into a bucket of water. The shirts were then dipped into the water and hung on the clothesline to dry. After the shirts dried, they had to be perfectly ironed. Not even a small wrinkle was allowed. Everything I did had to be nothing less than perfect. That was Mable's law. I knew I would be in trouble if I made a mistake.

One day when I was ironing, I scorched a white shirt. I obviously wasn't paying attention to what I was doing. I held the iron on the shirt too long. When Mable saw what I had done, she slapped me and pulled my hair. She was in a rage and kept hitting me and hitting me. She then insisted that I do the shirt all over from the beginning until I got it perfect. So, I scrubbed the shirt by hand until the scorched area could no longer be seen. Then I refilled the washer twice to wash and rinse the shirt. I was so upset that I caught my arm in the wringer of the washer. It hurt, but I continued to finish my job. I starched the shirt and hung it on the line to dry. Finally, I ironed the shirt a second time. I was successful. I felt lucky that I had gotten the shirt back to new again. I wasn't sure how I managed to get it right, but I did. I guess it was fear that motivated me. I knew I would get into more trouble if I didn't get the job done perfectly.

Another time, Mable kept me home from school to clean the living room floor. The floor was a linoleum floor that took special care. I scrubbed the floor on my hands and knees until it was spotless. Then, I rinsed it well. After the floor dried, I applied Johnson's Paste Wax to the entire surface. This particular wax was hard to use. I applied it with a rag using a circular motion. When the wax dried, I buffed the floor with an old blanket to create a high shine. The entire floor was backbreaking work.

Mable was out of her head with cleaning. She was an obsessed fanatic who had a particular way of doing everything. No matter how hard I tried to do a job her way and please her, it was never good enough. She never displayed any patience with me. She pushed me harder.

One night Mable told me to go find Ray Jr. and bring him home. It was almost dark outside. Ray Jr. had not come home, yet. He had stopped over at a friend's house down the block from where we lived. However, I didn't know Ray Jr. was there. It was really cold outside. There was so much snow on the ground I could barely wade through it. The air was frigid. I looked and looked for Ray Jr. I could not find him. I knew I would be in a heap of trouble if I didn't bring him back with me. I was scared to go home. My hands, toes, and feet were nearly frozen before I gave up the search and came home. I had to go home. I was in tremendous pain. I was crying really hard by the time I got back to the house. My hands had to be put in warm water to thaw them out. But worse than that, Mable beat me with my dad's fishing rod. She broke it on my back. It left welts on me for quite some time. When my dad came home, he saw that his fishing rod was broken. He was really angry, and he wanted to know what happened to his rod. Of course, Mable didn't tell him that she had broken it on me. She told him another lie.

Mable's bitterness towards me grew as time went by. She took every opportunity she could think of to hurt me physically. One morning as I was getting the kids ready for school and fixing breakfast, Mable intervened. I had just finished fixing some hot cocoa. Hot cocoa was my favorite drink. I gave each one of the kids a cup of cocoa. I told them to let it cool a minute before they drank it. It was very hot. I was going to drink what was left in the bottom of the pan after everyone had a cup of their own. Mable caught me just as I poured the last of the cocoa it into my cup. She didn't want me to have any. For revenge, she insisted that I drink every last drop of the hot chocolate. I was so scared that I drank it as fast as I could. Because it was so hot, I immediately vomited it all over the floor. Mable was livid. She slapped me as hard as she could and swung me around by my hair like a puppet. When she let go of me, she forced me to clean up the floor. Again, I was late for school.

During the year and a-half that I was in the hospitals, I didn't have any kind of schooling. The hospital didn't provide any tutoring for me. Therefore, I missed almost two year of school. I wanted to learn new things. I yearned to go to school. I knew I was behind in my class work. Also, I knew it would be very hard for me to catch up. But, I didn't care; I just wanted to go to school.

Mable only allowed me to go to school maybe once a week. The other days, I was kept home to clean house. Mable punished me by keeping me home from school. Repeatedly, it hurt me to miss out on the learning that I craved. I was getting older and depression started to set in. On the days I was allowed to go to school, class was already in session when I got there. I was embarrassed to walk into the classroom late. All the kids stared at me. I felt very self-conscious. I didn't want to be in this position. I felt overwhelmingly sad and out-of-place.

One day when Mable sent me to school late, I just couldn't go. It was really late this day and school had been in session a long time. When Mable finally set me free, I ran out of there like the house was on fire. I was so depressed I didn't know what to do with myself. I decided to skip school. I couldn't face the students and teachers. Instead of going to school late, I chose to walk up and down the alleyways until the time school would normally be let out. I walked and walked. Then I started crying. I was so sad. And, I was hurt that I had to live like this. Mable treated me so bad, and I didn't want to be in this situation anymore. I wished that I could die! I was desperately depressed and so miserable I could hardly stand it. God was the only one I could turn to. I prayed and prayed.

"Please get me out of this place. Please do something for me," I asked God. "I am afraid Mable will kill me!" My only hope was that God heard my prayers.

My depression continued to be so obvious that my teachers and the principal of my school, Mr. Cromwell, started to take notice. Mr. Cromwell called me into his office.

"Dottie, I don't know what is going on at your house, but I am going to have a talk with your dad," he told me. "I want you to tell him about the abuse you are suffering in the hands of your step-mother."

"I am not allowed to speak to my dad," I told Mr. Cromwell.

Mr. Cromwell told me he was going to call my dad to the school so I could have a conversation with him. In addition to calling my dad, the principal also had already called in the authorities that took care of abused children. They arrived at the school before my dad.

The group of authorities the principal called in wanted to talk with me. They told me they were there to help me. However, they could only help me if I ran away from home. If I ran away from home, the authorities would pick me up and place me in a foster home. This sounded really good to me. I was ready to do what they instructed. Anything was better than the hell I was living in. I only hoped my dad would agree to let me run away from home so these people could help me.

As we waited for my dad, I was asked questions about my home life. I was told exactly how many days of school I had missed. Also, I was told how many days I was late for school. They noted the many times the school nurse had come to our house to see whether or not I had a problem that prevented me from coming to school. The nurse had told them how callously Mable had treated her. The authorities and the principal seemed to know exactly what was happening in my life.

My dad worked across the street from the school. He was working on the furnace in the adjacent building. He came to the school and sat in the principal's office and heard the same things I had just heard. Then, the principal asked me to tell my dad what was going on at home. I was afraid to tell him about Mable. She had warned me many times to keep my mouth shut. But, I knew I had to speak up this time. I proceeded to tell my dad about the many times Mable kept me home from school to work in the house. Also, I explained how viscous Mable always treated me. Then, I told my dad about the authorities plan to help me. I told him I had to run away so they could pick me up and place me in a foster home. I would be able to live in a new home with no abuse. I told him everything I could to convince him to allow me to do as the authorities asked.

Everyone listened as I spoke. Unfortunately, my dad wasn't thinking along the same line as everyone there in the room.

"No, no, no, Dottie, don't do this. Don't tell these people a thing. Don't do what they told you to do," he commanded. "They will put you in a place that you wouldn't want to be. You hang in there." Then, my dad surprised me by saying, "Mable is sick, and she is going to die someday soon!"

I was absolutely heartsick. My own dad wouldn't help me. He didn't understand all I had been through living with Mable. His solution was for me to bide my time until this evil woman passed away? What else could I do? There had to be another solution to this problem. I thought about running away.

I didn't have one place to go and no one who wanted to take me into their home. I didn't know where I could hide if I did run away. I felt like I was doomed to a life of torture.

It really hurt me to think my dad didn't care about my welfare. He ignored the fact that Mable abused me physically and mentally. He wasn't on my side! He didn't care about me at all! It made me sick to think my own father was so callous towards me. This reinforced the fact that no one wanted me and no one cared for me.

Shortly after my dad and I had the conversation at school, I realized that Mable was indeed sick. At first, Mable assumed she was pregnant. Her stomach grew bigger and bigger. So, she visited her doctor. After he examined her, he told her that she was not pregnant. Her stomach was growing larger because of the tumor he found inside her stomach area. The doctor recommended that the tumor be removed right away. Mable made the appointment to have the surgery. Within a week, the tumor was removed.

The doctor tested the tumor and determined it to be cancerous. Obviously, it had been there for quite some time. After more testing, the doctor determined that the cancer had spread throughout Mable's entire body. Her chance of surviving the cancer wasn't good. She was surely going to die.

As the cancer progressed, Mable began to lose quite a bit of weight in a short time. She complained of being extremely tired. Most of the time, she just lay in her bed and rested. She continued to get sicker and weaker. Her pain level progressively increased. There was no doubt. Mable was going to die from the cancer ravishing her body.

I thought that this terrible turn of events would change the way Mable thought. But, it didn't. She continued to be as mean as ever. Her hatred towards me never eased up. Actually, she was even more hateful than usual. The days that Myrtle was able to get out of bed, were always bad for me.

Many times, Mable put me in the closet and locked me inside. The lock was only on the outside of the door. She usually locked me in the closet when everyone else was out of the house. She didn't want any witnesses. Mable told me that I had to go into the closet, because she didn't want to look at my face. I had to stay in there until she told me I could come out. I sat in the darkness and waited for that moment. There were no lights in the closet. The darkness enveloped me. Some days, I had to be in there half the day. And other times, I only had to stay one hour.

One particular night, Mable sent all the rest of the kids to the movies. She wouldn't let me go with them. After all the kids left, she locked me in the closet. However, this night I got a reprieve. My dad came home. He was going to take Mable to the hospital because she was getting sicker. He came directly to the closet to get his coat. As he opened the door, he saw me sitting in the closet floor. It startled him. He jumped like it scared him to death.

"What are you doing in here?" he said.

"Mable locked me in here," I explained to my dad with a quiet voice.

"Where are the rest of the kids?" he asked.

"They all went to the Ritz to see a movie," I told him while hoping that I could go to the show with the rest of my siblings.

My dad handed me fifteen cents, and said, "Go catch up with the other kids. Go to the show."

I grabbed the money and ran to the movie as fast as I could. I just wanted to get out of there! I wanted to enjoy the movie with the rest of my family.

My dad took Mable to the hospital that night. She ended up staying there for a few days. I was relieved to hear that she wouldn't be back right away. But now, the household responsibilities were place squarely on me. I was in charge of the younger kids. Ray Jr., Beth Ann, Fiona, and Rena all were still at home. I had to clean, iron, take care of the kids, and do whatever else needed to be done. Although Rena was older than me, I still had to do her ironing along with the other clothes. She was always too busy outside of the house. I felt like I was a slave. Work was all I ever did.

Daily, I went to the cob house and filled the bucket with corn cobs to burn in the stove. As I gathered the cobs, I prayed. I prayed out loud. I said, "Please God, get me out of here. Please give me a different life." I knew that God was the only one who could get me out of this mess. I was so miserable living in a place where no one wanted me, unless they wanted to use me.

Just when I thought it couldn't get any worse, it did. Mable's son Dickey came home from a camp where he stayed. It was called a CC Camp. He worked and lived at this camp most of the time. He only occasionally came home. He had been gone a long time. I was afraid of Dickey. He always tried to violate me. He was older and bigger than me. When I went to the coal shed to get our daily supply of coal, Dickey would seek me out and molest me. He would make me perform oral sex on him. At this time, I didn't even know what this type of sexual behavior was called. I just knew that it made me feel dirty and violated. He did it because he could. He trapped me like a caged animal. I had no one to protect me from him. These episodes of sexual abuse were heartbreaking to me. I my only hope was that he wouldn't be home very long. He finally left. However, the next time he came home, he continued the abuse. I had nowhere to run. I was a nervous and tense most of the time. I felt terribly sick inside.

For the next two years, my life spiraled in a downward trend. Mable got home from the hospital and seemed to be less sick for about two months. Then, she suddenly became totally bedridden. She lost more weight and complained all the time. She was wracked with pain. It soon became my job to take care of her every need. My workload grew bigger and bigger. I never rested.

Rena left home shortly after Mable became bedridden. She married her boyfriend just so she could get away from home. I was envious of her. I wanted to leave, too. I was fifteen years old, and now, I was overburdened with all household responsibilities. But most of all, I was stuck here taking care of my wicked step-mother.

The first thing I had to learn was how to give Mable her pain medication. My dad taught me how to administer the morphine to her. He taught me to crush the morphine tablet between two spoons to form a powder, add some water, and draw the liquid into the syringe. Then, I had to pull Mable's skin up and put the shot into that area. The morphine controlled her pain level.

Mable began to require more and more care. So, my dad hired a nurse to come to our house. Mable would not let the nurse touch her. Mable demanded that I continue to do everything for her. The nurse ended up sitting in a chair and watching me do her work. I had to bath Mable, administer morphine, and take care of her every need. I couldn't contain my resentment. This wasn't right!

Mable's mother, Grandma Lee, lived close to us and tried to help with the care of her daughter. Again, Mable would not allow it. She only wanted me to take care of her. So, Grandma Lee gave me some sort of antiseptic type solution. She told me to wash my hand with this solution every time I touched Mable. Grandma Lee thought the cancer was contagious, and she wanted to protect me from getting it. I did as she asked me and used the solution on my hands every time I did anything for Mable. I didn't want to get the cancer, too.

Mable lingeringly continued to get sicker and sicker. Her body wasted away. I could see her bony skeleton through her skin. She had no fat on her body. I had an eerie feeling every time I looked at her. I hated having to take care of her. But, I gritted my teeth and did what had to be done.

Over time, Mable required more and more morphine. The higher doses caused her to have hallucinations. She began to see things that weren't there. She acted like a crazy person. In addition to that, she had fits of anger and frustration. She beat her fists on the window beside her bed to get my attention so I could attend to her needs. I found myself resenting her more and more as time went by.

Once, I thought I saw a glimmer of hope. I thought Mable might actually see the error of her ways. But, my hope died instantly.

Mable called me to her bedside and said, "Dottie, you are the only one who has ever taken care of me."

I was speechless. I thought this might be her way of thanking me for all I had done for her. She was showing me appreciation? In the past, Mable had never given me a good word.

Then, out of the blue, Mable hit me so hard with her forearm that it threw me across the room! I fell to the floor in pain. Mable had caught me off guard. I didn't know where she got the strength to hit me. I laid there in a daze.

I thought, *"Boy, I was wrong to think this woman had any heart at all."*

I lifted myself off the floor. I moved away from Mable and didn't come close to again after that day.

Soon after that episode, Mable's jaws locked. She could no longer open her mouth to eat or speak. I have to admit, I felt a certain amount of peace knowing that she couldn't yell at me anymore. Now, it was necessary for me to squeeze a straw between Mable's teeth to give her a sip of water. I sensed that the end of her life was near at hand. I was right. Right after her jaws locked, she was taken to the hospital where she died that same week.

Chapter Six
UNKNOWN TERRITORY

When Mable went to the hospital to die, I was elated. I felt like I had been let out of prison! This was the first time that I felt really good for a long time, if ever. A weight was lifted off my shoulders. And, I felt like I could walk on air. I was truly happy. Unfortunately, this wonderful feeling lasted only a short while.

The day Mable passed away, my dad sent me to stay overnight at Grandma Lee's house. I felt comfortable staying with her. I liked her very much. She had always treated me well. Thank God, she was nothing like her daughter Mable.

The next day, my dad took me to stay with some people I barely knew. He told me I was going to stay with them for a short time. Their last name was Newberry. They were Dickey's wife's parents. They were very kind religious people, and I liked that. I attended a church with them in Champaign, Illinois. It was a Pentecostal Church. The choir sang beautifully. Their voices echoed throughout the church. The music lifted my spirit all the way to heaven. Mr. and Mrs. Newberry told me this church was what they called a Malatya church. I wasn't sure what that meant, so they explained it to me. They told me that many of the people in this church were half black and half white in color. That was fine with me. I enjoyed worshipping there with them.

I felt safe with the Newberry's. They seemed to like me pretty well. They said they wanted to continue to keep me, but my dad said that wasn't possible. He had already made a decision to sign all of his kids away. However, I didn't know that fact, yet. I only knew that I wasn't allowed to stay with these nice people.

Mable's funeral was quickly arranged. I was not allowed to attend. I didn't mind that, I was glad she was gone out of my life. However, even though I knew she was gone, I still had a deep seated fear of her. That fear manifested itself into nightmares which continued for years to come. I had the same nightmare over and over.

I dreamed that Mable was in a casket on a large cliff. She rose up out of the casket and came running after me. I ran as fast as I could to get away from her grasp. I knew beyond a doubt she meant to harm me in some way. She tried to grab me. So, I ran faster. I was afraid she would catch me. I thought she would kill me! I suddenly woke up screaming so loud that I woke up everyone in the house. In my heart, I thought that Mable was so evil that she could come back from the dead and hurt me, or worse, kill me! I thought she was the devil. And, I was still deathly afraid of her.

In addition to the nightmares, I didn't know what would happen to me next. In the past, my dad gave me to whoever would take care of me. Consequently, I was apprehensive about my future. I sensed that my life was going to change in a big way. I had learned over time to trust my gut instincts. They were usually right. I was headed into unknown territory.

Within days after the funeral, my dad went to the courthouse and signed the papers to give all of his kids away. He didn't want us. The only kids still left at home was me, Ray Jr., Fiona, Beth Ann, and Chick. My dad had gotten Chick out of the home in Lincoln a few months ago. Chick had only lived with us a short while.

All of us kids had to attend a court hearing. The court was making the decisions on where we would all be placed. The judge addressed us a group. He told all of us that we could not all stay together; there were too many kids for one household to take in. It saddened us all to know our family was splitting up.

We were all split up and sent into different directions, except Chick and me. It all happened so fast. I didn't have time to think about my future. Ray Jr. was sent to a children's home in Assumption, Illinois, called Kemmerer Village. He was later adopted out. Fiona was sent to

Champaign, Illinois. She was adopted out, too. Beth Ann went to live with her sister Kathleen. Chick and I were left for last. The court didn't know what to do with us. We were the oldest children. In the end, they decided to make Chick and I wards of the court. That meant that the court had the power to make decisions concerning our welfare.

Chick was mentally challenged. He was eighteen years old. He was now able take care of himself. However, there were times that he needed some help. Instead of sending Chick to a special home where he could be taken care of properly, the court sent him to live at a nursing home in Springfield, Illinois. It was called Mrs. Bards Nursing Home. It was located on South Grand Avenue West. The nursing home looked like a large house that sat back a distance from the road. Chick was given permission from the court to live at the nursing home and work for his keep as best he could.

I was fifteen years old, too old to be adopted out, and too young to be on my own. So, I was also sent to Mrs. Bards Nursing Home. This particular nursing home often took in wayward girls that were wards of the court. The nursing home was now responsible for my care. They gave me a room that I shared with a girl who was close to my own age. Her name was Maggie. Maggie and I both worked for out keep. We did whatever was asked of us. At times, the worked seemed like it was just too much.

I had several problems at Mrs. Bards Nursing Home, and going to school was one of them. I was almost sixteen years old. I had only completed a fourth grade education. During the time I was allowed to go to school, I had missed so many days that I couldn't comprehend what was going on in any subject. I was never able to keep up with the rest of the class. The school the nursing home sent me to only taught fifth and sixth graders. They were all lumped together in one classroom. Without a doubt, I was scholastically behind everyone else in the class. I couldn't understand any of my lessons. I tried to study harder, but I couldn't catch up. I felt hopelessly lost.

All of my subjects were beyond my scope of understanding, and mathematics was my worst subject. I didn't understand numbers at all. The multiplication and division problems totally stumped me. I had never seen anything like this before. I began to get very stressed out until

I was near a nervous breakdown. I was scared. When the teacher asked me to go to the board and write out a math problem, I panicked!

My teacher called on me to go to the front of the classroom and work a math problem on the blackboard. I didn't have the vaguest clue where to begin. So, I told the teacher I didn't know how to do this problem. The teacher became very angry with me. She insisted I try. I resisted, I knew I couldn't do the problem. I was almost in tears by now.

"I don't know how to do this problem!" I cried. I didn't know how else to get this point across to her. I had no idea where to begin

"Yes, you do know how to do this. You get up here and get it done!" the teacher yelled.

I was almost hysterical by now. I started to cry in front of everyone. I was embarrassed. I felt helpless, and I was angry with my teacher for not showing me more compassion for my ignorance.

"I don't know how!" I yelled back at the teacher.

The teacher responded by sending me directly to the principal's office.

When I arrived at the office, the principal proceeded to have a talk with me. Obviously, the teacher had told him about my lack of progress.

"Dottie, you are so far behind that it is not right for you to be here at school," he said. "Your birthday is tomorrow, and you will be sixteen years old. You have missed so much school that you can never catch up with the rest of your class." Then, he sympathized with me. "The class work is too hard for you. You just don't understand what is going on here," he stated as fact.

I knew he was right. But, it felt like he was calling me stupid. I felt stupid. I couldn't help the fact that I had so little education. It wasn't my fault. It hurt me to think I was of no use here.

The principal confirmed my thoughts as he continued to say, "I think it is best for you to quit school." He waited for my response.

A chilling thought hit me as I registered the principal's words. *Now what will I do? And, where would I be sent to this time?*

Right after the decision was made for me to quit school, I met Mrs. Piddle. I liked her right away. She was a motherly kind of woman. He voice was very soft spoken. Her body was a bit large in size. However,

I thought she was good looking. Mrs. Piddle told me she worked at the courthouse in Taylorville. The State of Illinois paid her to be a truant officer. She was the person who went out and picked up delinquent children when they skipped school. After picking them up, she placed them in either foster homes or work environments. She explained that it was her job to regularly check on these children to insure they were properly taken care of. She told me I was one of the children she was assigned to look after. I was now in her care. If I needed anything, I was to come to her. She explained, again, that I was a ward of the court, and she was my caretaker. But for now, I was to stay at the nursing home. I listened carefully as she explained her position, then it was my turn to talk.

"I am not happy in this nursing home," I told Mrs. Piddle. "I am not getting paid anything for the work I do. I want a job where I can make money so I can start my own bank account." I continued to say, "If this can't happen, then, I will settle for being placed in a foster home. I just want out of this place! "

Mrs. Piddle listened as I spoke. Then she finally said, "I will try to find you a place to live." I believed her and was satisfied with her answer.

I waited and waited for a call that told me I had a new home. It didn't come. Nothing changed. I was getting more and more depressed. All I ever did was work and sleep. Many times, I didn't get much sleep.

I was still having the same nightmares about Mable chasing me. I always woke up screaming. I wandered if I would ever get past my fear of her. Between the work and the nightmares, I was constantly tired.

My jobs here at the nursing home were many. I scrubbed floor, changed bed linens, cleaned, and helped take care of the elderly. In addition to that, I worked in the kitchen. The cook allowed me to help her cook. Then, I set the tables with place settings for all the meals. The fact that I didn't get paid for all this work ate at me. I felt like I was being used. Work, work, work, that is all I ever did!

One night, I was awakened in the middle of the night to go take care of a patient who had fallen out of his bed. He passed away as he fell to the floor. It was my job to prepare him for the ambulance before it came to take him to the mortuary. The nurses had taught me how to tend to the deceased. First, I cleaned him up by bathing him. Then, I closed the deceased eyed and put quarters on his eyelids to hold them shut. Otherwise, his eyes would have popped open. At last, I called the ambulance to come and get him. Usually, I was mentally and physically exhausted after doing this job. I was called upon to do these tasks often. Many times, it would be after midnight before I was able get back to bed and get some sleep. By morning, I was still physically tired. I always got up early the next day to start my chores all over again. I rose early and helped with breakfast and set the tables for the patients.

My patience was wearing thin. I needed more than this. The only entertainment I enjoyed was going to church on Sunday and a movie twice a year. After a year of living this lifestyle, I realized this just didn't seem right to me. I felt used. I was old enough to be getting paid for this type of work. But, no money came my way. Frustration gripped me like a vise. Then, I found out the nursing home was getting paid to keep me. It made me furious to think about it! They were getting paid twice. They got money from the State and a slave to do their dirty work. I resented it all. I worked hard, and I was worth more than I was getting. I was miserable. And, I knew there had to be more to life than this.

Another problem ate at me, too. I was so gullible the nurses made fun of me. It hurt my feelings. I didn't trust that I was being told the truth. On one such occasion, the nurse sent me downstairs to the basement to get a closet stretcher. I looked and looked, but I couldn't find it. I went back upstairs.

"I can't find it," I told the nurse. "I don't know what I am looking for."

Everyone started laughing at me. They were making fun of my stupidity! I was the brunt of their jokes. I learned two things from this experience. First, never trust anyone. And, from now on, I had to be shown the truth.

It seemed I couldn't trust anyone, even my half-sister Claire. Claire called me at the nursing home to see how I was doing. I told her I was absolutely miserable, and I wanted to get out of here as soon as I could. Claire tried to calm me down by making promises.

"I am going to get you out of there one of these days," she promised. "As soon as I get things straightened out, I am going to come and take you out of there."

I knew she meant well. I hoped she would do as she promised. But, she never showed up to get me. Again, I waited and waited.

I worked hard during this time. One night I was up most of the night with a patient. I was really tired. My attitude was getting worse and worse. I was still angry about working for nothing! I didn't get much sleep that night at all. The next morning, I got up early and did my chores like I did every day. I set the tables and helped with breakfast. When breakfast was ready, I went to my room and told Maggie it was time to eat. I had made a decision sometime during the long night's work, but I kept it to myself. I decided I was going to leave here.

Chapter Seven
THE WALK THAT CHANGED MY LIFE

I made a decision sometime during the long night. I was going to walk out the door of the nursing home in the morning and keep on going. When morning came, I put on my new black patented leather shoes I had gotten only a week ago. I was ready to walk. I wanted to be free. I surmised that no one appreciated me in this place. They didn't deserve to have me here. I wasn't sure exactly where I was going or what I would do. I only knew the time had come for me to go.

I figured I would walk to Taylorville first. Then, maybe I would go to Aunt Lou's house. I didn't know how far Aunt Lou's house was from Springfield or how long it would take me to get there. I didn't care. I was free at last!

As I walked out of the nursing home, I decided to walk down the railroad tracks for a while. I guessed these tracks would take me to a main road that would lead to Taylorville. I started walking on the tracks and walked, and walked, and walked. After a long time, I started to get thirsty. I thought there must be a farmhouse close by where I could get a drink of water. Sure enough, I spotted one. A woman was outside the house. She had a lot of kids. She offered me some water as I approached her. I thanked her and continued on my quest down the railroad tracks.

Eventually, I came to a main road that looked like a highway. I kept thinking this must be the way to Taylorville. As I walked down the highway, I came to what looked like an Army post. The post had a gate and a small structure that looked like a little house. A man dressed in an

Army uniform was inside the little house. I decided to ask him for directions to Taylorville.

"Is this the way to Taylorville?" I asked the man inside the structure.

"No, this is Route 66," he said. "You are headed towards St. Louis, Missouri."

I couldn't believe I had walked so far out of the way. I was going the wrong direction. I had to think of something fast.

"Oh! No! It can't be! I told him. "I am trying to get to Taylorville."

I knew I couldn't tell this man the truth. I couldn't tell him I ran away. I was afraid he would take me back to the nursing home. That was the last thing I would want to happen.

"My mother is sick, and I have to get to Taylorville to see her," I said. I hoped this man would feel sorry for me and offer his help.

Luckily, my ploy got results. The man told me to get his Jeep, and he would take me to the main road that leads to Taylorville. Yeah! This was a success. I didn't hesitate to accept his offer. I hopped in to the Jeep. We traveled until we came to a crossroad. The man let me out of the Jeep, and wished me well. He told me to follow the road, and it would take me where I wanted to go.

My successful attitude didn't last very long. I didn't realize Taylorville was still so far away. I kept walking. I started getting really tired and hungry. It was so hot the sweat was running down my face. My clothes were sticking to me. I felt dirty and grimy from the dirt that blew on me when the wind picked up. I had walked all day. The sun was getting low in the sky. Most of the day was gone. I was so tired, by now; I could barely keep my eyes open.

A car approached me and stopped. A middle-aged man was driving the car.

"Do you want a ride?" he asked.

"Yes, I need a ride to Taylorville," I said. I gladly accepted the offer, opened the car door, and sat down on the passenger side of the car. I sat there only an instant and quickly fell asleep. The next thing I remember: the man was shaking my shoulder and telling me that I was at the Taylorville intersection. He told me that he would be on his way. I thanked him for the ride and told him how much I appreciated it. I felt like he had been my angel when I needed a rest.

I walked down the main road until I came to the downtown area. I entered the courthouse to use the bathroom. My feet were burning like they were on fire. I could hardly walk another step. I took my shoes off and washed my feet in the restroom sink. My feet were bleeding. My new shoes had worn blisters all over my feet. I was in a lot of pain. I knew I couldn't walk anymore. I felt defeated. I slowly eased my new shoes back on my swollen feet and decided to find someone who could help me.

I knew Mrs. Piddle had told me once that she worked in the courthouse. So, I went in search of her. I saw a lady sitting at a deck.

"Where can I find Mrs. Piddle?" I asked the woman.

"She is out of the building," the lady replied. "She has already gone home for the day."

I figured it probably wouldn't have mattered anyway. At an earlier time, Mrs. Piddle had promised to find me a new place to live, and it never happened. I didn't suppose I could depend on her anyway. Consequently, I left the courthouse.

My dad only lived a few blocks from here, so I wouldn't have to walk very far. I decided to go and visit him. When I arrived at my dad's apartment, I knocked on the door. My dad opened the door. He was clearly shocked to see me.

"Dottie, don't you know the police are looking for you?" my dad warned me.

"I don't know why they didn't find me," I told him. "I was walking on the highway. I was in plain sight." I acted like I had not done anything wrong.

I sat down in the living room. I was too tired to get excited about anything. Very shortly, Mrs. Piddle showed up. Someone must have called her.

"Dottie, you cannot stay at your dad's house," she explained. "Your dad is living with a woman that he is not married to. It isn't proper, so I cannot allow you to stay here." Mrs. Piddle took me to my Aunt Goodie's house. Aunt Goodie lived only a few blocks away from my dad.

Mrs. Piddle was in a quandary about where to place me. She made sure I understood that I was only going to be at Aunt Goodie's house one night. The next morning, she would come and pick me up. Also, she assured me that I must go back to the nursing home. No way, did I want to go back there. But for now, I kept quiet. I knew I was in trouble. I was too tired to argue with her. I needed to rest and take care of my swollen feet. I didn't want to think about what would happen tomorrow. Right now, I had enough to deal with.

My feet were a mess! I had blisters on top of blisters. I was mad at myself, because I should have known better. I realized what a stupid idea it was wear a brand new pair of shoes and attempt to walk so many miles. Those countless miles had taken its toll on me. My feet were swollen and still bleeding. Aunt Goodie bathed them in warm water. Then, she gave me a soft pair of house slippers to comfort my aching feet. After that, she fed me and put me to bed for a good's night rest. My head no sooner hit the pillow; I was sound asleep. The next morning I would have to contend with my fate.

Mrs. Piddle came bright and early to collect me. She was in a real dilemma about where to place me. Her only course of action was to take me to the courthouse, have me appear before the judge, and let him make the final decision about my future. I didn't like this idea. I knew my livelihood was in the balance. Also, I knew had no choice but to go with her. I was so scared when I walked into the courtroom.

The judge said several things that scared me even more. First, he berated me for running away. Then, he threatened me. He explained about a place called Geneva. Geneva was a prison for girls who had done wrong. He said I was going to be sent me there. I figured a prison must be a bad place to go to, however; I didn't really understand what I had done that was so wrong. In my mind, I had walked out of a situation that was very unfair to me.

"Why do I have to go to a prison?" I asked the judge. "I didn't do anything wrong."

The judge shook his head and said, "Dottie, you disobeyed the law. Now you must pay for your crime. I am sending you to Geneva."

The impact of what the judge said hit me like a ton of bricks. He said I was going to prison. Now, I was even more scared than I was before. Just when I was about to panic; fate was with me....

The Sherriff of Taylorville was in the courtroom listening as the judge spoke to me. The Sheriff's name was Elmo McGill. Mr. Mc Gill spoke up and told the judge that I could come and stay at his home. He and his wife needed someone to help in their home. They had an extra bedroom where I could sleep. Also, he told the judge he would pay me twenty-five dollars a month for my services. I was thrilled to hear this. I was thinking, twenty-five dollars a month and my own bedroom. This was truly a dream come true! I really didn't mind any work. I was used to that. I was ready for this opportunity. Thank God, the judge agreed to allow me to accept this offer. I was going to live at the Mc Gills.

I moved in with the McGill's and started doing various jobs for them. I cleaned their house, did their laundry, and I cooked their food. Another responsibility I had was answering the phone and taking messages and phone numbers from the people who called the Sherriff. I had a slight problem with that. I couldn't write very well. I didn't know how to spell the words to create the message that was being left for the Sherriff. I couldn't spell the words correctly. However, I didn't give up. Somehow, I did manage to relay some of the messages to Mr. and Mrs. McGill. They worked with me and helped me along the way. I so happy they cared enough to help me. I liked living with them although we had a different kind of living arrangement.

The McGill's lived in a house that was split into two levels. They actually lived in the lower level. The upper level was the county jailhouse. When I prepared meals for the McGill's; I also prepared the meals for the inmates that were incarcerated. The kitchen had a dumb waiter type elevator in the kitchen. I used it to send food upstairs to the prisoners. I was pretty content to do this work. In turn, I was given a little personal freedom.

I was allowed to go to a local band concert on the weekend. The concert was held in the downtown area. I really enjoyed this entertainment. But, little did I know, I was being watched every moment. The Sheriff made sure I was doing exactly what I said I was doing. He and his fellow police officers kept tabs on me. I found this out quite by accident.

One day, I was dusting an end table in the McGills's living room. I lifted the scarf to dust underneath it. I wanted to do a good job. Under the scarf was a piece of paper. On the paper it stated exactly where I was standing when I was at the band concert. That was when I realized for sure I was being watched. It didn't really bother me too much, because I knew I had nothing to hide. I knew for certain I wasn't doing anything wrong. I was just enjoying doing something that was fun for me. I didn't mind the cooking, cleaning, and laundry. But, I felt it was only fair that I have something I enjoyed.

I was doing such a good job that my workload spread to the McGill's oldest son's house. Their son was married, and his wife had just had their first child. Mrs. McGill asked me to go and do some of her grandchild's laundry. The washing machine was in the basement of the house. The new mother was not able to tackle the stairs so soon after having the baby. I was happy to do this for them. They were very kind people.

One day as I was folding clothes in the basement, I was called upstairs to come and drink a 7Up. I went upstairs and readily drank it down. After drinking the 7Up, I headed back downstairs to finish the laundry. As I worked my way down the stairs, I tripped. I tumbled head-first down the stairs. I held my arm straight out to brace myself. A large concrete pillar made contact with my arm as I fell. I screamed out in pain! I was immediately taken to the doctor that lived down the street from the jailhouse. He did an ex-ray of my arm and determined that it was broken in two separate places. One break was at the elbow, and the other break was higher on my arm. The arm had started to swell within minutes. So, I had to wait until morning to have a cast put on it. In the meantime, I was given pain medication and sent back to the McGill's house to rest. When morning came, I was taken back to the doctor's office. He then, put a cast on my arm.

After the cast was set, I returned to the McGill's house. I tried to do my chores. My arm was still in a lot of pain, but I ignored that. I had a job to do. I started by washing the dishes with my one good hand. As I was rinsing the dishes, Mrs. McGill came into the kitchen. She seemed to be discussed with me.

"Go to your room and read comic books," she demanded. "You can't do anything with one arm. You are useless!"

"Now, they don't want me," I said in a low voice that no one could here. I felt useless. I hung my head down as I walked back to my bedroom. The longer I was there, the madder I got. I could have washed those dishes. She didn't even give me a chance to try! I could have done something with one hand. I brooded about this all night long. Between the thoughts of feeling useless and the pain in my arm; I didn't get much sleep. I kept asking myself, "What am I going to do now?" Like before, I knew it was time to take action.

The next morning, I got dressed and approached Mrs. McGill. I wanted to tell her about a decision I made during the night. I held my head up high and proceeded to tell her my plan.

"I can't help you in the kitchen, so I am going to find myself a job!" I proudly said.

My pride had been hurt. I was determined to work. I felt like Mrs. McGill didn't deserve to have me here working for her. Now that I was in capacitated, she didn't have a use for me. I just wasn't going to allow anyone to make me feel useless! I left and went to St. Vincent's Hospital.

I knew most of the nuns at the hospital. I thought they might be able to help me. The nuns knew me quite well. We became friends during my six months stay at the hospital when I was burned so badly. I no sooner entered the hospital when I seen a familiar face. It was one of the nuns. I walked over to address her.

"I need help," I told her. "Also, I need a place to work and a place to live." I explained to the nun that Mrs. Piddle was my guardian.

Of course, the nun went directly to the phone and called Mrs. Piddle. I knew her call was necessary. I wanted to do this the right way. After the nun had a short conversation with Mrs. Piddle, she told the outcome. Everyone was in agreement. Mrs. Piddle agreed to allow me to live with the nuns. What's more, I was going to get a job at the hospital. I was overjoyed! There was no one that I felt more comfortable with than the nuns here in this hospital! Things were really looking up for me. I thanked God for this wonderful turn of events.

The sister's at Saint Vincent's Hospital knew me well. During the six months I was in this hospital, I had gotten to know many of them. They were my closest friends. Also, they were the only people I could turn to in a time of need. They had all shown me such great kindness. I trusted them, because they had an incredibly strong faith in God. Therefore, I knew the nuns would always do right by me.

The home the sisters put me in looked like a big house. It was located behind the hospital. The sisters lived in the lower level of the house. The upper level was like a dormitory that had several beds in it. Also, there were two separate bedrooms that had only one bed in each room. I was given a room with one bed. I had this bedroom all to myself. I was elated to have my own space! But most of all, I felt like the luckiest person in the world, because I was living in the same house as the sisters. They were like my family.

The sisters woke me up early every Sunday to go to the six o'clock mass. The church was only a short distance from the hospital, so we all walked to the church together. The church and the services were a solace to me. I thanked God every minute for this golden opportunity I was given. One of the sisters gave me a small round scarf to place on the top of my head like a hat. It looked like a doily that someone had crocheted. The sister explained that it was a matter of respect to wear this head cover when I entered the church. The nuns taught me well. I cherished this experience.

For the first time in my life, I had a paying job. Although my arm was broken, the hospital staff assigned me different tasks to do. My first task was to place paper placemats in each food tray. Later, these food trays would be passed out to the patients in the hospital rooms. The stack of trays was very big, but I managed to handle them without any problems. It was a snap. After I finished this job, I wandered into the kitchen to see what the kitchen staff was doing. My need to help was always present. No one had to tell me what to do. I just did anything that needed to be done. I noticed there were dishes by the sink that needed to be placed in the cupboards. I slid them up on my casted arm and put them in their proper place. I could only handle a few at a time, so it took me a while to complete this job. I felt good being useful again. My determination paid off. I was now earning a paycheck. This gave me a sense of accomplishment and pride in myself. After my arm healed and the cast was removed, I was given a different set of duties.

One of my duties was to scrub the floors. I did this with a zest that no one expected. I truly enjoyed the work. As I was scrubbing the floors on my hands and knees, I sang at the top of my voice. I didn't realize I was so loud, until one of the sisters had a talk with me. She discreetly pulled me over to one side of the room.

"Dottie, this is a hospital," she reminded me. "You must be a little quieter for the sake of the patients."

I laughed at myself, but I obeyed the sister. I just felt so good inside that I needed to rejoice. These were the best moments of my life!

My job at the hospital was to work. I loved it! In the mornings, I passed out ice water to the patients. This gave me a chance to socialize with each one of them. I always asked them if there was anything else I could do for them. I was happy to be of help. My other job was working in the kitchen. I helped prepare meals and do various cleaning jobs. The kitchen staff members laughed and joked with me while we worked.

After working at the hospital a year, I turned seventeen years old. Often, I was teased about not having a boyfriend. I resisted this idea completely. I was still a ward of the court until I turned eighteen. I didn't even have the slightest notion to date anyone. The girls in the kitchen teased me about hooking me up with someone.

"No! Way! I don't want a boyfriend," I told them. I was very content to work and live the life I was now leading. I had a sense of freedom that I had never felt before. And, I liked it.

One girl in particular, Ella May Cybil, teased me all the time.

"Dottie, as old as you are, and you don't have a beau?" she asked.

"No," I quietly said.

"I'll get you a beau," she insisted. "You can go on a date with me."

"Oh, no I won't," I always told her. Ella May was a black girl, and I didn't know what to expect from her. She was a more street smart than me. I was a little leery of her.

Another one of the girls decided to hook me up with a blind date. She told me that she would come and pick me up. I finally agreed to do this, because I got tired of being teased so much. My co-worker came and picked me up in her car. She had a date with her, and her date's friend was in the backseat. She introduced me to the guys, and I hopped into the car. Then, we all went downtown to a local bar. I ordered a 7Up to drink. I had never been in a bar before.

"Why is it so dark in here?" I asked the others.

"Silly, it is supposed to be romantic," one of the guys said. I thought to myself, *what's romantic?* I didn't want to sound stupid by saying that out loud. I was totally clueless. I didn't even realize this was a date. I just thought that we were all here together doing a group thing.

My blind date seemed like a nice guy. He was respectful. The whole evening was just OK to me. I enjoyed the evening, but I never seen my so-called date after that night. Still, in my mind, I didn't consider this a date. My new acquaintance didn't really interest me. My heart wasn't in it. I just wasn't ready to get involved with the opposite sex, yet.

I was still a naïve and a bit childlike in my own mind. My idol was Shirley Temple. I wanted to be just like her. I liked everything about her. I had poker straight hair, and Shirley's hair was wavy. I wanted to look like her. I really wanted to be her! Also, I loved cowboy and Walt Disney movies. The cost of the movie was fifteen cents, so I went as often as I could. Gene Autry was one of my favorite actors. And, of course, the movie always had a happy ending.

I also enjoyed other types of recreation. The sister's worked on different crafts, and I helped put them together. They recycled greeting cards that were thrown away at the hospital. We cut out the prettiest part of the card. Then, we placed plastic on each side of the card. After this was done, we crocheted around the outer edges. The sister's taught me how to crochet. I was very content to simply sit with them, crochet, and enjoy their company.

During the time I stayed with the sisters, other people stayed there, too. One person in particular, changed my life. Her name was Billie Sue Lowery. She encouraged me to get outside the home and socialize with kids my own age. She and I walked downtown together every evening.

We went to a local dinette for a piece of pie and a soda. The local teenagers hung out in the dinette. Eve, my old friend, was usually there when we arrived. I often talked with her while we were there.

Today, Billie came up with a new plan. She was on a mission. She wanted me to meet someone. She was always trying to find me a boyfriend. Billie had a boyfriend named James who had a brother named Nate. Billie wanted me to meet Nate. So, Billie set up a time for us to meet accidently, of course.

As we walked downtown one evening Billie stopped at the door of a local bar. Billie tried to persuade me to go into the bar. I told her I didn't want to. I didn't like bars, and I didn't think drinking alcohol was a good idea. So, Billie went inside the bar and brought the guys out to meet me. After the introductions, we all decided to walk a while and get to know each other. We ended up at the local dinette eating pie and drinking sodas. As it turned out, this was the start of my first romance.

I was immediately awed by Nate. He was a handsome devil. His hair was dark, wavy, and neatly combed. He was average height, about five foot ten inches. His physique was perfect. I likened him to a movie star. Also, he was charming. I was quite taken in by him. It didn't take much for him to sweet talk me into dating him on a regular basis. However, in the beginning, I resisted him.

I wasn't eighteen yet. I was still a ward of the court. I knew I wasn't my own boss, yet. I told Nate these facts, but it didn't stop him from pursuing me. He phoned the nun's home daily and asked to talk with me. I tried to avoid him. It didn't work. He called me anyway. Many times, I answered the phone myself and told him I wasn't home. I told him that he might see me downtown sometime. I lied because; I didn't want to disobey the laws of the court. But most of all, I was scared of the new feelings that had been aroused in me.

I was seventeen years old, and I had never had a boy-girl relationship. This whole dating thing was new to me. And, I knew I wasn't free to make any kind of commitment. I had been warned by Mrs. Piddle several times. She told me that I was not to get involved with any boys. I didn't want to get into trouble, again. However, Nate's persistence paid off. Since his phone calls were useless, he tried another approach. He came to my door step and waited for me to come home from work. That method worked.

I was walking back to the girls' home from the hospital when I seen Nate sitting on the door step. I knew he was waiting for me. He had caught on to the fact that I was fooling him on the phone. So, he decided to show up in person and wait for me until I got off work. I was really impressed that he made such an effort to see me. I figured he must really like me to be that persistent. Consequently, we started dating regularly. From that time on, Nate either picked me up in his car, or we walked downtown. I enjoyed his company and his attention. What's more, he introduced me to new experiences. I was so naïve that everything was a new experience.

However, the one experience I wasn't sure about was walking into a bar. I wasn't hip to this idea at all. I didn't think it was the right thing to do. I had never seen anyone drink an alcoholic beverage. This had never been a part of my life. Nevertheless, I went into the bar and gave into the urge to have one drink. I didn't like the taste of it. However, drinking beer gave me a new sense of freedom that I had never known before. It released my rigid thinking and allowed me to become more uninhibited. Nate and I laughed and danced to the music from the jukebox. I was really having fun. Probably, I was having a little too much fun.

Before I knew it, I was in love with Nate. He said he loved me, too. He kept asking me to marry him.

"Let's get married," He suggested. "I want to marry you," Nate was a man of few words.

I was overwhelmingly impressed. I felt so lucky that this handsome man wanted to have me for his wife. Me, I had always been a person no one ever really wanted. And now, he wanted me, and he needed me. He made me feel loved and needed for the first time in my life. He bowled me over with his charm. He made me feel worthy.

Marriage was sacred to me. I intended to be loyal to my partner until death do us part. I told myself, "*Whenever I say my marriage vows, no matter what happens, I will stick to them.*" I believed that God wanted it that way, too. I was ready to move forward with our love. I knew I loved Nate, and I wanted to marry him. So, in the end, I said, "Yes, I will marry you."

From the time my mother passed away, until I met Nate, no one had ever showed me the love that he did. No one ever put their arms around me and hugged me. No one showed me affection in a loving sort of way. Because of my upbringing, I felt that no one could ever love me. It was a learned behavioral trait. I always had with me. In addition to that, I thought I was a bother to anyone I had to live with. I believed I was in their way. Although I tried my hardest to please everyone, nothing was ever good enough. It was different now. Nate showed me kindness and affection. I never experienced this from a man. I was drawn to him like a bug to a light. He made me feel special.

Nate appeared to be a very gentle man. I liked that about him. And, his kindness extended outside of me. He was willing to help anyone in a time of need. Many times, he helped someone in trouble with no intention of getting anything in return other than thanks. I liked his generous nature.

I was quite entertained in Nate's presence. He loved music and sang along with the radio when it played a familiar song. Sometimes, he sang the song in a funny way just to entertain me. He raised and lowered his voice to make the song sound different than it was intended. He wanted to make me laugh. He had a great sense of humor. We laughed together all the time. Just being around him helped me look at the lighter side of life. This was all new to me. In the past, I rarely got a glimpse of what it was to be happy. I was enjoying this so much. However, there was a part of me that couldn't trust life in general. I was always on guard waiting for things to fall apart. So, I continued to resist getting married and taking the big step towards commitment.

Nate continued to be very persistent. He had no doubt that he wanted me. Also, he knew that he had to outsmart me to get me to marry him. Consequently, he developed a new plan. One night he picked me up for our usual date. Then he explained his new idea.

"I've booked us a room at the Blue Classic Motel," he proudly told me. "I have already paid for it!"

What could I do? He had already paid for the motel room. The thrill of the new adventure lured me in. I wanted to be with Nate. I knew beyond a doubt, I loved him and he loved me. I wanted to stay the night with him. After all, Nate assured me that we would get married the next day. Because I was still underage; Nate convinced me that this was the only way we would be able get married.

The next morning we decided to buy a wedding ring. Nate didn't have any money. So, I had to buy my own ring. I had a little money from my job at the hospital. I picked out a ring and paid ten dollars for it. Next, we needed a preacher.

Nate borrowed a car from a friend. We were going to a small town near Taylorville, find a preacher, and get married. Pana was a small town about five miles from Taylorville. No one would know us there. Nate figured he would look up a preacher and have him marry us right on the spot. We were both excited about getting married. However, neither one of us knew the first thing about getting the job done. We just knew the preacher was the starting point. We went to the first church we came across and found a preacher who was willing to marry us.

"Do you have the blood tests and marriage license?" the preacher asked.

"No, we don't have any blood tests or a license." Nate said, "How do we get them?"

The preacher explained to us that we couldn't get married without a particular blood test, and we must go to the courthouse to get a marriage license. Of course, we were disappointed. We left the church with a plan to go back to Taylorville and get the tests and the license that we needed.

We went directly to St. Vincent's Hospital. I figured this was the place to get our blood tests done in a quicker way. Now, we faced another problem. Neither of us had the money to pay for the tests once they were done. We were in a dilemma. Then, Nate told the hospital staff he would pay for the blood tests when he received his next week's check. We, obviously, were going to have to wait a week to get married. We both felt a letdown as we walked out of the hospital. But when, I looked down, I had the result of the blood tests in my hand. Because I worked at the hospital, the nurse naturally handed me the results of our blood tests. She naturally handed me the paperwork before it was paid for. I was thrilled! Here it was in my hand. Now, we were going to get married. Or so I thought.

We immediately proceeded to the courthouse to get our marriage license. The first question the man at the counter asked me was, "How old are you Dottie?"

"I am eighteen years old," I quickly said. I had to lie to him. I knew I needed to be eighteen to get married without consent.

"What day were you born?" the man asked.

"I was born October 7th."

"What year were you born?" he continued to ask.

Before I took the time to think about it, I blurted out, "I was born in 1930." The minute I said the date, I knew I had made a mistake! He just had to do the math to figure out I wasn't old enough to get married without consent.

"I think you should go and get your mother," the man told me. He obviously realized I was underage.

"I can't," I told him. "She's dead."

"Then, you better go get your dad. You cannot get married without his permission." With that statement, the man ended the conversation.

Both Nate and I knew we had no other choice but to go and find my dad. So, we left the courthouse. I prayed that my dad would agree to give us his consent and his blessings.

Luckily my dad didn't live very far from the courthouse. He lived in a rented apartment in the downtown area. As luck would have it, my dad was home when we arrived. Nate and I sat down and told him the details of our day. We also told him that we had spent the night together, so we were committed. At last, we told him that we needed him to sign the papers of consent in order for us to get a marriage license. My dad patiently listened as we explained all the details of our day.

"Well," he said. "You went this far, so I guess you can get married." After a little more discussion, my dad agreed to come with us with one stipulation. He asked that we get married in a church. We agreed. Then, we all walked back to the courthouse.

Nate was getting very impatient by this time. It had been a long day filled with setbacks. He leaned down and whispered to me, "If your dad hadn't agreed to come with us, I would have thrown him down the stairway!" I didn't want him to be mad at a time like this, so I tried to reassure him that everything was going to work out in the end. We were going to get married, today.

After signing the necessary papers and getting our Marriage License, we went to the Nazarene Church to get married. Hours had passed because of the delays, so it was evening by this time. Luckily, the pastor was having an evening get together in the church basement. The congregation was still there. Nate and I approached the preacher.

"Can you marry us right away," Nate asked.

"Yes," replied the preacher. "But, we need witnesses."

The preacher went to the basement and brought up several people to be our witnesses. My dad and his wife Eva stood by our sides as we took our final vows. Finally, after a few words from the preacher, we were married!

As we were leaving, the kids at the church, found some rice to throw at us to celebrate the occasion. It was raining outside, so the rice stuck to us. But, we didn't care. We were both happy! I was married to the man I loved, and he loved me. And, I received another blessing. I made my dad proud of me. He gave Nate enough money to pay for a motel room for our honeymoon. Our first night of wedded bliss was ahead of us. Life was good.

Chapter Eight
NOT-SO WEDDED BLISS

The morning after our wedding, it was business as usual. I rose out of bed and went to straight to work. No sooner had I gotten there; I had a visitor. It was Mrs. Piddle, and she didn't look very happy. News travels fast.

"Dottie, I don't know what I am going to do with you! You were supposed to get my permission to get married, not your dad's. I am your guardian," Mrs. Piddle said in an angry tone.

I kept my mouth shut. I knew I was in trouble.

Then, Mrs. Piddle threatened my new husband. "Do you know that we could send Nate to prison for contributing to the delinquency of a minor?" she asked.

I knew Mrs. Piddle was right. I was afraid of what might happen when I disregarded her previous warnings. Mrs. Piddle insisted that I go to the courthouse right away. I had to appear before the judge, again. My old feelings of doom were back.

Mrs. Piddle took me to the courthouse. Nate wasn't going with me. He decided to take our marriage license to Stonington, Illinois to show his dad and mom. After all, I was the one in trouble. I had disobeyed the law, again. There were going to be consequences for my behavior.

I was scared as I stood before this new judge. The judge appeared to be a smart man. He asked me only one question.

"Have you had sex?" He bluntly asked.

I simply said, "Yes."

The judge looked at me, and then he looked at Mrs. Piddle. He addressed Mrs. Piddle.

"I think we better leave things the way they are," the judge recommended. "They are married." The judge speculated that there could be a chance I was pregnant. In the end, he made a decision. He agreed that Nate and I be allowed to live together as husband and wife. My life was turning around. I was free at last to be my own boss. I was a legal married woman in the eyes of the law.

The next day, Nate and I set out to start our new life. We didn't have much money, so all we could afford to live in was a small sleeping room. It would be OK for now. We were still high on the fact that we could legally live with each other. And, I still had my job at the hospital to rely on.

Nate was looking for a job. He was just recently released from the Navy. He had been in the Navy for four years. So, he was able to draw unemployment compensation.

We didn't need much. With Nate's unemployment and my weekly paycheck from the hospital, we were going to survive financially. But right now, we were living on love.

A month or so after we were married, I started getting sick. Every morning, I woke up with an upset stomach and vomited. Sure enough, just as the judge had speculated, I was pregnant. I really wasn't ready for this. I felt it was too soon in our marriage to have a baby. I couldn't believe I was pregnant. The doctors at the hospital in Chicago told me I would never have kids. So obviously, I was shocked to learn I was pregnant. I was going to have a baby. It happened. The morning sickness was overwhelming. I had to quit my job at the hospital. Then, I got even sicker.

I contacted a terrible bad cold. As the cold worsened, I lost my voice. Nate found a job with a local cab service. He drove a cab. Because his schedule varied, he was able to come home in the middle of the day to administer medicine for my cold. Realizing I was getting worse, he decided to make a concoction that would make me feel better. It was an age old recipe. He called it a hot toddy. Nate made the hot toddy with honey, whiskey, and lemon juice. I was so sick. I figured anything would help. I readily drank it; although it tasted terrible. After drinking it, I immediately fell back to sleep. When I woke up the next day, I thought, *He could have killed me with that concoction. And, I am pregnant. It might have hurt the baby, too.* My basic mistrust was showing up again. But, I had to admit, I felt better. After a short while, I returned to good health.

We made a decision to move to a bigger apartment to accommodate the new baby. I was due to have it at any moment. Our new place was an upstairs apartment on Adams Street. It was small, but it was bigger than our first apartment. The new apartment had one bedroom, a living room, and a kitchen. We were dirt poor because Nate didn't keep a job. We couldn't afford anything bigger at this time.

Nate had just lost another job as a mechanic. This was his usual way. He jumped from one job to another. And, he seemed to be drinking more and working less. He obviously did not want a regular job. Nate's way of making money was different. He tried to make money any way he could providing it was on his terms. He often scrounged through the neighborhoods to find junk other people had thrown away. He either put the stuff to use, or he sold it for a little money for us to get by on.

My step-grandmother, Mrs. Lee and her husband lived across the street from us. This gave me a little contentment. I always liked Mrs. Lee. I knew that she would help me if I needed her. Tonight, Nate and Mrs. Lee were looking for junk to sell to make some money for us to live on.

Suddenly, my water broke. I knew the baby was coming. Nate was gone, so I was going to walk to the hospital. I panicked! I thought *what if I don't make it to the hospital on time?* I decided to go to Mrs. Lee and ask for her help. I explained to Mrs. Lee that my water had broken. She called a cab and went with me to the hospital to have the baby. She didn't want me to be alone. The labor pains were bearing down hard by now. In a very short time; I had a baby girl! It was an easy birth. My new daughter weighed six pounds and seven ounces. After I had her, Nate showed up at the hospital. Someone had found him and let him know that I was having the baby.

When I looked at my new baby girl, I thought, *this is the most beautiful baby I have ever seen.* She had black hair and an olive complexion. She was born, February 19th, 1949. She was born exactly nine months after Nate and I got married. I wanted to name this baby after my sister Rena. So we decided on the name Mary Rena Gentry. She and I stayed in the hospital for the next three days.

Mrs. Piddle came to the hospital to see me and the baby. She brought some new clothes for Mary. One of the items was a soft fluffy snowsuit to keep Mary warm. Mrs. Piddle was a caring person. I had formed a bond with her throughout the years we had known each other. She had always been the closest thing to a mom I had ever had. I adored her. And, I felt sure that she cared for me, too.

When Nate came to the hospital to pick us up, he told me we were going to stay at his dad's house in the country. His dad lived right outside of Stonington, Illinois. Stonington was a few miles north of Taylorville. Nate's dad had a large two story house a few miles outside of town. I didn't know what happened to our apartment, and I didn't ask. Obviously, we had lost it, because we didn't pay the rent. Nate explained that Mary and I needed to stay with his dad and mom a few weeks until he found another job and a place for us to live. He was headed to Peoria, Illinois with a few other guys to look for a job in that area. He told me when he got settled into a place to live; he would come and get us. I merely accepted this chain of events. I trusted Nate to do exactly what he told me he would do. He would find us a new place to live. I had to trust him on this. I knew I wasn't able to do anything to help at this time. In the meantime, Mary and I stayed with Nate's parents.

While I stayed with Nate's folks, I did whatever I could to be productive. But most of all, I didn't want to be a bother in any way. I appreciated the fact that they allowed me and Mary to stay with them. I did everything I could to be self-sufficient. I washed our clothes out by hand and hung them on the line to dry. At night, I fixed Mary a bottle and wrapped it in a baby blanket. Then, I put it in the bed next to our bodies to keep it warm. When Mary woke up in the middle of the night, the bottle was ready for her. She didn't have to cry for it. By doing this, I didn't have to go downstairs in the middle of the night and take a chance on disturbing my in-laws. I knew I was lucky that Mary was such a good baby. As long as I met her basic needs, she didn't cry at all. I loved her so much, and so did Mrs. Gentry.

Mrs. Gentry made me feel welcome in her home. During the two weeks I stayed with her, she made little dresses for Mary. She loved her granddaughter. Mr. Gentry was a kind, loving, generous lady. Many times, I shared a Coke with her. Coke was favorite drink. She always kept it on hand. We sat in the kitchen and drank our Coke's while we talked endlessly.

In Mrs. Gentry's home, it was customary to allow her husband to eat before anyone else did. She fixed the meal, and then, she waited in the living room until Mr. Gentry was finished eating. When Mr. Gentry finished his meal, we girls went into the kitchen and ate our meal. It seemed a bit strange to me that we never ate together. I didn't question it. I just accepted this was their routine.

Mr. and Mrs. Gentry rarely spoke to each other. It was like they lived in two different worlds, yet, in the same house. This gave me an uneasy feeling. However, Mr. Gentry spoke to me a little. He asked me how I and Mary were doing in casual conversation. I usually said we were doing well, and that was the end of the conversation. I figured he must be a really quiet man. And, I realized part of my discomfort was coming from the fact that I was living with people I barely knew.

After two weeks, Nate came and picked Mary and I up and took us to our new home. He told me he wasn't able to find a job in Peoria. However, he did manage to find a job in Taylorville. Our new home was no more than a shanty in the back of a house owned by an old lady called Mrs. Dexter. We lived in the back part of the house, and Mrs. Dexter lived in the front of the house. Our living space was very small, but we made do with what we had. I often sat Mary in a baby carrier on the kitchen table so she could watch me work. I enjoyed my new baby. I was oblivious to anything else.

Mrs. Dexter showed her mean side right away. One day I went to the front porch to swing Mary. As we rocked back and forth, Mary cooed and smiled as we enjoyed the moment. However, Mrs. Dexter put a damper on our fun. She came out of the house in a huff.

"Your baby looks like she is black," she commented. "I don't want you to sit outside on my porch with her!"

Mrs. Dexter hurt my feelings, but I kept my feeling to myself. She had no idea that Mary's complexion was due to a strong Cherokee Indian blood line. I didn't want to cause any problems. I complied with Mrs. Dexter's wishes, and I stayed inside the house. I wasn't happy. I didn't like living next to that old bat Mrs. Dexter!

A few months later, I found it necessary to get a job. I was lucky to find a job right away. I worked as a cleaning lady at a local hotel. I didn't have a babysitter, so Nate decided he would stay home and take care of Mary while I worked. It didn't seem quite right to me, but I knew we needed money to pay our rent.

My first paycheck was used to pay the rent. I gave the money to Nate. Instead of paying the rent, Nate used the money to go on one of his drinking sprees. He borrowed a car from a friend and went out drinking with one of his buddies. I wasn't sure where Nate went or what he was doing. He stayed out all night long. I was awake most of the night wandering and worrying about what Nate was up to. I was steaming mad by the time the sun came up.

The next morning, I went to work at the hotel. I had no babysitter, so I took Mary with me. I put her in the baby buggy and kept her near me while I cleaned the hotel. Nate's friend Karl came to the hotel and told me that Nate was in jail. And, Nate wanted me to come to the jail to see him. I stopped everything and ran to the jail. Nate informed me that he was being sent to a minimum security prison for six months. His crime, as he told it, was drunk driving. I was thoroughly disgusted with him. He lied to me, not once, but several times! He wanted me to believe that he had been out looking for a job. Job hunting was Nate's usual excuse when he wanted to go out drinking. Furthermore, Nate spent all of our rent money. What was I going to do?

Nate was facing a prison term. The truth always prevails in the end. I learned that Nate had been out drinking and driving. He foolishly ran a truck off the road. The incident was reported to the police. So, the police picked Nate up and hauled him off to jail. In addition to that, Nate had a fourteen year old girl in the car with him when the police picked him up. Of course, when I confronted him with this bit of information, he lied to me. He told me the girl was with his buddy Karl. Karl told the girl was Nate's girlfriend. Obviously, the latter was true. Nate was the one sent to a penal farm in Vandalia, and Karl got off scot free. Nate was convicted on several counts. Drunk driving, vehicular endangerment, and contributing to the delinquency of a minor were the charges filed against him. His sentence was no less than six months. I was so upset. All of this happened so fast that I couldn't think straight. I didn't know what to do next?

Just when I felt my life couldn't get any worse, it did. After the trial, I returned home to our little shanty. Mrs. Dexter had locked me out. She had boarded up my door and nailed it shut. I couldn't get in to my house. I walked around to the front of the house and knocked on Mrs. Dexter's door.

"Why is my door nailed shut?" I asked.

"You are not getting back in until you pay the rent," she said. Then she slammed the door in my face.

I was at a loss. I didn't know what to do. I didn't have any money to pay the rent. Nate had spent my whole paycheck. I didn't realize that our rent wasn't paid until now.

Mrs. Dexter would not let me in my house to get mine or Mary's clothes, diapers, and bottles. I was beside myself. I didn't know where we were going to sleep. And, I didn't know anyone who could help me. My mind was a blank. I needed time to think. I took off walking with Mary in the baby buggy. I headed for the downtown area in a daze.

Chapter Nine
LIFE IN A QUANDARY

I headed downtown pushing Mary in the buggy. I had to think. I knew walking would help me think more clearly. I needed to figure out what I was going to do. I had no place to live and no place to sleep. I was homeless. I kept walking until I came to the downtown area. I walked around and around the square that housed the downtown shops. Suddenly, a car approached me. I recognized the couple inside the car.

Mel and Ellen Brooks had been downtown shopping. Ellen was related to me through my dad's family. When Ellen spotted me, she stopped to talk with me.

"What are you doing Dottie?" She curiously asked.

"I am looking for a place to live." I told Ellen "I was kicked out of my house. Now, I am homeless." Then, I continued to explain, "Mrs. Dexter kicked me out, nailed the door shut, and I can't get back in." I was in tears by this time. I cried as I told Ellen the details. "I can't even get back in to get diapers and clothes for Mary!"

"What are you going to do now?" Ellen asked.

I shook my head from side to side as I said, "I don't know."

Ellen didn't hesitate, she told me, "Get in the car. Dottie, you are coming home with us." Ellen had a loving heart, and I appreciated her offer. I had no other options.

"Thank you," I told Ellen. Mary and I hopped in the car and rode home with them. Mel and Ellen's house was in Stonington. I sat quietly in the back see while we rode the five miles to their house.

All I could think of was, *God bless them*. I silently thanked God for sending them to me in my time of despair. Now, Mary and I had a place to live until I could figure out my next move. That night, we slept in Ellen and Mel's living room.

Ellen explained to me that I would have to go to the ADC and ask for financial help. The ADC stood for Aid for Dependent Children. It was an organization that was set up to help people who had children in need. This information was all new to me. I didn't know such a place existed. I decided to go the very next day. I didn't want to wear out my welcome with Mel and Ellen. They had been a life saver to me. Ellen gave me milk and diapers for Mary to tied us over until I could get our belongings from my house.

Ellen took me to the ADC the next day. After talking to a case worker for a while, she explained that it would take a little while before I could get any money. She told me I could get eighty dollars a month. This would be enough money to take care of my rent and buy some food. In the meantime, she gave me a food order to help us until I started getting my checks. I would have to stay with Mel and Ellen a short while longer. It was such a relief to know I could pay for a roof over our heads and put food on our table.

I started looking for a new place to live. There was no way I wanted to deal with mean old Mrs. Dexter as a landlord. Luckily, I found us a place on Ester Street. It belonged to a woman I called Granny. Granny was a nice old lady who chewed Kentucky Twist tobacco. Granny owned a small house that she basically cut in half. I rented the half that had a bedroom, a very small kitchen, and a toilet stool. I had to make this work. It wasn't much, but the rent was cheap.

I tried to go back to work at the hotel, but they told me they would have to let me go. I was fired. The manager didn't want me to bring my baby to work with me. He didn't want the liability. Also, I had an inkling that I might be pregnant again. I figured I was about three months along in the pregnancy. The hotel didn't want that liability either. So, I was out of a job. My ADC checks were barely enough to pay my bills. But, I had to make it on that small amount until Nate got out of the penal farm.

I felt compelled to go see Nate. I hated to admit it, but I missed him. I wanted to see him. But first, I had to get a babysitter for Mary. My dad and his wife lived across the street from me. I didn't like my dad's wife Eva. She was the kind of woman who talked nice to your face, but she talked bad about you behind your back. I hated to ask them to watch Mary, but I had to. I had no other choices. It hurt my pride to ask anyone for anything. In spite of this, I asked them to babysit every week so I could go and see Nate. It took a while to get to Vandalia on the bus. I felt obligated to visit Nate. I was his wife. It was my duty. I knew that financially this weekly trip would drain me of what little money I had. But, I needed to see my husband.

Nate needed to see me, too. He needed money for cigarettes and candy bars. He explained that he needed these two luxuries in order to survive the hell hole he was in. I felt sorry for him. So, I gave him the money even though I had very little to give. After a short visit, I took a cab back to the bus station to ride the bus back home.

I never had enough money, not ever. It seemed to go as fast. Nate didn't seem to understand the hardship I was experiencing. He expected me to come every week no matter what. It did occur to me several times that I shouldn't make the weekly trip. However, I didn't want to disappoint Nate. I was all he had to look forward to. He begged and pleaded with me to come every weekend.

Many times, I got really angry at Nate for the mess he had gotten himself and his family into. However, I got over it when he sweet talked me into seeing things his way. I let go of the anger, because he loved me. I understood Nate better than anyone. I knew he had a rough childhood. I could relate to that. I understood his feelings as if they were my own. I guess I cut him some slack because I felt sorry for him. Nate never confided into anyone but me. I was his life. This made me feel needed.

Nate told me about his childhood. When he was a year old, his mom developed a goiter and had to have surgery. She couldn't take care of him, so she sent him to live with his Aunt Annie. Aunt Annie lived way out in the country in a two story house with a wrap-around porch. She lived a quiet simple lifestyle. Nate really loved his aunt, and he liked living with her. In turn, Aunt Annie loved him and spoiled him terribly. She had never had children of her own. Therefore, she treated Nate like he was her own child. He had all of her attention, and he liked it. Nate wanted to live with his aunt forever.

Aunt Annie taught Nate many things to prepare him for life. She taught him good manners and the proper way to behave. She taught him to be kind and helpful. And, she always made sure he was spotless in his appearance. Aunt Annie taught Nate to comb his hair having every hair in place. And, she bought him new clothes so he would look more polished.

After living with his aunt for six years, Nate was sent home. He was devastated and unhappy about this turn of events. When he came home, life was terrible for him. His four brothers teased him all the time. They laughed at him because he was neat and clean. His brothers were always dirty. They bullied him. Obviously, they were jealous of him. Nate hated their treatment of him; therefore he carried a chip on his shoulder. He held a grudge against them. This only made matters worse.

While Nate was gone, his mother became pregnant. So, Nate had a new little sister. She had been born while he was living with his aunt. Her name was June. It was now Nate's job to babysit June most of the time. He bonded with her immediately and became very close to her. Nate was a sensitive young man with a kind, loving heart. He enjoyed having his little sister around.

Since Nate was away from home most of his young life, he never developed a relationship with his dad. Nate's dad never took the time to listen to him and show him any love. He never bonded with him. Therefore, Nate had an angry attitude towards his dad. They argued all the time. Finally, at the age of seventeen, Nate went into the Navy. He spent four years in the service. He had just gotten out shortly before we met.

I understood Nate's unhappy childhood. I sympathized with him. I somehow wanted to make up for all his unhappiness by showing him how much I loved him even if I suffered myself. I went to the prison faithfully every week to see him.

Months passed this same way. I went to Vandalia every weekend. I tried to make it easier on myself, but somehow it never seemed to work out for the best. One time in particular, a guard stopped me as I was leaving the prison. I was very pregnant, by now, and I was as big as a barn. The guard realized how hard it was for me to get to Vandalia and back home every week. He lived in Taylorville, too. He asked me if I wanted a ride home. I knew this would save me some money to live on, so I agreed to ride with him. He told me it was no problem. He was going home anyway. I was happy to accept his kind offer. When we got to Taylorville, he dropped me off at my dad's house. I thanked him for the ride, and continued on his way home.

The next weekend when I came to see Nate, I told him the guard had given me a ride home. Nate was furious. He threw an angry fit. He ranted and raved for a long time.

"There is no way I want you in a car with another man." Nate yelled. "I don't want you to do that. I want you to ride the bus!"

"The man didn't want anything for the ride. And, I saved money to live on," I explained.

Nate didn't seem to be concerned about my welfare. I knew he wasn't thinking straight. I thought he was out of line with his jealousy, but as always, I obeyed him. I was only thinking about surviving from week to week. It hurt me that Nate didn't have my best interests in mind.

I was struggling to take care of Mary and myself. If it hadn't been for my good friend Joy Elliot, I would have been lost. Joy made feel like I wasn't in a struggle to make ends meet. She also helped to buy my weekly food. I didn't have a car, so Joy took Mary and I to the grocery store, bought the food, and took us back home. And, she helped me do whatever I could to survive the cold winter months. Many times, she and I walked down the alleyways of the town to find something to burn in my wood burning stove. We found coal or anything wooden that we could burn to get heat. I couldn't afford to buy coal or wood. I struggled from week to week. I was just trying to get by until Nate came home to help me.

I had no one to help me, but Joy. Nate's brother drove a taxi cab for a living. When I asked him to give me a ride home one day, he turned me down with no hesitation.

"There is no way I want the likes of you in my cab!" he said with anger. I was very pregnant and having trouble walking. That didn't seem to matter to him. He showed me no compassion. For some reason, he blamed me for Nate going to prison.

"You are the one who drove Nate to be put in prison!" he yelled. Then he drove off.

I didn't understand why they blamed me for Nate's problem. I wasn't the one who poured beer down Nate's throat and made him act stupid. This thought made me mad at Nate all over again. I tried to let go of the anger that had a grip on me. I decided to ignore the whole issue and slowly walked back home. I had been wrongly accused; I had no doubt about that. Also, I knew Nate would be home before very long. He was due to come home January 9th. This thought alone helped me to persevere.

Gil, Nate's other brother, also gave me a hard time. He came by my apartment on day. He was drunk and causing an uproar. He banged on my door and started yelling.

"I want to talk to you. You are the one who sent my brother to the State Farm," he raved. I wouldn't answer the door.

The lady who owned the apartment came out and told Gil, "Get out of here. Or, I'll call the police!" Gil left and that was the last I saw of him. I wanted all of this to be over. I held on to the hope that Nate would be home soon.

I didn't know how Nate would get home. I was not able to go to Vandalia to get him. My second child was due in a few short weeks. I had faith that Nate would find a way to get home. As it turned out, the prison gave him a one way bus ticket to Taylorville. Nate arrived home January 9th exactly as he promised.

Nate was home a few weeks when I bore our second child. I was only in labor a short time. I had a boy who weighted almost seven pounds. He was born January 26th, 1950. Nate wanted to name him Harris. I didn't really like the name, but I gave in and agreed, although I wanted to name him Nathan after his dad. So, I decided to use Nathan for his middle name. In the end, we named him Harris Nathan Gentry. When I gazed upon his face, I noted that he was wrinkled and looked like an old man. He had Nate's face. Harris came out crying and never seemed to stop.

Harris had several problems. First, he had colic. His tummy ached all the time. Therefore, he cried frequently. Also, he wasn't able to sleep for any length of time because of the pain. The only thing that seemed to help him was for me to hold him close to my body. I guessed the warmth of my body soothed him. But, when I put him down, he started crying all over again.

Another one of Harris's problems was Nate himself. Nate had no patience with this baby at all. For some reason, Nate did not want a boy. He was jealous of the time I spent taking care of this baby. Unfortunately, he took his anger out on Harris. He yelled at him all the time making Harris cry more. The crying got on Nate's nerves. He yelled at Harris compounding the problem. Harris cried harder and longer. He was tense and nervous around his dad. I felt bad for the way Nate treated his own son. Therefore, I picked him up and held him more often. I wanted him to feel safe. Of course, this only made Nate get angrier. We began to fight all the time.

I also had a physical problem associated with Harris's birth. While I was in the delivery room, I was given a type of gas. Obviously, I was allergic to some kind of material in the gas mask. My face broke out in a circular rash where the mask had come into contact with my face. The rash was painful, and my face itched like crazy. I had to go back to the doctor's office to get medicine to relieve the itching and pain.

While I was at the doctor's office, I begged Dr. Lane to fix me so I couldn't have any more kids. I had a plan to accomplish this.

"Please help me," I begged the doctor. "I read about a type of a birth control device called a gold button. I understand that it has to be inserted by a doctor. I believe it would prevent me from getting pregnant." I told him. "Can you do this for me?" I asked.

Dr. Lane shook his head and said, "No, I will not. This birth control method has been known to cause cancer."

I wasn't going to give up. I had another idea.

"Could you insert a diaphragm," I asked. I knew other women who used this method of birth control.

Dr. Lane laughed and shook his head from side to side. Then, he said, "The surest way to avoid having more kids is to run your own man away from home."

This statement made me mad! Didn't he understand how desperate I felt about not having any more kids? His answer wasn't a solution to my problem. I was discussed by his attitude. He gave me no other options to prevent further pregnancies. I didn't know what else I could do. I left Dr, Lane's office and went home in a huff. I needed to take care of my rash and my two kids.

I wanted to enjoy my family. I always wanted one, or at the most, two children. I always thought, *what is a family without children?* Because I never had the feeling of a family; I wanted to create that for myself. I made up my mind years ago. I only wanted to have no more than two kids. Now that I had a girl and a boy, my family was complete. This was my ideal of what a perfect family looked like. I was satisfied. I didn't want any more kids.

One of my worst fears was to have a lot of kids and not be able to properly raise them. I wanted to be able to financially take care of my own kids. When I thought back to when I was young, I saw what my dad had done to his kids. He gave them away, because he couldn't or wouldn't take care of them. He didn't feed them well, he never had enough room for them, and he never gave them the attention they needed. Altogether, he had five girls and five boys of his own. My dad's youngest boy was the only one who lived with him until he grew up and left home. My dad was looked down on by other people because he didn't take good care of his kids. I disrespected him for that. He didn't understand what it meant to have a family. I knew beyond a doubt, I didn't want to have a bunch of kids and not be able to raise them. This is why I diligently searched for a way to limit the amount of kids I had. However, my search for birth control was not realized. All the doctors I talked to gave me reasons why I could not use one method or another. No options were offered to me. Consequently, I kept having kids.

Mary was the bright spot in my life. She was a great baby. Most of the time, she was no trouble at all. I was happy to say, I didn't even have to potty train her. She did that job herself. This helped me out a lot. Now, I only had one baby in diapers.

Life went on and actually improved for a while. Nate got a job at the coal mine. His job was laying tracks. He was making good money. Consequently, we were able to buy the things we needed to live a better life. First, we bought a car. And, Nate was able to buy the tools he needed to work on the car if it needed repairs. The job at the coal mine was a good one, but Nate hated it. He didn't like the idea of working underground every day. I anticipated that Nate would become tired of the job and quit before very long.

I was thankful Nate worked long enough to buy us a car. It was a model A. When I was eighteen years old, I learned to drive in this car. Nate taught me how to drive. I didn't know the first thing about a car. It was all trial and error. My first lesson came when we were out late one night. It was around midnight. I got into the driver's seat and somehow managed to back the car into a ditch.

Very calmly Nate said, "You put the car in the ditch, you get it out."

I tried to get the car out of the ditch. I couldn't manage to back it onto the road. So finally, we got out of the car and manually pushed it out of the ditch. I drove off feeling relieved to be back on the road again.

I drove as much as I could to get the on the road experience. Soon, I felt pretty comfortable under the wheel. I drove for five years without a driver's license. I didn't know I needed one until Nate's sister June clued me in. She came to our house and asked to borrow our car so she could take her driver's test and get her official license. I realized right then and there that I must need a driver's license, too.

I was mad at Nate because he didn't tell me I needed one. I complained to him by saying, "You never told me that I needed a driver's license!"

He laughed and told me, "Go with June and take your test. You can get your license the same time she does."

June and I went to the Driver's Examination Building and took our tests the same day. The test was easy for me, because I had plenty of experience. I returned home with my new license in hand. I was proud of myself. Now, I could legally drive. I felt more confident now that I was within the law.

I was pretty green about most issues in life. I had not been taught very much as I grew up. And, I knew nothing about men. Nate taught me everything. The rest I learned the hard way. Experience was my best teacher. I learned the most when I did something wrong.

Nate came home from work one day and said, "I quit my job." He had had enough. Nate's brother Ben had gotten him his present job at the coal mine. Ben thought he was doing Nate a favor by putting in a good word for him. He recommended Nate for a particular position. Ben had worked at the mine all his life. When Nate quit, Ben was angry with him. Ben thought Nate was ungrateful and felt like he was too good work in a coal mine like he did. Ben was upset and viewed the whole incident as a personal insult.

Nate, on the other hand, didn't care what anyone thought. He pretty much did what he felt like doing. The fact that he had two kids and a wife to support didn't carry much weight with him. He moved us like nomads from place to place until the money ran out. And now, we were getting ready to move again.

Nate moved us back into old mean Mrs. Dexter's house, and he found another job within a week. He was hired by the railroad. Nate and his buddy Clyde worked together laying railroad ties. It was backbreaking work; so needless to say, Nate didn't work there more than a few weeks. He always wanted the easy way out, so he was always searching for something else to do. Nate and Clyde had gotten together and come up with a new plan. They decided that we needed to move up north where the jobs were more plentiful. Or so, that's what Nate had been told.

While Nate was in Vandalia, he met a friend. His name was Skip. Skip had told Nate that he could get him a job and a place to live. But first, Nate needed to move up north to Spring Valley. Because Skip was older than Nate, I thought he might know what he was talking about. It all sounded pretty good at the time. Nate told Skip he would think about his proposal.

In the meantime, Nate's mom and dad came to visit us. Harris was three months old, and they wanted to see him and the rest of the kids. They also wanted to ask us to come visit them in Stonington. We enjoyed their visit and planned to go see them in the near future. We were unaware at this time that this was going to be the last time we saw Mrs. Gentry alive.

On their way home, Mr. and Mrs. Gentry had a terrible care accident. They had a head on collision that turned out to be fatal. Mr. and Mrs. Gentry were in the front seat, and June was in the back seat. The force of the collision threw Mrs. Gentry forward in the seat. The compartment door sprung open during the crash, and it cut Mrs. Gentry all the way across her abdomen. She died instantly. Nate's dad and sister were also hurt in the accident. They were taken to the hospital and later released. When we found out what happened, we were so sad for the loss of such a lovely lady.

Right after the funeral, Nate was quite anxious. He made a decision to go to northern Illinois. He wanted to move there. He wanted a fresh start. This was going to be a new adventure. Nate's friends, Clyde and his wife, wanted to start over too, so they decided to go with us. We were all young and dumb. Nate and I started this adventure with flair. We dressed in matching shirts and blue jeans. We packed up a few clothes for the kids and ourselves, and we left in search of a new life. We were going to find a place to live, then, come back and get our furniture. We traveled about three hours before we got to Skip's parents house. Skip still lived with his parents. He was home when we arrived, but his parents were gone on a vacation. However, Skip told us we could stay there with him until we found a place of our own.

The house Skip lived in was bigger than any house I had ever seen. We were absolutely in awe of it. It was beautiful and looked like a mansion. To us, it was like lifestyles of the rich and famous. The house was equipped with a central vacuum system that pulled out from each wall in every room. It also had a laundry chute that sent dirty clothes to the basement. Skips' parents had a laundry service they used. This service sent people to the basement to collect the dirty laundry; they washed and folded it, and returned it to the house. I couldn't believe that people actually lived that way. I was totally impressed. And, we were going to stay here. We were all thrilled! So, the guys all decided to have a party to celebrate.

The party started. It was held in the back yard. We were all in a festive mood. We had homemade wine to drink. I personally didn't want everyone drinking alcohol, so I put lady bugs in the wine. I thought this would detour them for drinking it. No worries, Nate and Clyde strained the lady bugs out of the wine with a piece of cloth. Then, they kept on drinking. No one seemed to mind. I thought it was funny. I didn't tell them I had put the bugs in the wine. I kept that secret to myself. I didn't drink any of the wine. But, I was having a good time watching everyone else. We were having a party!

Soon after the night of the party, Skip set us up in an apartment near his own house. He also paid our first month's rent. It was an upstairs apartment. On the outside, it looked like a big house. The house was split up into different apartments. Two families lived downstairs. Half of the downstairs belonged to a man, his wife, and four kids. The other half belonged to the owner and his wife. They were an older couple who had a thirty five year old son living with them. This was our new residence.

We made a quick trip back to Taylorville to get our belongings. We borrowed a truck from Nate's dad to haul everything back up north. We had very little furniture, so one truckload held everything. We had a baby crib, another small bed, a pullout couch, and a kerosene stove that we used to cook on. We loaded everything in the truck, and we were on our way to set up our new life!

Chapter Ten
LIVING UP NORTH

The town we now lived in was very small. It was called Arlington. The town consisted of the house we lived in, a Post Office, and a tavern. The closest grocery store was thirty miles away in the town of Mendota. Needless to say, jobs were few and far between. The idea of finding a good job here looked rather bleak. There were none in our small berg. So, Nate had to travel to Mendota to find work.

At first, Nate found a few temporary jobs working about three days a week. He dug ditches, laid cable, and worked in a clock factory to name a few. He didn't keep a job very long. The little bit of money he made didn't go very far. Our rent never got paid. Most of our money was spent in the tavern. Nate's drinking came first.

I accused Nate of being an alcoholic. He denied it completely. And, he didn't want to discuss it any further. I wanted to help him, but he wouldn't allow it. He began to drink more and more. Therefore, he was working less and less. I rarely saw him without a beer in his hand. And of course, his mood swings became a constant problem. He began to have fits of anger. If he wasn't angry, he was high and acting like a fool. But most of the time, he stayed in his own little world oblivious to his family's needs.

In the meantime, I was making all the decisions concerning the kids. My biggest problem was feeding them. We had no money for food. We were literally starving to death. Harris cried almost non-stop because he was hungry. I couldn't afford to buy baby food. Beans and potatoes were the only food we could afford to eat. Harris's little stomach had a problem digesting these foods. I thought these foods caused him pain. That was the reason he cried so much. But, I had no other choice but to feed him what we had on hand. We had so little food in the house that it was unbelievable that we survived. I had lived with hunger before, but it was different now. My kids were starving. Of course Nate managed to bring a little food home, but it wasn't enough to last. I didn't know what to do. I thought about getting a job myself. However, that idea was squashed when I started getting sick again.

I woke up with morning sickness, and soon realized I was pregnant again. I experienced terrible morning sickness with all my kids. My new pregnancy was no different. In addition to the morning sickness, I had fainting spells. I could barely get off the couch to take care of Harris and Mary.

Emotionally, I was a wreck. I was devastated every time I thought about having another baby. I didn't want any more than two kids. I was satisfied with my family. I felt sure I could take care of these two kids if I had to do it alone. I had lived with a lot of kids all my life. I knew how hard it was to feed so many of them. I knew what it was like to go hungry. And, I didn't want my kids to face starvation. Now, here I was with two kids and one on the way. I had no way to feed them. This was one of my deepest fears. Daily, I faced it. I was getting more depressed, disappointed, and angrier as time went by.

Nate seemed to be experiencing morning sickness right along with me. Every morning Nate and I were sick when we woke up, so we decided to take a walk around the block before we attempted to eat. Then, we came back to the apartment and ate saltine crackers to keep from getting sick all over again. Pregnancy was no fun at all for either one of us.

Nate and I started to fight like cats and dogs. We fought because he drank so much. And, we fought because there was no money for food. The tension was too much for him. So, he left the apartment for days at a time. He didn't come back until he was ready to. I didn't know when or if he would come back home. Sometimes it was only a day. Other times, it was a week at a time. We were at this desolate place, and I knew we needed to change our lives. There was no way we could continue to live like this! In my mind, we needed to go back to Taylorville. I knew I could find a job there after I had this baby. But, Nate wouldn't listen to me. I became very sad and lonely. I didn't have anyone to turn to. And, I couldn't rely on Nate.

I made friends with the lady that lived close by. Her name was Mary. She was a rather odd person, but there was no one else I could talk to. Mary had four kids. Also, she and her family were dirt poor, so I had something in common with her. Mary's husband was an over-the-road truck driver who was gone most of the time. My husband was gone most of the time too. Mary and I often consoled each other as we discussed our many problems.

One day I went to Mary's to talk with her while my kids were taking their afternoon naps. Mary was giving her baby a bath when I arrived. As I stood there watching her, I realized the baby was dead. Mary didn't seem to notice this fact. It made me feel instantly sick inside. I ran to the nearby tavern and asked the owner to call someone who could help her. I didn't have a clue as to whom to call. The tavern owner, named Rob, knew what to do and made a call. I was overwhelmed with what I had just witnessed. I left the tavern and hurried back home to take care of my kids. Both of them were crying when I walked into my apartment.

After I calmed the kids down, I watched out the window for someone to come and help Mary. A car pulled up in front of the house. A man got out of the car and went in Mary's front door. He looked like a doctor. After a short while, the doctor came out of the apartment. He had wrapped the baby in a blanket, carried it under his arm, and put it in the car with him. Then he left. I was devastated. My only thoughts were *what if that was one of my babies? How would I feel?*

I was very pregnant and ready to deliver my third baby very soon. During my pregnancy, I never went to see a doctor. We had no money at all. We could barely afford to eat, let alone, pay doctor bills. I knew that I needed to take vitamins and calcium to make sure the baby and I were healthy, but I didn't have any money to buy them. In the past, the State had paid for both of my other children. Also, the fact that I was eating so little was not good. We ate only beans and potatoes for months. I felt undernourished. I felt physically weak. I was afraid I would need blood transfusions when the baby was born.

My labor pains finally started. It was time to go to the hospital in Mendota. I knew our junky car would barely make it the thirty miles to the hospital. The car was old and worn out. We had only had one gear left in the car and no reverse. But, somehow we managed to make it to the hospital in time.

The hospital looked like a big brick house. It was very small inside. At first, they had no room available for me. Several people were left in the hallway to wait for a room. I sat in the hallway in labor for a short while until a room became available for me to deliver the baby.

I didn't have a regular doctor during my whole pregnancy. Dr. Hay introduced himself to Nate and me. He was the doctor who would help deliver our third baby.

"You are going to have this baby, too." Dr. Hay told Nate as he handed him a lab coat. "Put this coat on." Nate was surprised. He had never been in the delivery room when I delivered my other two kids. And, the truth was, he didn't want to be here now. This was going to be a whole new experience for him. Nate was unsure about this experience, but he complied and put the lab coat on.

"Women are made to have babies, and we're going to have this baby now," Dr. Hay said. "I want you to grab your thighs and push." I did as he told me. I pulled my legs back towards my body. After a few attempts, the baby came out.

Nate walked over to the window like he was running away, and said, "Nooooo." He didn't see what was happening. He told me after the delivery, "If I hadn't been three stories up, I would have jumped out the window!"

My third child was born January 25th, 1951. It was a girl. She weighed about six pounds and seven ounces. She was born exactly one year and one day after Harris was born. She didn't have any hair. All my other kids had lots of hair. Immediately after her birth, the nurses rushed her out of the room. I barely had time to see her. Then it dawned on me; I had not heard her cry! I naturally assumed that she was born dead. Something was wrong with her. Half of her body looked black and blue like she had been beaten. She looked strange because this coloring was only on one side of her body. However, it continued down the whole length of her body.

"Why is she so blue?" I asked Dr. Hay. "Was the cord wrapped around her neck?"

"No, the cord was not wrapped around her neck," he said. "There are some things we just don't understand. We don't know why this happened. It is a mystery." He assured me that everything would be fine. My baby would need to be put in an oxygen tent for a few days, because she wasn't breathing well. After a few days, the oxygen should take care of the baby's problem.

Our new baby had another slight problem. She had an extra finger on her left hand. It was located next to her little finger. Dr. Hay assured me this was not all that rare, and they would take care of it as soon as possible. He explained that a silk string would be tied tightly around the baby's extra finger. After a little while, the finger would fall off on its own. We didn't quite understand this, but we accepted his explanation. After I gave this rarity some thought, I remembered one of my family members also had an extra finger. This must be genetic.

I named our third child, Jeannie Marie Gentry. I named Jeannie after the movie, I Dream of Jeannie. I thought it was a beautiful name. Also, I liked the name Marie.

After three days, the nurse brought my new baby into my room. Jeannie's body still looked a little blue, but it wasn't as dark a blue as it was before. The blue coloring had faded to a light green. It now looked like a bruise that was disappearing. Also, her extra finger had indeed fallen off. I felt relieved that Jeannie was doing well. Now, I was ready to go home.

Having a new baby should be a happy occasion. But, it wasn't for me. An extra child was more of a hardship. Now I had another mouth to feed, and no food to accommodate this newborn baby. I had my hands full. I felt terribly overwhelmed thinking about how I would take care of this child.

Before we left the hospital, Dr. Hay wanted to have a serious conversation with both Nate and I. We sat down and prepared to listen.

"Dottie is having babies too close together," Dr. Hay told Nate. "This is taking a toll on her body. She has had three babies in less than three years."

Nate listened as the doctor continued.

"It is now time to stop having babies," the doctor said.

I was elated to hear this! Even more, I wanted Nate to hear what the doctor said. I didn't want any more kids. I discussed this with Dr. Hay a few days ago. I asked him to talk to Nate. I thought Nate would listen to a doctor quicker than me. I begged Dr. Hay to fix me so I wouldn't have any more kids. I told him Nate was against this idea, and I hoped he might be able to sway Nate into changing his mind. I needed his consent to have the surgery. I already had one more child than I wanted. I was adamant about not having any more kids. I was happy Dr. Hay did as I asked.

"When this baby is six months old, I want you to bring Dottie back to the hospital, and I will surgically fix her so she cannot have any more children," Dr. Hay continued to speak directly to Nate.

Nate only comment was, "Yeah, yeah." I thought he was agreeing to do as the doctor asked. I thought he would bring me back to the hospital in six months and have me sterilized so I wouldn't get pregnant ever again. Now, I was ready to go home.

I stayed in the hospital three days. I needed to go home. Mary and Harris were staying at my neighbor's apartment. I didn't want to impose on them any longer than was necessary. Also, I knew we couldn't afford the higher hospital bills for an extended stay. I really wasn't ready to go back to our dismal lifestyle, but I had no choice.

When I went home, Nate was in a rage. He thought about the procedure Dr. Hay wanted to do on me. He hadn't brought the subject up until now.

"I am not about to take you back to that hospital and have you fixed so you can't have any more kids," he said. Then he added insult to injury by saying, "You'd be nothing but a whore! I will never sign those papers."

Nate really hurt me with his nasty words. I stewed about bad attitude for a long time. I couldn't let the hurt and disappointment go. The more I thought about it, the madder I got. Nate confirmed my feeling about him not having my best interests at heart.

My anger continued to build. Our apartment was so cold inside, it was almost frigid. Our stove had not been lit in a while, because we had nothing to burn in it. It made me mad that our kids were freezing to death. And, there was almost no food in the apartment. I realized just how destitute we were. Mostly, I blamed Nate for this mess we were in. I didn't even want to talk to him. The last thing I needed right now was a visit from Nate's brother.

Nate's brother James had brought a friend up to visit us. James lived in Taylorville. He and his friend were hungry and wanted me to fix them something to eat. All I could fix was a few beans and potatoes.

"Is that all you have is beans?" James asked me.

"That's what we have been living on," I told him. It was like a slap in the face to admit how poor we were. James wasn't any help. He was broke, too. He barely had enough money to get back home. He didn't stay very long to my relief. I was in no mood for company. I wasn't sure why James had made the trip.

I was feeling quite overwhelmed with my life in general. I was uptight and tense all the time. I couldn't feed my kids. Harris cried all the time, because he was hungry. I didn't have any baby food to feed him. I blamed Nate for not supporting his family. Furthermore, Nate and I continually argued. Most of the time, we argued about sex.

I was angry and disappointed with Nate, and I couldn't hide it. I was mad because I didn't want to have any more kids. I had not had a period three months. I was afraid I was pregnant. I put all the blame on Nate. It was his fault. I did not want to have any more kids! It pissed me off that he wouldn't take me back to the hospital to get the necessary surgery. Apparently, the only way to prevent a pregnancy was to have no sex at all. Well, the truth was, I didn't like Nate right now. I didn't want him to touch me let alone have sex! I held out on him. I wanted to get back at him for not giving his consent for the surgery. And, I knew I would get pregnant again if I consented to have sex. The fact that I refused sex only made things worse. Consequently, we argued and fought all the time. I was depressed and at the end of my rope. Something had to change.

Nate retaliated by being obstinate. He wouldn't work half the time. He was gone more and more. He came home only when he decided to.

He seemed to have no compassion for the fact that his family was literally starving to death. I no longer could deal with all of fighting and my nightmares, too.

My ongoing nightmares about Mable had to stop! It had been years since she had died, and I was still have the same nightmare. I was going crazy thinking about all the terrible things she had done to me. I just wanted the nightmares to stop. But first, I had to come to terms with the hatred still harbored towards her. Every time I looked at the scars on my body, I felt loathing and hatred for the woman who cause it. I blamed her. She wanted me to die, and I hated her for that! I reasoned in my own mind telling myself, she was an adult. She should have known better than to tell a twelve year old to light a match near gasoline! I hated Mable for the constant mean treatment that she imposed on me. I didn't deserve to be treated like that! I always tried so hard to please her. I was wallowing in my anger towards her. There was no justice for what she had done to me all those years. The anger was eating me up like a cancer, and I knew I had to make amends in order to move past it.

So, I got down on my hands and knees and prayed.

"I forgive Mable for what she had done to me!" I prayed to God. "I forgive her." I meant it. I knew I had to feel forgiveness in order to overcome my fear of Mable, and also to get the nightmares to stop. I cried, and I prayed until I was exhausted. In the end, the nightmares stopped. This alone lifted a weight off of my shoulders. I had been carrying this weight around with me for a long time. My prayers were answered. I never experienced the awful nightmares after that time.

I had to deal with one problem at a time. Right now, I had to deal with three kids. Mary was two years old, Harris was one year old, and I had a baby that required constant attention. Harris was fussy all the time. Also, he wouldn't try to walk. Every time I put his feet down on the floor, he drew them up and refused to stand on them. He was able to crawl anywhere he wanted, so walking wasn't a problem for him. He crawled anywhere he wanted to go, and he continued to be adventuresome.

Nate came home one day with a different car. He wanted me to come outside to take a good look at it. When I walked outside, I waved to my neighbors who where in the front yard. All of a sudden, my neighbors were pointing their fingers up towards the roof of our house! My bedroom window was open. Our apartment windows were large and reached all the way down to the floor. Harris had crawled out the opened window onto the roof. He was looking over the edge of the roof to see what I was doing outside. It scared me to death! I thought he was going to fall off the roof. I flew up the stairs as fast as I could run. I went to the window and said, "Come here, honey, come to Mommy." Harris responded to my voice. He crawled back through the window and crawled into my arms. I was so happy he was safe.

A few months went by before Nate came up with a new idea. He came home one night and wanted me to go to an old man's apartment. Obviously, he had just met this person. I gathered up the kids and went with him to meet this guy. It was snowing really heavy outside. This didn't stop us. Somehow we managed to get to the little town this guy lived in. The town was called Spring Valley, Illinois. I met Nate's new friend, and he offered us a place to stay for the night. His house was warm and full of food. We were all hungry, so I accept the invitation. Rarely did we have this much food to eat. I was in heaven and so were the kids. We nestled in for the night. The next morning it had snowed so much that we couldn't get the front door open to leave.

As it turned out, this man had planned on leaving his apartment. He was already packed and ready to leave. So, Nate and I decided to move in immediately after his new friend left. The apartment was on the lower level of the house. And, it had an artesian well. The water was so refreshing it tasted almost sweet. It was wonderful. This was a definite improvement in our living arrangements. Now, we didn't have to climb so many steps. We decided to move in right away. We lived there for about three months.

Overall, our destitute life didn't seem to get any better. It was no good living in this area. There were no jobs. That meant no money, which meant, the rent didn't get paid. I had finally had it. I had three kids to feed. Mary was two years old. Harris was a little over a year old. And, Jeannie was two months old. I had my hands full with no help from Nate. I was totally upset most of the time. I began to realize I was going to have to depend on myself to support these kids. But, right now, I was in no shape to get a job. I was so unfamiliar with this area that I didn't feel I could find a job here. So, I told Nate, "Get me back to Taylorville." I was familiar with it. I knew I could find a job there. I knew life could be better there than it was here. I had to find a way to make him understand that it was time to go back home.

My sister Claire and her husband Will came to visit us in Spring Valley. They lived in Virden, Illinois. Virden was a small town a few miles from Taylorville. I told Claire that I wanted to come back home. When Claire and Will saw Jeannie, they fell in love with her. Claire knew how overwhelmed I felt. She wanted to help.

"Oh my, Dottie, let us take Jeannie back home with us," she insisted. "You can come to Virden on New Year's Day and stay with us." Claire's suggestion sounded like a good idea to me. This would ease our burden a little, and get us out of this black pit we were in. I knew I could find myself a job in Taylorville. I always did before. That was my goal, and this was a way to achieve it. This sounded like an answer to my prayers. I agreed to let Claire take Jeannie home with them.

When New Years came, we went to stay with Claire and Will. They were happy to see us and suggested Nate find a job in their area.

"You can stay with us until you get back on your feet," Claire offered.

I immediately said, "Yes." I couldn't even think about going back up north. I wanted to stay in this area, and Nate agreed. So, the next day, he set out to find a job.

Luck was with us. It didn't take Nate long to find a job and a new place for us to live. A friend of his, named Evert Nation, hired him. We found a house in Taylorville. It was a little yellow house on Huston Street. I felt comfortable here. I was home. But first, we had to go back up north and get our furniture.

Nate and I took Mary and Harris with us to get the rest of our things up north. Jeannie stayed behind with Claire and Will. I had my hands full with two kids. Also, I realized at this time, I was pregnant again. I wasn't too happy about that. Nevertheless, it was a fact, and I had to deal with it.

The drive up north was grueling. It was cold and icy. It was the last week of January. The roads were slick and treacherous. I worried for our safety all the way there and back. We managed to get Spring Valley all intact, loaded up the furniture, and headed back to Taylorville. It was hard to keep the truck on the road. The wind was very strong. It whipped us back and forth. Something flew off the truck, but we didn't stop to see what it was. We wanted to get back home. Later on, we realized that our missing item was our stove pipe. The good news was we made it back in one piece. I was elated to be home at last.

After we settled in to our new house, we went back to Claire and Will's to get Jeannie. Claire was gone, and she had taken Jeannie with her. Will told us they were over at his brother's house. We left thinking that we would come back at another time.

A while later we went back to collect Jeannie. Again, she was not there. I knew that Claire and Will doted on Jeannie. They took good care of her. Actually, they treated her like she was their own flesh and blood. The truth was they wanted to keep her. However, Nate and I didn't like the idea that they were deliberately keeping Jeannie from us. We didn't like the cat and mouse game they were playing with us. Claire and Will sensed our feelings, but they weren't willing to give Jeannie back to us. What could we do? We left their house without confronting them.

We decided to go talk to my dad about this problem. He told us that Claire and Will intended to keep Jeannie until we came up with some money. They wanted to be paid for the time they had kept her. This really made me mad. Claire was my sister. I thought the world of her. I accepted her exactly like she was. I knew she drank too much, but I still loved her. And, all this time, I thought she wanted to do something good for me. I was really disappointed in her. Of course, I was getting this message second handed, but I believed my dad.

I came up with a plan to go to Will and Claire's house and somehow steal Jeannie away from them. I was going to grab her while she played outside in Claire's yard. Then, we planned to drive off with her. There was no way I was going give Claire and Will any money I didn't have. So, we tried to implement our plan, but it didn't work. We failed.

Then, out of the blue, Eva, my dad's wife, called and said, "Come over to our house and get Jeannie. She is here with us."

I was perplexed. Claire and Will must have figured my dad's house was neutral ground. They didn't want to talk to us face to face. We drove over to my dad's house right away. Claire and Will had brought Jeannie to my dad's because she had a problem, and they didn't know what to do about it.

Will always worked on his brother's farm. After the corn was taken out of the fields, Will gathered leftover corn for the birds. Will and Jeannie were walking in the cornfield. At two years old, Jeannie was not always so sure footed. The cornstalks were jutting up in all directions. Consequently, Jeannie tripped and fell on a cornstalk. It stabbed her right eye. Her eye became infected to the degree that it needed medical attention. It scared Claire and Will to think they would be liable for this accident. Also, they wanted us to get her treated for the infection. So, they brought her to my dad's house so we could take her to the doctor.

I was boiling mad when I seen how bad the infection was in Jeannie's eye. I told my dad to tell Claire and Will they better never come on my property again. I meant it. I would put them under a peace bond if they tried to bother us. I didn't want to deal with them. They didn't try to communicate with me after that day. I didn't see them again for years.

Chapter Eleven
MY FOURTH AND FIFTH CHILDREN

When we moved to Taylorville, I was about six months along in my pregnancy with my forth child. I went to see the same doctor who delivered my first two kids. I felt secure that he would take good care of me. I was still very upset about having another child. I wanted to do something to end these pregnancies. I did not want to have any more kids! I was overwhelmed with the thought. However, the doctor talked me out of doing anything. He tried a different approach.

"Oh, you will have the prettiest little girl," he assured me. "Wouldn't you want a baby girl?"

I got the message. He wouldn't do anything to help me. I was going to have four kids weather like it or not.

My fourth child was born, April 15th, 1952. It was a boy. He weighed close to six pounds and seven ounces. The labor and birth was quite easy. When I went into labor, I expected to have a girl. My doctor had convinced me of that earlier in my pregnancy. Instead, I had a boy. I had to admit, he was a beauty. I could see the Indian blood in him. He was dark skinned and had a full head of almost black hair. His eyes were dark brown. I thought he looked like a Mexican baby. When Nate worked at a bakery up north, his boss's name was Bobby. Nate liked that name and wanted to use it for our new baby boy. I picked his middle name. My sister Rena's husband's name was Lee. I liked that name, so we agreed to call our boy, Bobby Lee Gentry.

I had to admit to a little disappointment when I realized I had a boy. All through my pregnancy, I thought I was carrying a girl. It took me a while to accept this fact. Now, I had two girls and two boys. My family was complete.

A few days after Bobby was born, we went to Nate's brother's house in Stonington, Illinois. We were there to visit and show them our newest baby. Lily, my sister-in-law, knew I was dead set against having anymore kids. She clued me in on a new product that prevented further pregnancies. She took me into her bedroom so we could talk between ourselves.

"Dottie, I've got something here that will keep you from getting pregnant," she told me. "I have used this product for years.

Believe me, I was all ears. I didn't know a product like this existed. All those times I talked to different doctor about not having more kids; not a one of them suggested a product like this. It made me mad all over again just thinking about that! I would have used this product years ago, if I had known about it.

"Good. Show me what the product looks like," I told her. "I don't want to get pregnant again."

Lily gave me a tube of something called vaginal jelly. She explained that I would have to insert the jelly prior to sexual activity. I was happy to try this or anything else. Life was tough, and I couldn't afford another mouth to feed.

After that day, I remained faithful to my new birth control product. It was a good thing because we moved from one place to another. Nate didn't keep a job. Therefore, we couldn't pay the rent. And, we were still struggling to feed everyone. For six years, I didn't have any more kids. I was grateful that I wasn't pregnant during that time, and I thought maybe I was done having kids.

While Bobby was a baby, we moved in with my brother, named Tim, and his wife Madge. They lived just a few miles from Taylorville. They had six kids of their own. Nate and I were at a desperate stage in our lives. We had no money and no place to live. So, Tim let us stay in one of his bedrooms. The bedroom only had a mattress on the floor for a bed. I put Bobby on the mattress and he crawled off it. That was the first time I knew he could crawl. Tim allowed us to stay with him until Nate found another job. Then, we could find ourselves another place to live.

Nate went looking for a job. He found one at Borg Warner in Decatur, Illinois. Somehow he always managed to get a job. It was keeping it that was the problem. He just wouldn't work for very long. He obviously liked to play more than work. And, drinking beer was more important to him than his family.

One day, I packed Nate's lunch for work. He left for work that morning as usual. However, he didn't bother to go to work that day. He decided to play hooky. I found this out after the fact. I had a feeling in the pit of my stomach that I couldn't quite put my finger on. I believe it was disgust. I figured Nate had taken off work to go drinking. I knew him well. I think he had planned this in advance. Nate met up with his sister June and her friend Eve. The three of them were driving around drinking beer all day. I went looking for him that day. He wasn't at work just as I expected. I had a real good reason to find Nate. I needed him to take me to the doctor.

I was so sick I could barely get to the doctor. I was jaundice. This caused the whites of my eyes and my skin to become yellow. And, I itched all over. In addition to that, I couldn't eat anything because it gave me diarrhea. I had gotten so tired and weak I could barely stand it. I tried to think about what caused this problem. Then, I remembered drinking some water from a well in the back yard. The water must have been contaminated. That was the only reasonable explanation for the jaundice.

I went to see Dr. Lane. He gave me some sulfur tablets to take. Also, he threatened to put me in the hospital. I told him that was impossible. I was living with my brother, my kids were at his house, and I had to get back home to take care of them. Not to mention the fact that I couldn't afford to go to the hospital. Finally, the doctor gave in. He insisted that I go home and merely rest. I told him I would do that. But first, I was on another mission.

I had to find Nate. I walked to Nate's sister's apartment. The neighbors told me she had left with her brother. Then, I walked to Eve's house on Cleveland Street. Eve left with June and her brother. So, I put two and two together. I figured Nate was having a fling with Eve.

I was really pissed off by the time Nate finally decided to come home. It was late and I was already in bed. When Nate came into our bedroom, I attacked him.

"Where have you been?" I asked him.

"That's none of your business!" he flatly said.

I yelled back at him saying, "Yes, it is my business. You didn't go to work today!"

Nate was furious because he was caught red-handed. We started to fight. Then, Nate decided he was going to have sex with me. I boldly refused.

"You are not touching me after you have been out screwing around!" I accused.

This infuriated Nate. I then accused him of being with Eve. He became brutal. He shoved me down on the bed and forced himself on me. I struggled to get free with no luck.

"I am going to take you any way I can get you," he warned me. "You are my wife and my property. He held me down so I couldn't struggle to get free. He began having his way with me.

My brother heard us arguing. He came to our bedroom door.

"Sis, are you having trouble in there?" he asked.

Tim wanted to protect me. He knew how sick I had been. We had lived there long enough that he had become disgusted with Nate's drinking, too. He sensed I was having a problem with Nate. He wanted to help me. I felt guilty for waking him up. This was his house. Also, I was embarrassed at Nate's behavior. I didn't want Tim to get involved, so I lied.

"No, we're not having any trouble," I told him through the door. I did not want him to know what was going on in that room. And, I didn't want any more trouble.

Tim gave up. He decided to allow me to fight my own battles. He knew Nate and I fought quite often. And, although we lived in constant turmoil, I was going to stay with him. Tim knew he would be fighting a losing battle. Soon after this incident, we found another place to live.

When we returned to get our furniture, Tim had put everything in one room. I think he was ready for us to move. He had already moved another family into the bedroom we had just left. He didn't say anything to us: we just knew he was done helping us.

I had other reasons to distrust Nate. Not long after I accused him of being unfaithful, I saw other clues that condemned him. Eve had asked us to take her to Nate's dad's house to see June. We agreed to give her a ride. I was driving, Eve was in the middle of the seat, and Nate was on the other side of the car. Nate leaned over and put his head on Eve's breasts. Then, he put his hand on her. I was livid! I didn't say a word until we left Eve at her destination. Then, I lit into Nate.

"I don't like what I just seen you do!" I accused him. "I saw you put your hand on Eve."

"You're a liar!" Nate said. "You are just making that lie up as you go along!" He denied my wrongful accusations.

Yeah, I admit it. I was jealous. But, I had ample reason to be. Another time, Eve asked me to ride along with her to a bar in Stonington. She had won a case of beer there and needed to pick it up. Nate was not a home. He was gone most of the time. He usually left without telling me where he was going or how long he would be gone. I agreed to go with Eve to keep her company. When Eve and I walked into the bar, Nate was there. He was sitting at a table with a woman named Maxine. He didn't expect to see me in this bar. So much so, he walked right past me with his arm around this woman. They walked arm in arm out the door and left together. Nate and Maxine got in the backseat of Maxine's car. Maxine's husband got in the front seat and drove them all away. I just stood there like a fool with my mouth hanging open. I couldn't believe what I had just seen.

The next day, I brought the episode to Nate's attention. "I saw you at the bar with your arm around Maxine," I told him. "You walked right past me."

"You were just seeing things. I didn't do that!" Nate said. He didn't believe I was at the bar. He never admitted doing anything. But, I knew I wasn't crazy. I had seen him with my own eyes. For some reason, I felt that by just bringing the matter up; I was handling it.

Many times, I had seen Nate kiss other women. He kissed them on the lips. I knew I wasn't just seeing things. But, he acted like it was normal behavior. He just laughed it off when I said anything about it. My feelings didn't seem to matter to him. He ignored me and did whatever he wanted to do.

These episodes made me feel defeated. Nothing was ever resolved. I played the martyr. I told Nate, "Yeah, you really love me don't you!" I knew deep inside I felt if a man really loved a woman he wouldn't treat her like this. And, I always felt that I loved Nate more than he loved me. I didn't feel worthy of his love. My own insecurity was stopping me from taking any further action. Other times, I was forced into action.

On one such occasion, Nate had been out all night drinking. I was so mad at him for his lack of responsibility towards his family. I hated the fact he drank so much. He was supposed to be working to support his family. When he came home this particular morning, I launched an attack.

"Where is the money for groceries?" I asked him. Those few words were all it took to start a major fight. Nate immediately grabbed a butcher's knife off the kitchen table. He thrust it towards me and backed me against the kitchen window. Then, he put the knife to my throat!

"I ought to put this knife in your gut," he threatened. "You are so mean. I am going to tie you to the bed."

I was enraged at his threat. How dare he treat me like this when he had been out drinking all night and doing who knows what! I retaliated in a flash. I grabbed him by hair, threw him down on the floor, and I sat on top of him. We wrestled until we were halfway down the basement steps. I pinned him down so he couldn't get up. The kids were all screaming and crying as they watched this fight unfold. I hated to upset the kids. I wanted this fight to end.

"You better tell me you will never do this again," I told Nate. "I will let you up if this fight stops right here!" Nate conceded. He agreed to stop fighting so I let him up.

I never wanted the kids to see Nate and I fight. I hid most of it from them. I never talked about the problem Nate had with alcohol. Most of the time, I swept the unpleasantness under the rug and refused to talk about it. I knew I couldn't count on Nate to be available to us. He constantly brought chaos into our lives. I was always braced for battle, because I knew I had to fight for everything. Even my best efforts couldn't tame him. My kids and I never knew where we would be living tomorrow or whether or not we would have food to eat. Most of the time, I had to look within myself to survive and thrive. I hid what money I could for food. I did whatever I could to make our lives better.

It took me a long time to realize it didn't matter how loving, kind, or how good I was; when alcohol was controlling our lives, love didn't help. It was never enough. However, I didn't' give up. I diligently worked to smooth out the rough spots and make our lives a journey that got better and better. That was my goal.

I overlooked Nate's weaknesses and served him like he was a king. I waited on him hand and foot. When he was drunk, I helped him get sober. Every day I pushed him to get out of bed. And, I pushed him go to work. Many days, it was a struggle to get him out the door, because he was hung over. He was like a child, and spoiled brat at that. He constantly resisted. However, in the end, he complied with my wishes. I knew we could only prosper if he worked regularly and brought in a weekly paycheck.

I knew how dysfunctional we lived, but I tried to override that with pride and dignity. I wanted other people to believe we were upstanding in the community. Also, I wanted to preserve the illusion that out household was just like other households, and everything was fine.

I took pride in our home. It was always clean and neat. And, I kept our yard immaculate. My kids were always clean and neat with much effort. I proudly held my head high. In all these ways, I felt like I was protecting my family. I had dignity! And, no one was going to talk bad about my family. Little did I know at this time, I was about to have more kids to protect.

As it turned out, I was in for a real surprise. One day while I was scrubbing my floors, I passed out. After I came to, I went to the doctor. The doctor found a cyst on my breast. He decided to cut it out. When he did this procedure, he found that the milk ducks in my breast indicated I was pregnant.

"Did you know you are pregnant?" he asked me.

"No! I can't be pregnant," I cried. "My last baby was six years ago." I had not done anything different. I was using the same birth control product for six years.

The doctor confirmed his speculation. Without a doubt, I was pregnant again. I still don't know how it happened. I hadn't changed a thing. I thought I was protected from further pregnancies. But, I was wrong.

The year was 1958. My youngest boy was six years old. So many things were going well in our lives at this time. Nate was working every day, and so was I. We could finally afford to have food on our table. Being pregnant was the last thing I wanted to happen.

Some things had not changed. We were still moving quite often. We were looking for another place to live when I met my first really good friend. Her name was Mattie Larks. Mattie just happened to be pregnant, too. We were due to have our babies at the same time. Mattie, her husband Earl, and their five children lived in a house in Hewittville. This was a small village at the south end of Taylorville. Mattie and Earl also owned a house on the lot next to them. They rented this house to Nate and I for next to nothing. I think they sensed our dire state of affairs.

The house we rented from Mattie and Earl contained only three rooms. It had a combination kitchen and living room, and two bedrooms. Also, it had no water inside the house. We had to go to Mattie's house and get water from the well in her back yard. We carried it back and forth in a five gallon bucket. In addition to this minor inconvenience, the toilet was an outhouse in the back yard. Although we were cramped for space, we decided to stay here because the price was right.

The Larks family was really great to have as landlords and neighbors. They always planted a large garden. Because they were such giving people; they supplied us with fresh vegetables. They gave us green beans, turnips, turnip greens, and potatoes. They also gave us fresh grapes from their grape arbor. In return, I help them pick the beans, dig the potatoes, and get them ready to can for the winter. I ended up getting canned food all winter long. And, as a special bonus, we all considered each other friends.

Mattie and I became best friends. She was typically a good old country girl from Alabama. I likened her to a hillbilly. She had a heart of gold. Her kindness was always genuine. And, she never met a stranger. She loved everyone. People were her main concern. As a special bonus, Mattie loved my four kids as if they were her own. My kids often played at Mattie's house. They ate grapes from a huge grape arbor in the back yard. Mattie always welcomed them at any time.

Both mine and Mattie's kids acted like they had known each other all their lives. They played well together. Mattie had four girls and was pregnant with her fifth child. Likewise, I had four kids and was pregnant with my fifth one. I had two boys and two girls. I was happy all the kids got along so well.

Not only was Mattie my best friend, she helped me out financially. Mattie's house was very messy with piles of stuff everywhere, but it didn't bother her. House cleaning was not one of her priorities. I volunteered to help clean Mattie's house. She agreed only if I allowed her to pay me for that service. Needless to say, I was grateful. We needed the money. So, we had a deal. I agreed to come and clean for her once a week. I looked forward to doing the job for her and her family. While I cleaned the house, Mattie sat at the kitchen table and talked about anything and everything. We both felt good about what we were doing for each other. I took pride in the fact that her house was clean. And, Mattie felt good that she could help me buy food for the family.

When Mattie's husband came home from work, he always complimented me on how nice the house looked. His compliment made me feel good to be of help to them. Mattie and Earl were fine people. I cherished every moment with them.

After I finished cleaning, Mattie and I sat down at the kitchen table and shared a cup of coffee. We talked for hours on end. It was good therapy for both of us. I needed someone to share my problems with, and Mattie was a good listener. I often confided in her about the problems I was having with Nate. Also, we shared stories about our childhood days.

Mattie always made me laugh. She had a good since of humor and a quick smile. I never saw her in a bad mood. She was happy all time. I loved spending time with her. I felt truly blessed to have her for my friend.

She was truly one-of-a-kind. She was always patient and sympathetic as she responded to my constant problems. I was lucky to have her positive input.

Nate was always my main problem. Drinking beer was his passion. He drank habitually every day. His excessive drinking usually caused me trouble, because he had no boundaries. The more beer Nate drank, the worse he behaved. The chaos caused me a great deal of anxiety. I constantly had something negative to deal with.

While I was pregnant with my fifth child, Nate made a big mistake. He told me he was going to the store to get a quart of beer. He left, and I waited and waited for his return. He didn't come home. So, I decided to go look for him. I figured he was up to no good. But first, I had to walk over to the babysitter's house to see if she could watch the kids for me. Frankie was a 17 year old girl who usually babysat for us. When I got to her house, Frankie's mother told me that Nate had already picked her up two hours ago. Now, I was really worried. I went back home and waited for Nate to come home.

The truth was, Nate stopped by a convenience store and bought some beer, picked up Frankie, and took her out into an isolated area of the country where he could be alone with her. He lied to her. He told her he was taking her to our house to babysit. He didn't have good intentions on his mind. He drove up a long lane that led to a deserted old farmhouse. He stopped the car.

"I want to talk to you," he said as he leaned towards her. He put his arm around her.

"I can't talk to my wife," he complained to get her sympathy. "But, I know you will listen to me."

Frankie panicked. She wasn't sure what to do. She was very upset to think that Nate might try to take advantage of her.

"No! Take me back to town!" she demanded as she opened the car door to get out.

Nate knew right away that he had made a mistake. Suddenly, he realized how scared the girl was, so he decided to take her home.

"Get back in the car. I'll take you back to town," he promised.

Frankie was apprehensive, but she climbed back into the car.

Nate took her home, dropped her off, and went about his drinking spree.

When Frankie got back home, she was still upset. She told her mother what had happened in Nate's car. She explained that Nate had scared her. He didn't touch her in any other way.

Frankie's mother went into a rage. She wanted to file charges against Nate. However, instead of the truth, she wanted to create a lie to make sure the police put him in jail. Her plan was to file rape charges against him and have me testify that her lie was the truth. She called me and told me her plan. She knew Nate had not raped Frankie, but she didn't care. She wanted justice! He had scared the life out of her daughter. She appealed to me. She wanted me to go to court and testify against Nate, so she could put him in prison. I just couldn't do that. I wasn't stupid! I wasn't going to lie. I was really mad to find out what Nate had done, but I knew telling a lie wasn't right. I had to deal with this in my own way.

When Nate finally came home that night, I was waiting up for him. I had seethed with anger all night. I was almost due to have my fifth child, and I was as big as a barrel. The physical stress on my body was nearly as strong as the emotional stress brought on by my husband's latest escapade. I just couldn't trust him. When Nate walked in the door, I confronted him with the story Frankie had told her mother.

"Frankie's mother called and told me that you harassed her daughter," I said. I wanted him to know I knew the whole truth. What's more, I believed what I had been told. "She wants me to go to court and testify that you raped Frankie."

Nate was enraged to think anyone was going to tell lies on him! But, I didn't let his ire bother me. I knew the truth, and he was going to hear it.

"I know what you attempted to do to Frankie," I continued to tell him.

Immediately, Nate went into a fit of rage. Somehow through his drunkenness, he thought I had betrayed him! Of course, he retaliated. He shoved me down onto the bed and put a pillow over my face. He pressed so hard I couldn't move. I kept struggling to get out from under the pillow. I fought and fought. I thought he was trying to kill me! Finally, he let me up. It didn't matter to him that I was pregnant at this time. He had only thought of himself. This thought shook me up. I walked away from Nate. I didn't want to have anything to do with him. I wouldn't talk to him for over a week.

This fight was over, but it was only one of many more. My trust in Nate was completely gone. I questioned everything he did from that time on. I had good reason to. The struggle within myself caused me feel tense all the time.

Whenever Nate drank too much, I never knew what to expect from him. He did some radical things. Once, he told me that he was going to lay on the railroad tracks and wait for a train to come and kill him. He left the house with this intention. Of course he was drunk at the time, so I believe he would go through with his stupid plan. I panicked. It scared me. I loved him, and I didn't want to lose him. This time he was so drunk I figured he really might kill himself. I gathered up the kids a few minutes after he left and went after him. Sure enough, he was laying on the railroad tracks waiting for the train to come. He was so drunk. He looked like he was in a coma. He was sprawled out across the tracks oblivious to anything in the real world. The kids and I dragged him off of the tracks. He couldn't even walk. We actually had to manually carry him back home. I was so mad at him; I could have killed him myself.

I was mad at him for several reasons. First, I was mad because he drank so much he was in a stupor. I was mad because he didn't have any respect for himself. But mostly, I was mad because he put me and his kids through this ridiculous experience. He was a terrible role model for his kids. Also, I was mad because he constantly embarrassed me. But the worst of all, he did it again.

He attempted suicide several times. Once he threatened to jump in front of a moving train. Another time, he had a small knife that he held to his own throat. I finally had enough of this stupid behavior! I was tired of his drunken antics. This time, I didn't argue with him. I went to the kitchen and came back with a large butcher's knife. I handed the knife to him and said, "If you are going to kill yourself, do it good!" Nate was very shocked at this turn of events. So much so that he put the knife down and walked away. He no longer had an audience. After that episode, he didn't threaten his own life again.

Later, I told myself that I should have reacted this way the first time Nate threatened to kill himself. But, I couldn't. I was too scared. I was afraid he might actually accomplish the job. And, I didn't know how to handle any situation that concerned him. He was too volatile. However, I learned from past experiences. It was all trial and error. I had been too easy on him. I needed to toughen up and not allow Nate to manipulate me.

Somehow we managed to get past all that conflict, and I had my fifth child. I started out having very hard labor pains. We had been at the races in Macon when I started having a terrible bad back ache. I was ready to deliver the baby any minute. Therefore, I had the suitcase packed and already in the car. I was prepared. My backache didn't let up. I decided the backache must be related to labor pains, so we left the races and went directly to the hospital. We went to St. Vincent's Hospital in Taylorville. After we got to the hospital, the labor pains continued for a long time. I walked up and down the hallways. Then, I sat in the shower and let the water ease my pains. For some reason the baby wouldn't come. Finally, the doctor decided to take steps to encourage my birth process. It appeared that the baby was too large for me to deliver the regular way. The doctor had to use forceps' to spread my pelvic area wide enough to accommodate such a large baby. Thankfully, the forceps helped me deliver the baby.

I delivered a boy. He was born on Mother's Day. It was May 11th, 1958. He weighed 8 lbs and 11 ounces. He was the largest baby I ever had. He looked like he was a month old when he was born. He wasn't even wrinkled. When I seen him the first time, he had his little arms up in the air like a prize fighter. His fists were clinched and his little arms looked like they were well muscled. I thought he looked like a prize fighter.

So, I decided on the name Mackie. I told the nun at the hospital the name I had picked out for the baby.

"Mackie is not a name," the nun said. "Don't name him Mackie."

"I wanted his name to be Mac," I explained to the nun.

"Mac is a good name," the nun replied. "I like the name Mac.

So in the end, I named my new son Mac Flynn Gentry. But, I still intended to call him Mackie.

Mackie was a red haired baby with a crooked smile, and he smiled all the time. He was a happy baby. The older kids liked to play with him. They made him laugh all the time. Even the neighborhood kids liked to entertain him. Because the other kids were older, they pretty much took care of him. They all treated Mackie like he was a new toy. Someone wanted to carry him around all the time. This was a big help to me.

One of the neighborhood girls playfully told me Mac's future. She said he was going to ride a motorcycle and wear a black leather jacket with Mac written on the back of it. We all laughed. The kids enjoyed this baby. It was a pleasure for me to watch them interact with Mackie.

I really enjoyed having this baby. I had not had a baby for six years. I felt as if I had to learn how to take care of a newborn all over again.

Nate surprised me. He enjoyed this baby more than any other. He carried him around all the time. He fed him, played with him, and diapered him. This was a first! I was happy for the change. I figured it was because Nate was getting older and more mature. It gave me a warm feeling when I saw how well he interacted with his latest son.

Mattie became pregnant at the same time I did. And, our neighbor to the right of us, named Carol Tomlinson, ended up pregnant, too. It seemed like an epidemic. We all joked with each other and commented that there must be something in the water that made us all conceive!

We continued to live in Mattie and Earl's rental property for almost a year after Mackie was born. Our already small house was getting even smaller. We needed more room. Our bedroom was packed with our bed, a baby crib, a television, and a chair. And to my surprise, before the year was over, I was pregnant, again. This was totally unbelievable! There was certainly no room for another crib. So this prompted us to look for another house. Mattie and Earl understood this, and I felt sure Mattie and I would remain good friends.

Chapter Twelve
MY LAST CHILD

We found a rental house in Taylorville located behind a pizza parlor. It was called Johnny's Pizza. We could smell fresh baked pizza every day. It was irresistible. Needless to say, Johnny's Pizza got some business from us, too. Many times we enjoyed having pizza for dinner. If we didn't have the money to pay for it; Johnny kept a tab for us. We paid up every Friday when Nate received his check. Because it was a family owned business, we became friends with Johnny and his family.

Our new rental house was small, but it had two bedrooms, a living room, and a kitchen. The kitchen contained an iron pump that we used to get cold drinking water. If we needed hot water, we had to heat it on the stove. At least, we had water inside the house. We also had an inside bathroom. This was definitely an improvement. And, we had an old wringer-type washer to wash our clothes. It was still a primitive life style, but we were going to make it work for us. After all, it was better than the house we lived in before.

Our wringer-type washer was an electric Maytag. The people who lived in the house before us left the washer behind. I was grateful for this convenience, although it was still quite an ordeal to do the laundry. The water had to be heated on the stove and poured into the washer. Then, after the clothes were washed, the washer had to be drained. Fresh water was then added to rinse the clothes. After the clothes went through the rinse cycle, we ran them through the wringers to get the excess water out.

Several times, one of the kids got their hands caught in the automatic wringers. Fortunately, no one broke any bones because of it. The final process was hanging the clothes on the line to dry. If the weather was bad, we hung them all over the inside of the house. The kids always helped me to accomplish this long ordeal, because we had a tremendous amount of laundry with seven of us in the house.

I made most of the clothes the kids wore. I used an old treadle-type Singer sewing machine. I used my foot to move the treadle back and forth to make the machine sew. I made Mary and Jeannie look-alike outfits out of scrap material my sister-in-law Eve had given me. Eve worked at the Simplicity Dress Factory at this time. She often brought me material from the factory and helped me make the clothes for the kids. We made shorts, shirts, and dresses. One of the girl's outfits had blue tops with pink, stripped, flowered shorts. We finished them up by embroidering each girls name on them. Because the outfits were alike, many people thought Mary and Jeannie were twins. We also tore old clothes apart and used them for patterns. I also used my sewing machine to repair the kid's clothes when they were torn. There were always repairs to do.

I was very depressed thinking about having a sixth child. I knew I had to do something to stop getting pregnant. Nate's sister June gave me some good advice.

"Dottie, you must go see Dr. Mathew in Blue Mound, Illinois. You tell him this is your sixth child. He will find you a doctor who will fix you so you won't have any more kids," June suggested. "And, you do not have to have Nate's consent."

I didn't waste any time. I called and made an appointment. I had not seen a doctor for my pregnancy yet, so this was a good time to do it. When I called, I told the receptionist that I needed to talk to Dr. Mathews as soon as possible. She made me an appointment for that same week.

When I went in to see the doctor, I told him, "Dr. Mathews, my husband is an alcoholic, and this is my sixth child. I don't want any more kids. I want to be fixed so I can't have any more."

"I can't do that for you, but I can call another doctor in to do it right after you have this child." He continued to say, "You will have to go to

Decatur to have this child, because the doctor who would do your surgery only does it at the Decatur hospital."

I agreed to do as the doctor asked, because I knew our insurance would pay for the surgical procedure. I was grateful to think I was never going to get pregnant again.

Dr. Mathews was rather upset with me that I had not seen a doctor earlier in my pregnancy. I was almost eight months along by now. I knew I couldn't afford the doctor bills. However, Nate had just gotten a job at Caterpillar. I now had insurance. So, I felt a little freer to make an appointment. Dr. Mathews took some blood tests. He wanted to see if I was anemic. As it turned out, I wasn't. But, the doctor made me promise to come for regular checkups until the baby was born. I agreed.

I was happier knowing Nate had a paycheck coming in every week. I had medical insurance for the first time. Because I was already pregnant when Nate got his job at Caterpillar, the insurance would pay for the delivery and the baby's care, but not for my hospital stay. I was willing to pay my part of the bill. What a wonderful relief this was for me to have some of the financial burden taken off us. Also, the insurance paid the doctor bills for both me and my baby. In the past, all of my other kid's delivery bills had been paid by the State. I wasn't happy about that. It always made me feel like we were a charity case. Now, that we had insurance, I felt much more comfortable going to see the doctor.

We finally had some stability in our lives for the first time in years. The kids regularly attended the Nazarene Church which was a few blocks from our house. They all sang in the choir. They also attended Bible School during the summer months. The kids really enjoyed the activities offered at Bible School. They did crafts, made wooden objects, and other projects that they took pride in. During the month of December, my kids participated in the church's Christmas Programs. I wanted them to be active in the church. But, most of all, I managed to have a few moments to myself. I accrued a break from the chaos of five noisy kids and a demanding husband.

Of course, I was growing bigger all the time with this pregnancy. By the end of the day, I was exhausted. My family took all my time and effort. There was always laundry, dishes, cooking, and cleaning to do. And,

Nate was like having an extra child who wanted attention every waking minute. I was really looking forward to having this baby, so I could have a few moments to myself while I was in the hospital.

I was cooking a pot of navy beans for our Thanksgiving Day meal when I went into labor with my sixth child. I had no doubt my time to deliver was near.

"You have to take me to the hospital in Decatur," I told Nate. "I am going to have this baby today!"

Nate took the kids to a friend's house, and then took me to St. Mary's Hospital in Decatur. I had already called Dr. Mathews so he could meet me at the hospital. I wasn't in labor very long when I had a baby girl. Dr. Mathews suggested that I should call my new baby Faith. I had told him all through the pregnancy that this baby was going to be a girl. That way, I had three boys and three girls to even the score. He said I had faith that I would have a girl. Sure enough, I was right. It was a girl. She weighed close to six pounds and seven ounces. She was born, November 26th, 1959.

When I first saw my new baby, they were holding her upside down. Bubbles were coming out of her mouth. I asked Dr. Mathews, "Why does she have bubbles coming out of mouth?"

"She was born with bronchitis," he said.

Also, my new baby had a scar on the side of her neck. Dr. Mathews couldn't explain why the scar was there. He wanted to put the baby in what he called cold storage for a while. They needed to isolate her from the rest of the babies until they figured out what the scar was. It turned out to be just a scar with no explanation for it.

As I looked at my new baby, I saw that she was so skinny and little. I thought she looked like a little bird. Her tiny little mouth was wide open, and I thought she looked like a little Robin waiting for food from her mamma. Right away, I laughingly wanted to call her Robin.

"Robin Alexandria Gentry," I exclaimed. "That is going to be her name." But after I gave the name more thought, I decided the name was too big for such a little baby. So in the end, I decided on the name Robin Gentry. Her first name was so long that I decided to forgo a middle name. When I lived up north, the bar tenders name was Rob. He had given us food when we had none. I had planned on naming one of the boys after him, but it never fit them. But, Robin seemed to fit this baby.

I thought Robin was a beautiful baby. She was so small that she looked like a doll lying on the bed. Her eyes were dark and so was her hair. Also, her skin was dark like she already been in the sun and developed a beautiful tan. She looked like a typical Indian baby. I was so proud of her. And, I felt lucky that she was such a good baby. I made up my mind. I was really going to enjoy this baby, because she was my last child.

The next morning after the birth, I was prepared for the sterilization. The doctor came into my room and explained that he would not only tie my fallopian tubes, but he would burn the ends of them so I could never be pregnant again.

"Does my husband need to sign the papers for me to have this procedure done?" I asked.

"No. This is your sixth child; you sign right here," the doctor said as he indicated the line I needed to sign on.

I readily signed the papers. I was relieved that I didn't need Nate's consent. I knew he wouldn't agree to allow me to have the sterilization. And, he wasn't at the hospital at this time.

I was taken into surgery the next morning. The doctor completed the sterilization procedure on me. Afterwards, I silently thanked God for this procedure. I was finally done having kids. Soon, I would be taking my last child home.

When I woke up from the surgery, Nate was in my room. He had been out drinking all night long. He knew that for the first time, I had control over my own body. And, he was not happy about that change. I went against his wishes. He was still mad at me. It looked to me like he was on a real drinking spree. Furthermore, he planned to continue drinking the rest of the night. There was nothing I could do about that. I wasn't coming home until the next day.

Little did I realize the hell I would be experiencing when I got home? Life as I knew it was about to change. I was about to experience a whole new mindset that would stay with me the rest of my life. Because of a painful experience, I would grow up and take control of my own life.

While I was in the hospital having my last child, Nate stooped to the bottom of the bucket. As far as I was concerned, he could rot there! He was angry because I was getting fixed so I couldn't have any more kids. Also, he was mad because I made up my mind to do the surgery even though he was against it. So, he was too busy to come and spend his time with me at the hospital.

In retaliation for Nate's anger at me, he decided to spend his time with an old bar fly who, in the end, gave him gonorrhea. Of course, he didn't bother to tell me this unfortunate truth. It took me a while before I found out the whole ugly story.

When I came home from the hospital, Nate was quite indifferent to me. He was distant. He didn't' hug me or kiss me at all. He pushed me away when I attempted to be affectionate. This was highly unusual for him. He wouldn't touch me or get close to me at all. In the past, he was all over me physically. I never turned him down when he wanted to have sex. I always felt that I was his property, and I didn't have the right to say, "No."

In the past, Nate was always after me to have sex. Sometimes, I just wanted him to get the act over with because he wanted to do it so often. Many times, he came home in the middle of the day for the same reason. No matter what I was doing, he expected me to drop everything and focus on him. He was selfish in this way. I always obeyed him and did what I had to do. I felt it was my responsibility to satisfy his every need. And, he always wanted to have sex right away after each one of my kids. Usually, he never gave me time to heal. But this time, he abstained.

"Why don't you want to have sex," I asked Nate.

"I want to wait until your six weeks are up, "he told me. "That way you will be healed."

I knew something was very wrong, but I wasn't sure what the problem was. Later, I found out the truth.

Nate made an appointment with a doctor. The doctor was in a small town outside of Taylorville. I was suspicious.

"Why are you seeing an out-town doctor?" I asked.

"I am having a problem with my back," Nate explained. "My back hurts all the time."

After seeing the doctor, he informed me, "The doctor doesn't want me to have sex until my back gets better."

For some reason, I didn't believe Nate. He was still going to work every day. Usually when his back hurt, he used it as an excuse not to work. I was really leery of his behavior. Again, my mistrust reared its ugly head. Also, Nate wouldn't allow me to go into the doctor's office with him. That caused me to be really suspicious, so I decided to find out for myself exactly what Nate's problem was.

One day, after Nate got out of the doctor's office, he decided to stop and have a beer at a local bar. I decided to stay in the car and wait for him. I had a plan. As I sat there with my own thoughts; curiosity got the best of me. I walked back to the doctor's office and asked to see the doctor who had taken care of Nate. When the doctor came out, I started firing questions at him.

"Why is my husband doctoring with you?" I asked. "And, why is he taking medicine?" I didn't give the doctor a chance to answer. He looked perplexed as he patiently waited for me to get it all out.

"My husband was just here, and he said that you gave him a shot for his back," I further explained.

"His back?" the doctor asked. "No, I am not treating him for his back. I am giving him penicillin shots for gonorrhea."

I really wasn't sure what kind of disease gonorrhea was.

"Could you explain what having gonorrhea means? "I asked the doctor.

"It's also called, the clap," the doctor replied.

Now, I had heard of that before. I also knew that the only way a person could get it was through sexual intercourse. I remembered that penicillin was an antibiotic used to treat venereal diseases. That was all I needed to know. Now it all came together for me. I understood why Nate had been so distant and unapproachable. My only consolation was that Nate had not given it to me. My blood was starting to boil. I left the doctor's office with all the ammunition that I needed. I was furious! Nate had really done it now. This was the final straw that broke the camel's back. In my mind, I was done with Nate. I had had enough shit from him! I had taken all I could handle.

I walked back and sat in the car in a rage. The minute Nate got into the car; I told him what I had learned.

"I went to see your doctor," I told him. "You are getting penicillin shots for gonorrhea!" I continued on, "You had sex with someone else and got the clap."

Of course, Nate went into a violent rage. I thought he was going to hit me, but he didn't.

"You had no right to go to the doctor's office and check up on me," he yelled.

"Yes, I did. You have been lying to me all along," I exclaimed rather loudly.

Nate didn't deny anything I said. But he did try to turn the argument towards me as if I were the one doing something wrong. We continued to yell at each other for quite some time. Then, I just shut up. It was like I turned off a switch. I felt numb.

Nothing would ever be the same. I no longer cared what Nate had to say. This was the last straw! I had always suspected him of infidelity in the past. But now, I wasn't guessing. I caught him red handed. This was a turning point in my life. I lost something that day I would never get back. The love and admiration I had always felt for Nate was gone. I felt very empty inside. From that point on, I would not go into a bar with him when he wanted to drink. I stayed home. I distanced myself from him. I didn't know if I could ever get over his blatant infidelity.

Nate knew that he had lost something precious. He slowly began to change. He still went for a beer, but he came back sooner than before. He acted like a dog that had been beaten. And of course, he was the only one he could blame. His guilt ate him up. He tried to get close to me. But, I was mentally unavailable. It took Nate a long time to open the door that I had so thoroughly closed off.

The truth was, Nate had gotten the clap from an old bar fly who hung out in his favorite bar. The whore Nate had slept with was the stepdaughter of my step-mother Eva. We called her Slimy Slim. She was disgusting. She was ugly and dirty. And, she would have sex with anyone. I couldn't stand to be around her before this happened. And Now, I could have bit nails in half thinking about her having sex with my husband! I never wanted to see her again. It made me sick to my stomach every time I thought about it. And, I didn't want to look at Nate. He discussed me, too. I didn't want to be in his presence. But, the worst part was, he was screwing that woman while I was in the hospital having his baby! It was time to take action. I was done.

The next day, I went downtown to the courthouse to speak to Mrs. Piddle and to turn the whore in to the police for spreading her nasty disease. That was my justice. I, then, found Mrs. Piddle and asked her for help.

"Mrs. Piddle, I need your help," I told her. "I kicked my husband out of the house, and he won't leave. I don't know what to do." I only hoped that she had some answers for me. I continued to explain my reasons why I needed help. "I have suffered humiliation and abuse from Nate, not once, but many times. I want out, but I have six kids and nowhere to go. I need your help."

Mrs. Piddle was the only mother figure I had ever known. I trusted that she would lead me in the right direction. She was my only hope. I anxiously waited for her reply.

"Dottie, you have got a big family, and those kids need a dad," she explained. "Honey, you can make things good again. Go back home and try to work this out."

I was heartsick when I heard her say that. She offered me no choices. She wanted me to go back home and stay with him. She took away my hope for getting away from Nate. I didn't want to go back to him. But, I could see that I had to. I was not going to get any help from Mrs. Piddle. I left in a daze. By the time I got home, my anger and rage had resurfaced.

I felt so violated and angry. In the past, I would have crawled on my hands and knees for this man that I loved so much. I was always good to him. I had treated him with nothing but respect. Not anymore. I hated Nate for what he had done to me. And, I questioned everything he had done in the past. He violated our marriage not once, but many times. Also, I resented the fact that I had done so many things for him that he could have done for himself. I had been a fool. But more than that, I felt that he had never loved me. He was trapped into staying married to me, because we had so many kids. And now, I wanted him out of my life. I felt defeated. But, I was not going to give up on the idea of leaving him.

When I returned from the courthouse, I told Nate, "Get out! You are going to give me money to take care of these kids, but you get out!"

Nate knew I was dead serious. For the first time in my life, I really didn't love him at all. I felt cold inside. I just wanted him out of my sight. In my mind, I had lost something that would never return. This was a real turning point in my life.

I drove Nate out to his dad's house to ask his dad if he could stay with him. The minute Nate opened his mouth, he lied to his dad. "I am not making enough money to suit Dottie, so she kicked me out," The minute Nate got the lie out of his mouth, I blew up. I decided right then and there to use my new found voice.

"You want the truth?" I asked Nate's dad. "Nate was out having sex with another woman when I was in the hospital having his baby!" I poured out the story of Nate's lewd affair. "To top it all off, he got the clap." Then I told his dad, "I am done with him; he wants a place to live, and he wants to stay here."

Mr. Gentry didn't mince words, he said, "No. Go home, both of you, and work this thing out between the two of you." That was the end of it. Nate had no choice but to go back home. Nate continued to live with us, but it was never the same.

When we got back home, I threatened Nate. "When my kids grow up and my youngest one turns eighteen, I am out of here! I will not live with you another day!" I was serious. What's more, Nate really believed me this time.

After I calmed down, I told Nate, "I don't think you ever loved me. No man would treat a woman he loves like this."

"But, I do love you, he assured me. "I will show you I can be different. I promise." After that day, Nate tried to convince me that he indeed loved me. But, I needed more.

Nate never, ever, said he was sorry. I may have felt better if he had at the least apologized to me. Then again, maybe I wouldn't have felt better. In my mind, I had already left Nate. I still felt the pain deep in my soul. My anger constantly nagged at me. Right now, I just couldn't let it go.

I felt dead inside. The numbness stayed with me for a long time. I often thought about leaving Nate. But, I had six kids, and I didn't have a job. And, I knew no one who would take in seven people. I felt really trapped. But, I did learn something from the whole experience.

This was a major turning point in my life. I had lost something precious and replaced it with a power I never knew I had. This power felt good to me. I was now in control for the first time in my life, and I knew it. I had never felt this kind of power before. And, I liked the feeling. I now had a voice, and I intended to use it. It was an awakening. Also, I made up my mind that I would never be hurt like this again. It was a plan. Unfortunately, my anger was just below the surface waiting to be released. I didn't feel that I had anything to lose anymore. I was bolder in my pursuit for justice even in small matters. Nate and I experienced a role reversal.

Nate knew that he had wronged me for the last time. He began to change. I knew he loved me in his own way. It was the only way he knew. Mostly, he showed his affection in a sexual way. Sometimes that offended me. All I needed was a simple hug. Nate tried to prove his love and please me as best he could. I believe he finally made a decision not to violate our marriage from this time forward. He never went anywhere without me. Consequently, I would know where he was and what he was doing all the time. He wanted to rebuild my trust in him in this way. He did not want to lose me, and he was going to prove his love. He also wanted to prove that he could change for the better.

Nate was working nights at Caterpillar at this time. He worked from 3:18pm to 11:18pm. He wanted to prove that he could be responsible, so he worked regularly. The regular paycheck did change our lives. The lack of financial pressure helped my attitude. I began to feel a little more at ease. Nate usually slept late in the mornings. Therefore, we didn't go anywhere in the evenings for quite some time. We stayed at home for several months.

I began to work for my half-sister Rena. I cleaned her house in the mornings while Nate was asleep. I got up early, bathed Robin, and put her in her bassinette. Then, I got her bottle ready for when she woke up.

Mary and Jeannie were my babysitters. Mary was almost eleven years old, and Jeannie was almost nine years old.

"You kids must stay quiet while your dad is asleep," I ordered them. "When Robin wakes up and starts to cry, give her the bottle I have ready for her. I won't be gone very long."

The kids were all mature enough to follow my orders. They always did what I asked them to do without question.

I went to Rena's and scrubbed her floors on my hands and knees. This was the cleanest way to do the job. I liked helping Rena. Actually, it helped both of us. She liked a clean house, and I liked having a little extra money. I cleaned house for her once a week.

I idolized Rena. She was a beautiful woman. We were almost the same age. Rena had lost her leg in a car accident. Her leg did not heal well. She had developed cancer in that leg. She eventually had the leg taken off up to the hip area. This caused her to walk on crutches. Although she had prosthesis for that leg, she didn't wear it. Since Rena was not able to do her own cleaning, so I worked for her.

Many times, when I returned home, Robin was still sleeping. As long as she was fed, clean, and had on a dry diaper, she was happy. She was surely a joy to me. And, the other kids took care of her very well. Robin was like having a live doll to play with. Everyone enjoyed her.

Nate came home one night and told me his hours at work had been changed. He would now be working the day shift from 7:18am until 3:18pm. This was going to be a big change in our lifestyle. Now, we were going to have a social life again. We could go out in the evenings. Of course, our entertainment was going to the local bars. Nate was going to always drink beer. But, just as he promised, he wanted me to accompany him. I didn't drink, but I finally agreed to go with him. Mainly because, somewhere in the back of my mind, I knew he would get into trouble if I didn't go along. And, I needed a little socialization, too.

Nate's favorite local bar was called Big Mo's. This was a small town bar where the locals hung out. Nate was a regular there. We both knew the owners of the bar, Big Mo and his wife Colleen. Mo was a really big man, hence the name of the bar. If any trouble arose in the bar, Mo could handle it. Colleen was always friendly and easy to talk to. I enjoyed sharing stories about our kids, husbands, and family. This was my social time, too. So, I kind of looked forward to coming here with Nate.

Several years passed, and life was definitely getting better all the time. Nate and I were both working, so we had a little extra money. The kids were getting old enough to take care of themselves. Therefore, we had less pressure in our lives. Often, we went to several different bars for recreation and socialization. We danced to the music that was playing on the jukebox. We entertained ourselves with a game of shuffleboard. But mostly, we got to know more people with whom we could socialize with. Our lives as a whole were on an even keel. We liked it this way.

I tried to forget the pain of our past experiences and move forward, but the past did come back to haunt me. One evening, Nate and I decided to go to Big Mo's tavern. Usually, when we went there, we sat at the bar to talk with Mo and Colleen. However, on this particular evening, Nate steered me towards a table in the corner of the room. I thought this was a bit strange, until I realized why he had done this. When I looked towards the bar, I saw old Slimy Slim sitting up on the bar stool. In a flash, my fury rose to the surface like a tidal wave. The memory of Nate being with her while I was having his baby came to me like a demon. Something inside me snapped! Nate had never really admitted that she was the one he slept with. But, a small voice inside told me that she was the one. I rose from the table and walked directly over to her. I grabbed the scarf around her neck and twisted it as hard as I could. I was choking her. I was out of control.

"You bitch!" I yelled. "You slept with my husband while I was having his baby!"

Slimy Slim was clearly shocked by my boldness. But, I saw guilt written on her face. She blinked and shuddered several time. She was stupid, and I knew it.

"Dottie, I only did it that one night," she excused herself by saying.

Nate suddenly appeared by my side. He heard the confrontation. He addressed the whore.

"You bitch!" he called her. Nate looked mad as he confronted her. "You would sleep with anybody." He told her. "You are nothing but a whore, and you gave me the clap."

The truth finally came out. I suspected it all along. Like this was supposed to make me feel better. Well, it didn't. This whole scene just made me feel sick all over again. I was ready to not only leave this bar, but Nate, too.

As we left the bar, my anger was still blazing. Evidently, I didn't get all my anger out.

"You better never violate our marriage again." I added, "If this ever happens again, you won't get out, but I will! My kids are getting older, and they can take care of themselves." I didn't hold back. I had to get it out. This anger had been brewing inside me for a long time. I no longer felt trapped in this relationship, and I wanted Nate to know it. I could get by without him. Now, that Nate knew where I stood, I was able move forward.

I finally began to show Nate I still loved him. I never stopped doing the things I had done before. I cooked, cleaned, took care of the kids, and I showed him the affection that a wife shows her husband. My life was still devoted to him. Yet, deep inside, I felt a void that was like an emptiness that couldn't be filled. Life would never be quite the same. I felt like I was experiencing grief.

Along with that grief, my half sister Rena passed away. Her death devastated me. I loved her so much. Her presence was such a total loss for me. I had grown very close to her in the last few years. I envied her. She always took great care with her appearance. I remembered her sitting up in her bed pinning her hair in curls even when she was very sick. She was a strong lady. I looked up to her. And, I wanted to be like her. She had always been my mentor and friend. Now, she was gone. I felt very alone. This added to the turning point in my life. I was growing up and seeing life more clearly.

When Robin was starting to walk, we were forced to move again. Caterpillar had gone on strike, so we were almost completely without money. We couldn't afford to pay our rent. So, we found a small house on a farm in Morrisonville, Illinois. The farm belonged to a man named Primo. Primo allowed us to live on his farm for free room and board. In turn, he asked that we take care of his pigs. Our job was to husk the corn by hand and feed the pigs daily. Also, we had to keep them warm in the winter so they wouldn't freeze to death. We hauled straw up to the barn to keep them warm. As a bonus, the kids enjoyed taking care of the pigs. The pigs were pets to them.

The house had two bedrooms, a large living room, and a big kitchen. The whole house was heated with a wood stove. We couldn't afford to buy wood for the stove. Therefore, we had to go to the timber and cut our own wood to burn. The stove I cooked on was also fueled with wood.

Primo loaned us a gun to hunt our own food. I always hid the clip with the ammo in it until we needed it. I often took the gun and went looking for a rabbit or squirrel to shoot for our dinner. I didn't find either of them. But, one day, I saw a bird running on the ground. I aimed the gun and fired. My aim was good. I killed the bird, cleaned it, and baked it for supper. My family feasted that night. Later, I found out it was a pheasant. I certainly enjoyed eating that bird!

Nate often cut down trees on Primo's farm. He used a chainsaw to accomplish this task. One day he was cutting down trees and cut right into his knee. He came up to the house with blood gushing from the wound. I was shocked when I seen so much blood.

"Fix it!" Nate told me.

I examined the wound and saw the gash was deep. I knew it probably needed stitches, but we couldn't afford a doctor or hospital bill. So, I proceeded to clean the wound with peroxide. Then, I used duct tape to hold the skin together. I wrapped the tape around Nate's leg several times. I continued to wrap the duct tape around his entire knee.

"You are going to have to stay in the house and keep this elevated in order for it to heal," I told Nate. "Otherwise, it will get infected."

Nate did as I told him. However, his leg no sooner healed when he went out and did the same thing to his other knee. We went through the same process all over again. Of course, he had been drinking both times. Otherwise, he would have been smarter and safer with the chain saw.

Another time, Nate drove the tractor out into the timber to smoke out a ground hog. He attached a hose to the exhaust pipe of the tractor and placed it into the ground hog's hole. Of course, he had been drinking a lot of beer. It was late at night. After he was finished with this nonsense, he and Harris rode the tractor back up to the house. Nate couldn't see very well through the darkness. There were no lights outside our house. As he drove into the back yard, the clothesline caught him under the neck and jerked him off the tractor. Harris stayed on the tractor until it hit our car and pushed it into the house. The tractor was grinding the car against the house with its motor still running. The sound of the car grinding against the house scared me to death! Nate came running up to the house in dark, hopped on the tractor, and shut off the engine. But, the damage was already done. Needless to say, I was livid! This was just another one of Nate's drunken antics.

Primo didn't help Nate out with his drinking problem. He encouraged Nate to drink while he was on the job. Primo owned a liquor store near the downtown area of Taylorville. Nate worked in the store doing odd jobs for Primo. He often painted or cleaned in the store. For lunch, Primo offered Nate warm beer to drink. Of course, he drank it. He kind of liked that part of his job.

We didn't live at Primo's for very long, but it was a memorable time. The kids really enjoyed playing with those pigs. They often cornered one of them and rode them like a bucking bronco. Also, they learned what it was like to live on a farm. All too soon, we moved on.

We then rented a house on a hill about three miles east of Taylorville. Nate was still on strike. So, we had no money for food or gas for our car. Many times, I didn't know where our next meal was coming from. But something always came up, literally. The kids knew how to scrounge for food. They dug dandelions greens out of the front yard. Also, they hunted pasture mushrooms, picked blackberries and apples, and cracked open hickory nuts, black walnuts, and hazel nuts. We knew how to find natural foods before it was so popular. Also, Nate provided us with rabbit, turtle, and frog legs. We all worked together and did whatever we could do to get by. We somehow managed to survive the tough times.

After the older kids left for school, I took the two youngest kids and walked three miles into town. The kids and I walked to Mattie's house. I still cleaned house for her once a week. I made enough money to buy a few groceries. After I finished cleaning, I walked the three miles back home.

Through the grapevine, I acquired more cleaning jobs. On Monday mornings, I cleaned Millie Riley's beauty salon. The salon was closed on Mondays, so this was a perfect day to clean it without interruptions. Millie trusted me to be there alone and was quite pleased with my work. She passed the word on to other people who needed a good trustworthy cleaning lady.

Colleen Hall came to my door one day. She needed an honest person to clean her house.

"Dottie, Millie Riley told me that you do housework." Colleen said. "My husband and I both work at the Hopper Paper Mill. If you will clean my house once a week, I will pay you seventy-five cents an hour."

"Yes, I will be happy to clean for you." I told Colleen. "But, right now, I don't even have enough gas in my car to get to your house."

That was not a problem for Colleen. She immediately gave me ten dollars for gas and set up a time for me to clean for her on a weekly basis.

I liked having that weekly money coming in. I liked it so well, I found another job. I started working at the G&R Café. I worked in the kitchen washing dishes. Also, when the owners were on vacation, I cleaned the café from top to bottom. One job led to another. Soon, I was working every day. At least I could now feed my kids. They were my first priority. My house rent was my second priority. The rent was cheap, so we stayed right where were we were for a few years.

The house we now lived in was on a hill overlooking a highway. It was a small house that had only four rooms. It had a living room, two bedrooms and a real small kitchen. Our four older kids slept in a double bed in one of the bedrooms. And, Nate, Robin, Mac, and I slept in the other bedroom in a double bed. The small house was crowded.

Our current lifestyle was rather primitive. In the wintertime, we closed off the bedrooms and the kitchen. We only heated the living room. The kitchen was so cold that icicles hung off the cabinets. Also, the house had no electricity, because our power had been turned off. We couldn't pay the bill. Therefore, we used an old kerosene lamp for light in the evenings. Usually, we went to bed early. In addition to our other inconveniences, our water came from a pump outside the house. We had no inside plumbing. Therefore, we had an outhouse in the back yard. It sure was cold in the winter. Unfortunately, we couldn't afford anything better than this.

Because we were so poor, the State offered us food called commodities. Commodities were a variety of foods like cheese, rice, canned meats, and butter. While Nate was on strike from Caterpillar, he was given a slip of paper that allowed us to get this food free of charge.

We managed to live on the hill for four years. Things got better over time. Nate went back to work at Caterpillar. So, we were able to live a little better. However, because our rent was low, we continued to live the same house. We still had left over doctor and hospital bills that we were trying to pay off. We were trying to get back on our feet again.

Nate continued to drink, and sometimes did stupid things. One day he decided to use the only tub we had to clean a motor that he was working on. After cleaning the motor, he started the engine while it was still in my tub. The motor went crazy! It ate a hole clean through the bottom of the tub. It ruined it. I was hopping mad. Now, we had to buy a new tub.

After Nate was back to work about a year, he was called into his bosses' office. Nate was worried that he might lose his job. However, his boss had a different problem.

"Nate, your debtors are trying to get the money you owe them." He told Nate. "They threatened to garnish your wages." Nate boss had a recommendation. "I suggest that you go see a lawyer and file for bankruptcy."

"I think that is a good idea," Nate told him.

Although filing for bankruptcy would affect Nate's credit for many years, he could see no other way to solve this problem. His debt at this time was $3,000. He just didn't have that kind of money. So, Nate went to see a lawyer the next day and declared bankruptcy on the amount he owed. This gave us a chance to start over.

Nate's brother Gil, and his wife Fanny, had come to visit us and told us about a house that would change our future.

"Dottie, I've got a house for you." Fanny told me with excitement. "The newspaper ad says free rent for upkeep."

Fanny had gone to look at the house herself. She had considered the house for herself and Gil. Stonington was Gil's home town. He and Fanny rented a small apartment on Main Street in Stonington. They often thought about buying a house, so they considered the house they told me about on Livergood Street. But in the end, Fanny decided the house would take too much work she and Gil to handle. They were getting up in age and didn't want the headache of remodeling.

"Dottie, you could turn this house into a real doll house." Fanny said with confidence.

I was impressed; free rent! This was truly a dream come true. It seemed like we were never able to pay our rent. This house sounded real good to me.

"Yeah, I could keep that house up." I told Fanny.

Fanny continued to explain more about this particular house. I was getting more excited about it the more she talked.

"The house has three bedrooms, two upstairs and one down. Also, it had a large living room, kitchen, and an inside bathroom. This house has a furnace inside a corner of the kitchen. Off of the kitchen there is a small closed-in back porch. Along with that, it has an attached one car garage and a front porch." Fanny said as she described the house.

Wow! This was sounding better all the time. This house was huge compared to what we were living in. I was really excited about this opportunity.

Fanny told me the house number and said it was located in Stonington, Illinois. It was on Livergood Street. Nate and his family had grown up in the country outside of Stonington. So, I was familiar with the territory. According to Fanny, the only money we needed was fifty dollars to pay for back taxes. It sounded too good to be true! The next day we decided to go look at this house.

When we went to look at the house, I understood why it was rent free. This house was a mess! The hedge in front of the house was taller than me. No one had cut it for a very long time, so it was at least six feet tall and four feet wide. The weeds in the yard had grown up so high that it overtook the grass. Also, the yard was littered with junk that included and an old baby buggy, bricks, large rocks, a large old bed spring, and more. I realized it would take a long time to get the yard in shape. We would probably have to do that first.

This house had obviously been abandoned for a long period of time. Many of the windows were broken. And, the front porch needed to be completely redone. The boards had rotted away with age, and it had a large whole directly in the center of it. The outside of the house was covered in what looked like sheets of green shingles. Actually, the outside of the house didn't look too bad. I could tell from looking at the whole picture, this was going to take a lot of work. However, it might be worth it if we could get it rent free.

We peaked through the windows to see the inside the house. This had to be the filthiest house I had ever seen. I had lived in some dumps before, but this one took the cake! I am sure it had not been cleaned in years. The walls literally had human fecal matter smeared on them. I found it hard to believe that anyone could have lived here in quite a few years. In addition to that, every room was filled with paper, garbage, pieces of furniture, and more filth. As I looked from room to room, I spoke out loud saying, "What have I gotten in to?" Then the thought of it being rent free came back to me. I had to stay focused on that thought.

Nate and I discussed how large an undertaking this would be for us. We both were accustomed to hard work, so that didn't bother us. And, our kids were plenty old enough to help. They were all good workers, so we had plenty of help. We understood what we were all in for. The work on this house would be grueling. However, in the end, we decided that we could turn this house into a nice place to live. We decided to go for it!

The size of this house was perfect for all eight of us. In the past, we lived in dozens of houses since we had been married. They all had been rental properties. Most of them were so small we barely had room for the kids to sleep. In this house, the kids could have a lot more space. The three girls could have their own room, and the three boys could have their own room. Also, the kids would have a big yard to play in. The entire yard was almost an acre. I could see the possibilities. But, best of all, we had an opportunity to own our own home. This was my dream. We needed to act now.

We contacted a woman who lived in Decatur, Illinois. This woman was supposed to be the daughter of the people who used to live in the house we wanted to buy. We met this woman and gave her fifty dollars for the back taxes. She accepted it and wished us luck. We were now ready to start the work to make this house our own.

Chapter Thirteen
OUR PROPERTY ON LIVERGOOD STREET

We were ready to start the work to transform this mess into a home. I dreaded the work, but I knew it was a new beginning for us. With a lot of elbow grease, we could make this a fine home. We could own property for the first time in our lives. I was prepared to make the sacrifice.

We tacked the yard first. We cut the hedge about one foot high with a chainsaw. It didn't' look very good, but I figured it was going to either be better because of this, or it would die. Either way, it was OK with me. Then, we took an axe and chopped down excess trees and bushes. Next, we used a sickle to cut the highest grasses. We picked all the junk out of the yard and hauled out to the alley until we could have it taken away. After that was done, we finally mowed and manicured the lawn.

The month was late July, 1963. It was so hot we could barely stand it. Sweat was rolling off of each one of us in a steady stream. The intense heat made the work ten times harder. Every one of us labored for three weeks before we saw results. I don't think I had ever worked so hard in all my life as I was right now. But, it was worth it. In the end, we had a beautiful lawn. Now, we were ready to tackle the inside of the house.

The inside of the house was the most pitiful mess I had ever seen. It was filthy. Also, it was full of useless stuff that needed to be thrown away. This stuff included papers, magazines, old furniture, and just plain crud. We opened a window in the living room. This window opened into the attached garage. Nate and I used a shovel to pick up garbage and toss it through the window into the garage. Because the garage had a dirt floor, we didn't worry about getting it dirty. In no time at all, we had completely filled the garage.

The City of Stonington agreed to haul truckloads of garbage away from our house. They made a deal with us. They wouldn't charge us for the cleanup. In exchange, we cleaned up the house. They had their jobs cut out for them, and so did we. They no sooner hauled off one truckload; they came back for another one. During the three months it took us to clean up the house; the City hauled away many truckload of garbage. We were happy that we didn't have to do this job ourselves. And, the City of Stonington was grateful that we were cleaning up the property. It had been an eyesore for the town for quite some time. After getting all the excess mess out of the house, we were ready to clean the inside.

The walls, floors, and bathroom inside the house were grimy. We used bleach and scouring cleanser on everything we touched. Both the kitchen and bathroom floors were so dirty, they looked black. I didn't even want to walk on them until they had been totally cleaned. The four foot by six foot floor in the bathroom took us hours to clean. We had to clean the bathroom first, so we could use the toilet stool while we worked. The entire bathroom contained a toilet stool, a sink, and a small mirror. The dirt was embedded into floor worse than anything I had ever seen. We cleaned all the floors first, and then, we bleached the walls inch by inch. We bleached every wall in the house from the ceiling to the floor.

We were trying to get our new house in shape before school started, but we were running out of time. The kids would start to school in late August, so we needed to get moved in before then. I had already enrolled Mac into Kindergarten. Robin was my only child who was not old enough to go to school. My oldest four kids were excited to be living here, and going to school in this town. Now, they would not have to switch schools. This thought alone brought stability to our lives. Also, the kids had already met some of the neighborhood kids and liked them. Therefore, everyone was happy about this house. But we were running out of time. We needed to find a way to get the remodeling done faster.

Nate came up with another plan. He used his vacation money from Caterpillar to get the job done faster. His vacation check was for one-hundred and thirty-five dollars. He paid to have new glass replaced in the windows that were broken. Also, he paid Louise Wiseman, a friend of ours, to put up new wall paper in our living room and lower bedroom. She was good at this job and did it regularly. We trusted her expertise. Not to mention the fact, she could get it done ten times faster than we could have. Louise wallpapered the lower level of the house. She used a pretty wallpaper to make our living room and bedroom look special.

Nate put up a new back door. It was a used door, but it was new to us. By doing these extras, our house was looking better all the time. Also, we were getting it done faster with extra help.

Next, I tore apart the furnace that was located in the corner of the kitchen. It was so dirty I had to take it apart piece by piece to clean it. After I washed and dried each piece, I laid them out into a pattern so I could put it back together the same way I took it apart. This was the first time we had a furnace inside a house. My hope was that when winter got here, the furnace would be operational.

After the cleaning was finished, we were ready do the finish work. We painted the rest of the rooms in the house. Then, we decided to replace the linoleum in the kitchen. After that, we put all new carpeting in the living room and lower bedroom. It looked really nice and clean. We were so proud of our efforts.

Our last major project was to fix the front porch. I had heard that someone in town was tearing down a house, and I had an idea. I went to the location of the house and asked the people working there if I could have the tongue and groove boards they were throwing away. Of course, they were glad to have someone haul them off. The kind people readily gave me as many boards as I needed. I piled them into the trunk of the car and brought them home. While I was doing that, Nate had already cleared the old boards off of the porch. There was only a skeleton of boards left around the perimeter However, it was getting late, and Nate was ready to quit for the night.

The next morning after Nate left for work, I decided that I could put the porch together myself. I got out the electric saw and started sawing the boards. It took me most of the day to get the boards the right length and nail them into place. I looked at what I had done so far, and it looked good. Now, I had only one board left to cut. Suddenly, the saw quit on me. The blade had somehow come loose. I felt lucky the blade had not flown off and injure me. I had to quit before I was finished. When Nate got home from work, he tightened the blade and finished the last board. I was proud of my work. The porch looked great!

We had finally accomplished our goal. The kids now had a place they could really call home. They had their own rooms, a big yard to play in, and only one school from now on. Nate and I now owned our own property. We put a lot of money and effort into making this place a nice home. This gave us a feeling of stability that was priceless. All our efforts were worth it. We had accomplished our goal! Our family had a real solid home.

I took pride in working in my new home. I was busy all the time. I always had something to clean. I cleaned house, ran the sweeper, dusted, did the laundry. Then, I went outside and swept the sidewalk and the dirt floor in the garage. If the car needed washed, I washed it on the inside and out. Next, I worked in the yard. I pulled the extra weeds out of my flowers to keep them neat. By ten o'clock in the morning, I had all my work done.

I had a little free time now, so it gave me time to think about my mother. I often thought of her. I had never been told much about my mother's life before she died, so I contacted several people who knew her when she was young. I had always been told that my mother died in childbirth. I wanted to know for sure how she died. So, I went to the courthouse and obtained my mother's death certificate. It noted her cause of death to be pneumonia. I also found out her full name. It was Flora Viola Fore Tiller. She was born in Freeport, Illinois. It listed her mother as Berta Winfield. Berta and Grandpa Fore lived in Freeport a while before moving to Taylorville.

I found out several things I needed to know about my mother. She was the youngest of the three children in her family. She had a sister named Mable who lived in St. Louis. I never got to meet her. I often wondered if she looked like my mom.

I also found out where my mom was buried. I never knew. I was told that she was buried in Oak Hill Cemetery. This was a very large cemetery on the outskirts of Taylorville. I went to the cemetery to find my mother's grave. I located the cemetery office and asked the caretaker for the location of Edie Dons. Edie was my mother's first husband. Supposedly, my mother was buried next to him. The caretaker told me to look for a concrete bench near Edie Dons. I would find my mother's grave there. I walked and walked. Edie had a military stone that looked like all the other military personnel, so it took me a while before I found his. I located my mother's grave.

Next to my mother's grave was a concrete bench. I often went to the cemetery and sat on this bench. This gave me a chance to grieve. I cried because I missed my mother. I wished she could wrap her arms around me and give me a hug. I wished she could tell me that she loved me. When I was feeling particularly sad, I went to the cemetery and talked with her. I talked to her as if she were right there with me. I knew beyond a doubt; she heard me. Somehow, it made me feel close to her just sitting on the bench near her grave. This was as close as I could get. Sitting by my mother's grave gave me a feeling of peace in my heart.

I always felt sad that no one placed a stone on my mother's grave. So, many years later, I purchased one myself. I needed to do this. It made me feel good. I was letting her know that I loved her and thought she was special. This was my gift to her.

Throughout my life I felt like I had been living a bad dream concerning my mother. I questioned whether or not everything I remembered was real. Then, one day I met an old neighbor of mine. Her name was Mrs. Riggers and she lived across the street from me when my mother died. I was happy to talk to someone who had actually known my mother.

"I knew your mother very well." Mrs. Riggers told me.

What a great feeling it was for me to talk with someone who personally knew my mother. I talked with Mr. Riggers for quite a while. I relayed my thoughts about the events that led up to my mother's funeral. I told Mrs. Riggers that I remembered how the chairs were placed in rows in my living room. And, I told her how I remembered the hearse taking my mother away.

"I thought the day of the funeral was a bad dream." I told Mrs. Riggers. "I wasn't sure if it was real."

"Dottie, everything you told me was not a dream." She told me as she validated the events leading up to the funeral. "You remembered exactly what happened. The funeral was real."

What a relief it was to me to know I remembered the past so well. Many times throughout my life, the thoughts of the day of my mother's funeral kept coming back to me. Now, I had a sense of peace knowing that it wasn't all a dream. I thanked Mrs. Riggers for clarifying the whole experience for me. I felt better knowing I remembered it all correctly. I was ready to move forward in my life.

I always got up at four thirty in the morning. I made the coffee. Then, I woke up Nate. While he was drinking his coffee, I fixed his lunch. I wanted to make sure he got off to work. He had to catch his ride at six o'clock in the morning. Sometimes, it was a chore to get him off to work. He usually came up with all kinds of excuses not to go. Many times, he complained about his back. I didn't know whether or not to believe him. He didn't look sick. And, I knew he just didn't want to work. He wanted to drink beer. I figured that's what made him sick in the first place! I didn't have patience for that. So, I did everything I could to make the transition to work easy for him. In the winter time, I even scooped a path out to the road so he wouldn't get his feet wet. I told everyone, "I had to sharpen my pitchfork to get him out the door." It was a running joke.

A whole year rolled by, and it was summer again. I had gotten to know my closest neighbors, and I talked to them almost daily. Dolly Emery lived across the street from me. I liked her right away. We often shared a cup of coffee and good conversation. One day as we were talking, Dolly mentioned that it was time to pay our taxes on our property. I didn't know anything about taxes.

"How often do you pay your taxes Dolly?" I asked.

"I have to pay them every year at this time." Dolly explained.

"Where do we pay the taxes?" I asked Dolly. This was the first time I ever owned a house. I was clueless about this subject. I didn't know taxes had to be paid every year. It kind of worried me thinking about it. Dolly had lived in her house for years. So, she suggested I go to the courthouse in Taylorville and ask about the taxes for the old Emerson place. The people at the courthouse could tell me what I needed to know about my property. I thanked Dolly for the information, and I decided I would go do this the next day.

Overnight, I had time to think about this problem. I thought about the woman I had given money to for back taxes. Her name was Maxine. She told me that was all I needed to live in my house. I thought I was done paying for anything associated with this house. I thought that was our agreement. But, after I thought about it, Maxine had not even come around the house to see what we had accomplished. Something didn't seem right here. I had an uneasy feeling about the whole deal.

The next day, I went to the courthouse. I gave the woman at the counter my street address in Stonington. I told her I wanted to pay my taxes.

The clerk looked up my street address and said, "Why honey, your house has been sold. It was sold last October."

"Sold?" I exclaimed. "The house can't be sold. I live in that house." I stood in awe, and I started to get madder by the minute. I was also hurt to think we had just put all that effort into this house, and someone bought it right out from underneath us.

"Sold?" I said again.

"Yes, it was bought by a Mr. Cumbersome who lives in Pana, Illinois. He works at the bank in Pana and often buys up houses for the back taxes." She continued to explain. "Mr. Cumbersome uses the houses for rental property."

I was just beside myself when I reflected back on what the woman in the courthouse told me. I didn't know what to do next. I left the courthouse in a tizzy. I was just sick about all this.

On my way home, I thought about all the good things that happened in our lives since we moved into our house. We were living well. Our lives were even more stable than a year ago. The kids were all doing well in school. And, my older girls were built in babysitters. This freed me up to look for work outside the house. Our lives were good. I just didn't understand why this had to happen at such a good time. We were living right. I thought and thought. Finally, I came to the conclusion that there had to be some way to resolve this problem. And, I was going to face it head on.

When Nate came home from work, I told him, "You have to take me to Pana to see a man by the name of Cumbersome. He has bought our house!" I continued to tell him, "We are in trouble. We put all this money into this house. We cleaned it up. And now the taxes are due. This man bought our house for back taxes!"

Nate knew I was upset. Straight away, we drove to Pana. We went to the bank where Mr. Cumbersome worked and asked to speak with Mr. Cumbersome. He approached us right away and introduced himself. Nate and I sat down at his desk to have a talk with him. I wasn't going to beat-around-the bush.

"I was told that you bought our house in Stonington."

"Yes, I did buy a house in Stonington." Mr. Cumbersome said after a little thought. "But, I haven't seen it, yet." Supposedly, he had bought our house sight unseen.

Nate and I told him about the work we had done to the house and how much money we had put in it. We were at his mercy. I only hoped he would realize that our blood, sweat, and tears had gone into fixing this house up. This was our home! After Mr. Cumbersome heard us out, he promised to come to Stonington to take a look at the house. He would talk more with us after he had done that.

Just as Mr. Cumbersome promised, he showed up unexpectedly one afternoon. I was in the kitchen washing dishes when I caught a glimpse of someone walking around our house. He was looking at the exterior of the house. The kids were all home from school, and they were curious about who this man was. I realized that it was Mr. Cumbersome. So, I invited him into the living room. He sat down in one of the chairs, and I sat in the other chair. Curiosity got the best of the kids. All six kids followed Mr. Cumbersome inside the house. The kids were taught to be well mannered, so they all lined up on the couch in the living room. They all sat quietly and listened. They wanted to hear what this man had to say. They were old enough to know our future was at stake.

I started to explain to Mr. Cumbersome the events that took place prior to us moving into this house. I told him about giving the fifty dollars to Maxine to pay the back taxes before we moved into the house last year. I had been told that she was a relative to the people who lived in the house before us. I contacted her, and gave her fifty dollars for the back taxes. I thought it was a done deal. I thought the house was ours.

Mrs. Cumbersome listened very carefully as I told him how much money and work we had put into this house during the last year.

"The woman you gave the money to had no connection to this house at all." Mr. Cumbersome informed me. He then waited until I had time to absorb this bit of information.

He glanced around the living room and said, "You have gotten this fixed up pretty well. It is nice and clean. Were you figuring to buy this house?"

I didn't hesitate, I said, "Yes."

"What kind of collateral do you have? Do you have money in the bank?" he asked.

"No, I don't have any money." I told him.

Mr. Cumbersome thought about that for a moment, then he said, "What do you expect to use for a down payment?"

"Mr. Cumbersome, I can't put any money down on this house. I would just have to pay it like rent." I suggested.

"How much could you pay a month for rent?" he asked.

"I can afford twenty dollars a month." I truthfully told him.

"That's no money." He told me. "Let's say twenty-five dollars a month?"

I agreed. "Twenty-five dollars a month seems alright to me." I figured I could pay that amount every month.

"You need a down payment." He stated. "What kind of collateral do you have?"

"Mr. Cumbersome, I don't have anything!" I whined. Didn't he understand this? I was feeling desperate.

"I'll take whatever you have in your purse." He finally suggested.

Boy, he really didn't get it! I was heartsick to think that I might lose this house because I had no ready cash. But I didn't back down. I looked him straight in the eyes and said, "I don't have one dime in my purse." I was getting really frustrated by now.

"You must have some kind of collateral?" he told me.

I had had it! I pointed to my kids sitting on the couch. I told him, "The only collateral I have is those six kids sitting right there on that couch. And, they need a roof over their heads!"

Mr. Cumbersome laughed like he really got a kick out of that statement. He then proceeded to carry on a little small talk to ease the tension.

"I'll tell you what I am going to do." He told me after a while. " I paid one-thousand dollars for this house. I will sell it to you for that same amount. Also, I will write you a voucher for the down payment. Then, you can pay me twenty-five dollars a month until you get the house paid off."

"That sounds good to me." I said in agreement. It was obvious to me that Mr. Cumbersome was a good man. He didn't' expect to make a profit off of me. I was quite satisfied with our agreement. We shook hands on it. At this time, I didn't really know what a voucher was. All I understood was, I was going to own my own house as soon as I could pay it off.

Every month after that time, I went to the bank, purchased a money order for twenty five dollars, and sent it to Mr. Cumbersome. When I could afford a little extra, I increased it to fifty or seventy five dollars. Each time I tallied up my total. I was on a mission to pay this house off.

Nate and I had some really good friends. One couple was Bob and Linda. Nate met Bob when he worked at Caterpillar. He was looking for a regular ride to work. Nate didn't want to ride the bus. Bob drove a car full of guys to work every day. Nate joined them, and the friendship continued for many years.

Bob and Linda own a lot at the lake. When we wanted to relax, we went to the lake lot and visited with them. They were usually there every weekend. Linda and I became close friends, too. We talked for hour and shared stories about our kids.

We like Bob and Linda so much that we planned a vacation with them. They owned a real nice cabin down in the Ozarks. We went there for a week at a time. It was great fun! Nate and Bob drank beer and shared stories about work. And, Linda tried to teach me to swim. That was a lost cause. I ended up pulling her into the water with me. Later, Linda told me, "Oh, no, I will never do that again!" I was a little embarrassed. I was just too scared of the water. I didn't really like to get in the water. I was happy to just sit around and talk.

One weekend Linda made some mulligan stew and asked us to join them for dinner at the lake lot. They had also invited some other friends. It sounded like fun, so Nate and I agreed to come. I enjoyed talking to Linda. And, I was always ready to meet new people.

One of Linda's friends, named Jean, talked to me quite frankly. I told her that I cleaned houses for a living. I had several regular customers that depended on me to clean their house every week.

"Dottie, I don't know why you do housework when you could work in a factory," she said. You could make more money in a factory." Jean worked at a sewing factory in Taylorville. It was called Rootle's Sewing Factory. Jean told me, "The sewing factory needs an inspector and a clipper. You could do that."

"No, I couldn't work in a factory." I told Jean. "I only have a fourth grade education."

But Jean wouldn't give up. She continued to encourage me by saying, "Yes, you can do it Dottie. I know you can!" Jean had so much faith in me that I really believed I could get this job. I knew I would need help in learning the ropes, but I was ready to apply for the job.

Later I told Nate, "I am going to put my application in at the sewing factory, and I am going to get that job Jean talked about."

Nate immediately discouraged me. He told me, "I'll bet you ten dollars you don't get it. You don't have the education, and you have never worked in a factory."

His words kind of hit me wrong. But, this did not discourage me; in fact, I was even more determined to prove him wrong.

I went to the factory and picked up an application. I wasn't sure how to fill it out. Jeannie was in high school at this time. I asked her fill out the application for me. It didn't take her very long. As soon as she was finished, I took it to the owner of the sewing factory. His name was Mr. Rootle. He reviewed my application right on the spot. When he finished, he looked at me and simply said, "Set your alarm clock and bring your lunch to work tomorrow."

Wow! Just like that. I had a real job. I was really excited. I did it! I couldn't wait to tell Nate, and of course, collect my ten dollars.

I didn't have much time to think about this job, because I was starting my employment the next day. Mr. Rootle had told me that I would need to keep a record of my time and output. He said my job was called a piece-rate job. It occurred to me that I would have to do some math every day. This scared me. Math was like Greek to me. I was worried that I wouldn't be able to do that part of the job.

I went to work the next day and somehow managed to make over the standard rate every day that first week. Although it appeared I was doing a good job, I still struggled to keep that daily record. I was unsure of myself. I wanted to make sure I did my math right.

I went to my neighbor's house to have a talk with her about my fears. I was starting to panic. This neighbor was Nan Morrow. Nan was always honest with me. I valued her opinion.

"Nan, I need your opinion. I am really concerned. I am afraid that I won't be able to add my piece-rate right at work," I explained.

"Don't you worry Dottie," Nan said. "You are doing well; give it two weeks. I am sure your math will get easier."

I thanked Nan for her confidence in me and went back home with the idea that I would give myself one more week to get my math right.

One week marched into another. Everyone pitched in to help me with my time sheet. Eventually, I became more comfortable with the calculations. Also, I became more confident and secure with a regular paycheck. This was the only job I ever had where I had money left over at the end of the week. This was great! I loved this job. I was lucky to work here.

I had done housework most of my life. The little money I made went for groceries, kid's shoes, and clothes for the kids. There was never any extra money. I never had money left over for me. Now, because of this job at the sewing factory, I had a little extra money that I could put in a savings account. This was another dream of mine. But, my first priority was to pay off my house.

I started sending Mr. Cumbersome a little extra each month. I kept my tally of what I had paid every month, until I totaled it up to be one-thousand dollars. Finally, I finished paying off my house. I was thrilled and proud of myself! I sent Mr. Cumbersome a letter asking for my deed.

I was at work one day a few weeks later when my boss called me into his office. Mr. Cumbersome was in his office and had come to see me personally. I was certainly surprised to see him here.

"Mrs. Gentry, I brought the tax deed to your house, but you do not have the house paid off yet," Mr. Cumbersome informed me.

I didn't know what he was talking about. I knew I did the math right. I calculated several times.

"Every time I sent a money order, I figured it up and it totaled one-thousand dollars," I said with a surprised look on my face. I can't see where I made a mistake in my total.

Mr. Cumbersome pulled out the voucher he gave me for the down payment on my house. He explained, "You did not pay for this voucher. It was for twenty-five dollars."

I was embarrassed. I had forgotten all about that voucher. I guess I didn't realize I needed to pay him for the loan.

"Oh, I forgot," I quickly told him. "When I get my check at the end of the week, the twenty-five dollars will be in the mail."

Mr. Cumbersome handed me the deed with a big smile on his face. He knew I would send him a check at the end of the week. He trusted me.

When he received the money for the voucher, he sent me a real nice letter. It said, Mrs. Gentry, it was good doing business with you. If you ever need to buy another house, please contact me. I would be glad to help you. It was signed, Mr. Cumbersome. I was so proud of myself. What an accomplishment this was for me. This was my first business transaction. I was a success, and I had the deed to prove it!

We had nine and a-half wonderful years in our house on Livergood Street. During that time, we went through a lot of changes. Nate and I were both working every day. Having two paychecks really made a difference in our lives. We felt more secure financially. I even managed to establish that savings account I always wanted. And, Nate and I's personal relationship was on an even keel. We had both gotten older and seemed to appreciate each other's company more than ever before. Also, the kids were growing up. This freed Nate and I up to do more fun things by ourselves and with the kids.

I had always been a saver. I never spent a lot of money. Unfortunately, Nate was a spender. If he had ten dollars, he was going to spend twenty. When Nate figured I had a little money saved, he tried to find an excuse to use that money. I didn't want to use it. So sometimes, I hid my money from him. I was protecting myself from disappointment. I liked having a cushion to rely on.

Lack of food was no longer an issue for us. We went to the grocery store every week and bought enough food to last the whole week. It felt good to have plenty of food in the house. The kids thrived on it, and so did I.

Our Christmas holidays were really special. I usually made twelve pies. So, each boy had a pie of his own. I cooked up a feast. Everyone joined in on the preparation of the food. At noon, we all gave thanks to God and ate our food. When I was young, I never knew what a holiday was. No one celebrated Easter, Thanksgiving, or Christmas. I started having Christmas when my kids were little. I wanted to make Christmas special for them. We could never afford much, but we bought each kid a little something special that we knew they wanted. I enjoyed their happiness. Sometimes, it made me feel like a kid again. I thanked God for this special time.

God was my solace. I had no doubt that I was living right within myself. Each evening after supper, I read the bible to the kids. I tried to teach them the Christian way to live. As I read my favorite scriptures to the kids, we discussed each one of them. All the kids patiently listened. Then, they asked me questions about each one. Sometimes we quoted the passages to memorize them. We all looked forward to this special time. I felt peaceful and content. I like sharing the Lord's work with them.

Our house usually smelled of home cooking. I made most of our dishes from scratch. Homemade bread was specialty. I mix the ingredients, rolled it into a ball, and placed it in a glass bowl with a dishcloth over the top. It took all day for the bread to rise several times. When the bread swelled to the top of the bowl, I gently kneaded the dough back down. When it was ready to bake, I broke off pieces of dough, rolled them in balls, and then placed them on a cookie sheet. Then, I baked them in the oven until they were brown. To finish them off, I buttered the tops. I called them light rolls. I usually served them with ham and beans.

If I had any dough left over, I made cinnamon rolls, donuts, or Indian bread. I rolled the dough flat with a rolling pin, sprinkled it with cinnamon, sugar, and add pats of butter. Then, I hand rolled the dough into a long strip. I then cut the strip into one inch slices. I now had perfectly shaped cinnamon rolls. Often, I left the dough flat for Indian bread. I used an old Indian receipt. I flattened the dough into a thin patty, fried it in grease until it was brown on one side, and flipped it over to brown the other side. It was great. Otherwise, I cut donuts out using a small glass, and deep fried them my grease. The kids loved these treats, and so did I.

The kids all loved cookies, too. I made them regularly. Oatmeal cookies was everyone's favorite. Nate even liked them. I packed them in his lunch to take to work. I made sure the cookies were always available to him.

We were still eating beans and potatoes, but we had more variety in our diets. I fried potatoes with onions. And, sometimes we had gravy. My beans usually had a ham hock in them. And, since we had a garden, we had fresh vegetables. My vegetable soup was delicious. In addition to that, I made spaghetti and different types of pasta. I now had a choice of what I could cook. And, I thought the kids were healthier because of it.

I tried to make every meal special. Our dessert consisted of a leaf of lettuce placed on each individual's saucers with a ring of pineapple on top of it, and a dollop of cottage cheese to top it off. If I was feeling festive, I placed a maraschino on top of the cottage cheese. Another dessert was various kinds of Jell-O with fruit in it. I made Dream Whip for our topping. These were healthy desserts.

My life was always busy. I always felt like I was hurrying all the time. I had a lot of people to take care of. Many times, I felt like I was on a big Ferris wheel going round and round. I was hollering for help. But, I had no one to help me. I really felt like I was alone in my pursuit for excellence. I carried the weight of the household, the kids, and my husband on my shoulders. I took care of the kids, bought the groceries, cleaned the car, house, and yard, and whatever else came up. I even mowed and trimmed the yard like a professional groundskeeper. I didn't know how I managed to do everything I did.

As the kids got older, they were a tremendous help. I taught them how to cook and clean the right way. They all had chores assigned to them. Also, they were able to look after each other. I gave them room to grow, but I always kept a tight control over them. I was lucky. They were all good kids.

As time passed, one by one the kids started to leave home. First, Mary got married and left home. She flew to Turkey to be with her husband who was in the Air Force. Second, Harris and Bobby joined the Army within a few years apart. Then Jeannie left home two weeks after graduating from High School. Now, I only had my two younger kids at home. Life was getting a little easier all the time.

We lived very happily for seven years, until a catastrophe struck. It was springtime. The rainy season was heavier than usual. We didn't think the rain would ever stop. The water rose at least twelve inches. Our house looked like it was in the middle of a lake. It made me nervous as the water got higher and higher. I had just put new carpeting in the house, and I was afraid the water would get into the house and ruin it. Suddenly I heard a deep gurgling sound in my heat registers. I quickly took action.

"Hurry, go get some two by fours out in the garage!" I ordered the kids. "Or, get some bricks. I need them to put under the furniture to keep it dry."

The kids ran and got whatever they could find as fast as they could. We barely got the bedroom furniture up on blocks when the water came rushing into the house. It gushed in and quickly covered my new carpet. The water continued to come into the house until it climbed to about six inches on my walls. I was devastated. Everything was going to be ruined.

The water stayed for a week or so before it receded. Now, we had to fix the damage. The walls had to be redone. The woodwork along the base of the floor had to be replaced. Also, the floors had buckled and swelled from the dampness. Therefore, they had to be replaced. Of course, our insurance did not pay for flood damage, so we had to come up with the money to remodel. The only thing that was saved was the carpeting. We pulled the carpet off the floor, and draped it over the clothesline to dry. It took quite several days to completely dry. And, of course, the carpet did shrink a little. However, we were able to stretch the carpet back out enough to reuse it. It hurt me to see everything ruined. I knew I would never feel the same way about our house again. I was ready to move out of this area. Every time it would rain, I was nervous thinking the devastation would happen all over again.

I suggested that Nate start looking for a new house. It didn't take him long before he found a house he liked in Taylorville. The owner was asking six-thousand dollars for this property. Nate didn't mince words; he told the owner of the house he was asking too much money. Nate walked away from that particular house with the idea that he would look for another one. But first, he went straight to a local bar for a beer. While Nate was in the bar, the owner of the property he had just looked at walked in. He sat down by Nate. They knew each other, so they drank a few beers and talked aimlessly about whatever popped into their heads. The subject of the owner's house finally came up.

He made Nate another offer. "I'll take four-thousand five-hundred dollars for my house," he told Nate.

Nate didn't even hesitate, he told him, "You've got a deal. I'll go to the bank and get the money for the down payment." He then left the bar with the intention of bringing the money back to the owner of the house.

When Nate got to the bank, the bank teller told him that he needed his wife's bank book to withdrawal money. He didn't realize that he needed the bank book that was in my purse at work. This didn't set well with him at all. Earlier, he had gotten mad because I didn't have the account in his name, too. I originally put the money in my name only. I really didn't want Nate to be able to get into my savings without my permission. But, after a few fights, I gave in and put both our names on the bank account. However, he needed the bank book to get money out of the account. I kept the book with me at all times. I had saved fifty cents at a time for years to build my account to one-thousand dollars. I planned on using the money for a down payment on our next house.

Nate came to the sewing factory to get the bank book. I gave it to him and told him I would meet him at the bank after work. We could do this together.

After I got off work, I went to the bank to meet Nate. We then asked the bank to loan us the money we needed to buy the house. The bank agreed to loan us the money, but it would take a few days to get all the paperwork ready. We understood these things take time.

We withdrew a thousand dollars out of our savings account for the down payment; we looked up the owner of the house and gave it to him. We asked him for a receipt to prove he accepted our money. We didn't realize it at this time, but this man was not the owner of this house! The real owner was his son. We found this out when the son's children came to the house while we were there. They came to see the property they had just inherited. I thought we were going to lose this house before we even moved in it.

Nate and I went straight to a lawyer to get this whole thing settled. We showed the lawyer the receipt we had gotten for the down payment. After looking at the receipt, the lawyer advised us to continue our transaction with the bank. Then, he wanted us to bring the money to him to hold until the true owner could get together with us at his office. The lawyer set up the date for us to meet.

We weren't sure what was going to happen, but luck was with us. All sides met at the lawyer's office on the appointed day. After a short discussion, we reached an agreement. The son agreed that if we handed over the money for the property, it was ours. To be honest, I wasn't sure what I was getting in to. I hadn't had a good look at this house yet.

We went right over to the house, and I looked it over real good. My first words were, "Nate, you can't do this to me again!" This place was a mess. The wall paper was hanging off the walls. Many of the windows were broken out. And, it was dirty. All I could see was work and more work. However, Nate tried to reassure me.

"Don't worry. Don't worry, he assured me. "I borrowed enough money to get this place fixed up so it will be livable."

Needless to say, that statement only eased my mind a little. I knew I would have to do a lot of the work myself. It always happened that way in the past.

I could see that this house had potential. It had three bedrooms, a nice size kitchen and living room, a bathroom, and a basement. This would give us more room. And, the yard was nice and big. The outside of the house didn't look bad at all. Yeah, I figured this just might be nice after we did a little work to it. I was ready for the challenge.

Nate was true to his word. He hired a man to redo the walls. He contracted the job to Jake Bayfield. Jake was Mary's father-in-law. He lived in a small town outside of Taylorville. Jake knew what he was doing. He had done carpentry work for years. Lucky for us, he was able to start right away. He redid the plasterboard on the walls in no time at all. Then, he put up new paneling in the bedrooms. And next, he painted the walls in the rest of the house. It looked really nice when all the walls were finished. Now it was looking like a home.

We only had one problem left to contend with before we moved into the house. Honey bees had made their home under a portion of our siding. They were also inside the house. They seemed to like one corner of the living room. They kept coming back to that area. We weren't quite sure how to get rid of them. Finally, we decided to smoke them out. Nate attached a hose to the exhaust of the car and put it under the siding where the bees called home. Sure enough, it killed the bees. We were now ready to move in our new home.

I was really glad that we got the house ready to move into so fast, because I had already sold our house in Stonington. I sold it for two-thousand dollars. Actually, the house itself wasn't worth much. But, the two lots it sat on were. I sold each of them for one-thousand dollars apiece. The principal of the Stonington High School was interested in buying the property. He wanted to tear the house down, and build one of his own. I sold it to him. I was really proud of myself. I sold this property for twice as much as I paid for it. Now, that was good business!

We hired a moving van, and moved into our new house the next day. Now, this was the way to move! In the past, we always had to use a pickup truck. And, one trip was never enough. The moving van moved us the very same day. By that same evening, we were in the house and everything was put in its place. When things are meant to happen, they fall into place easily. I decided that this move was definitely meant to happen.

Chapter Fourteen
THE GOOD LIFE ON ENGLAND STREET

We moved into our new home, November 26th, 1971. Today was Robin's birthday. She was mad at us, because she felt that her birthday had been ignored because of the move. She cried and said, "Nobody loves me. Nobody said a thing about my birthday!" Nate and I felt bad that she was so upset. Later that night, we bought a birthday cake and celebrated Robin's special day. I had gotten a special gift for her. It was a musical jewelry box. When Robin opened the top of it, a ballerina popped up and danced as the music played. This gift delighted her. This day was a total success.

Everything went pretty smooth until the following summer. During the heat of summer, the bees came back. We decided that the only way to truly get rid of them was to tear the siding off of the house. The bees' nest was under the siding. So, we tore into the siding and found a large honeycomb. It was so hot on this particular day that the honey ran down the side of the house. We sprayed bee killer on everything. Of course, this enraged them. They swarmed around us. Nate and I were both scared of them. But, in a little while, the lethal spray killed all the bees, and we were able to tear out the entire honeycomb. As we were putting the siding back on the house, I knelt down to pick up a board. Sure enough, my knee came down on a bee. The stinger dug sharply into my knee. My knee immediately swelled up and stung like fire. However, I did not let the pain stop me. I continued to work until we had completely finished the east side of the house.

The next day I went to work in pain. One of my co-workers told me I needed to draw the stinger out of my knee in order for it to heal. She suggested I make a paste out of flour and water and place it on my bee sting. When I got home from work, I made the paste and applied it to my knee. As the paste dried, the stinger came out, and the swelling slowly went down. I was now ready for my next project.

When we bought our house, it didn't have a garage. Since we had an acre of property, we decided to build a two car garage. Nate decided to build this garage in my flower garden. He ran electrical wires from the house to the garage. He did it right. He ran the power from the basement, underground, to a hole in the garage. I thought that was pretty good thinking on his part. No outside wires mucking up the scenery. I was proud of him.

After the garage was finished, we redid the driveway. Instead of a straight driveway, we made it circular. We figured we could pull in one side of the driveway and out the other. We used several truckloads of rock to fill this area. However, it turned into a real pain after a while. I had a hard time keeping the weeds pulled out from between the rocks. I worked too hard keeping the driveway perfectly neat. Nate didn't want me to work that hard.

While I was gone getting my hair fixed one day, Nate had asphalt put down on the entire circular driveway. Some men had stopped by with some left over asphalt from a job they had just finished. They offered Nate a good deal. He didn't hesitate. He accepted their offer and had them finish the driveway before I returned home. I was pleasantly surprised as I turned into my new driveway. Nate had saved me a lot of time and effort. Now, I had more time to play.

My life was running real smooth and getting better as time passed. My last two kids graduated from High School and both moved out on their own. Now that my last child had left home, I was free. Nate and I were pretty content to have just the two of us to take care of. We fell into a pretty good routine of enjoying each other's company. We laughed and joked more, because we didn't feel any outside pressures. Also, we were older and mellower in nature. We didn't let the small things bother as much as we used to. We were more relaxed. Now, we had hobbies that kept us occupied.

I started making quilts in my spare time. A good quilt didn't put out too much fuzz like an ordinary blanket. I always had an interest in making my own quilts. Nate and I worked together on this project. I liked the teamwork. Nate made the templates and cut the quilt pieces for me. He always did the math beforehand. He figured how much material I would need to make a particular size quilt. After he cut the quilt pieces, I sewed them together by hand to make the quilt top. Then, I put the quilt top, the filling for the center, and the backing together. I based the three sections together with large stitches. Next, I did the hand quilting on the entire quilt. When the quilt was finished, Nate and I both took pride in our work.

From start to finish, it took me almost a year to complete an average size quilt. As soon as I finished the one I was working on, I started another. I often read quilting books, so I could get new ideas on quilt patterns and to learn how to better my finished product.

I made six different quilts to begin with. I made one for each of my kids. I couldn't decide which quilt I wanted to give to each child. So, I put six numbers in a cigar box. I had everyone draw a number out of the box. The six numbers correlated with a particular quilt. I felt this was the only fair way to make the choice. After each one of the kids drew a number and matched it to their quilt, I told them they could trade with each other if they wanted. No one wanted to trade. They were all happy with their luck of the draw.

After the kids had a quilt apiece, I gave my quits to family members. I would decide who the lucky person was going to be each year. Sometime during the yearly family reunion at Manners Park, I presented the quilt to the lucky person. But first, we had a potluck style lunch, played baseball, and sit around a talking about what happened in our lives during the last year. It was great family time. Usually at the end of the day, I presented someone with that year's quilt. No one knew who the lucky recipient was until that very day of the reunion. I kept it a secret. I felt honored to give my quilt to whomever I chose each year. Everyone waited anxiously until I presented my quit to that one lucky person. This was my way of leaving a legacy.

In the beginning phase of my quilt making, I bought material and clothes from the sewing factory where I worked. The factory sold material at discounted prices to any employee who was interested in buying. I bought up as much material as I could for further projects. Most of the material was multicolored which was great for making quilt tops. I used the multicolored patterns to make what I called a crazy quilt. Also, the factory sold very nice clothes at discounted prices. Dresses, blouses, and housecoats were some of the items available to me. It was great having this option to buy the products that we made every day. These were great perks.

After nine years of working in the sewing factory, the business closed its doors. I was out of a job. Although I still cleaned houses for a few of my old customers, I wasn't making the money I did at the factory. I was getting older, so I had cut down to just a few weekly cleaning jobs. Then suddenly, my life changed for the better through and accident.

I was washing walls and doing my spring cleaning. I used a ladder to wash the highest part of the walls. For some reason, I wasn't focused on what I was doing. I stepped backwards off the ladder as if it weren't there. I fell to the floor with the ladder on top of me. I was really mad at myself for doing such a dumb thing. Luckily, I didn't get hurt. However, this incident made me realize that I was getting older, and I was not thinking very clear. I was almost sixty-two years old. I had been working hard all my life.

When Nate came home from work, I told him about my silly fall. Of course, he told me I was working too hard and it was time for me to slow down. He had an idea.

"I don't know why you don't quit working and start drawing your Social Security checks?" Nate asked. "Most people draw their checks at sixty-two. Then he gave me the worst case scenario, "Some people die before they are sixty-five!" he added.

I hadn't thought of possibility that I might die before I reached the age of retirement. I decided to give Nate's idea some consideration. My mind was made up in no time at all. I was going to sign up for Social Security right away.

I signed up for my Social Security three months before I turned sixty-two. I was able to start getting my checks regularly. What a wonderful feeling it was to get a check every month. And, I didn't have to work for it! Now, all my time was all my own. I was free to do whatever I wanted. What a great feeling!

I enjoyed these precious moments with myself until a new phase of my life changed. Nate came home from work one day and told me, "I am thinking about retiring. I have been working at Caterpillar for over thirty years." He reminded me that he started working at Caterpillar in the year 1959. It was now 1987. When he told me he wanted to retire, I kind of panicked! We still had a car payment, and I was worried that we wouldn't be able to handle our payments if he retired.

"Why don't you work one more year, so we can pay off our car loan?" I suggested to Nate. I only thought this made good sense.

Nate didn't respond to my suggestion, but he seemed to be thinking about it. I thought that he must have agreed with me. I should have known better.

A few days later, Nate came home from work and told me, "Well, I am retiring tomorrow! I have it all fixed up. I just have to go to work tomorrow, sign the paperwork, and I am done."

I was really surprise. I had no idea he had made his mind of to retire right now. But, I knew when he made up his mind to do something; there was no talking him out of it. It was a done deal.

I now had to adjust to a new way of living. I had already started walking five miles every day because my cholesterol was high. Nate measured the distance with the car's mileage indicator. I walked from England Street, to Manner's Park, around the park, and back home. I figured Nate could walk with me now that he was retired. This would be good for both of us. Nate agreed to walk with me a couple of times a week. I was looking forward to the company.

After a few times of walking five miles, Nate came up with a faster method. He bought bicycles for the both of us. We now rode our bicycles the five miles twice a week. The hills in the park were pretty steep. Nate had a rough time peddling up several of them. Some days, I walked my bike and put my hand on his back to push him up the hill. Now, this was work! But, I enjoyed it. I liked the exercise and Nate's company, too.

We fell into a nice routine of enjoying our time together. We both had hobbies. Nate made knives and wooden objects, and I made quilts. Then, we sat and watched TV together. I worked on my quilt while we watched our favorite programs. We were both more relaxed after Nate retired, and we were enjoying the good life.

One day, I was doing my spring cleaning. I had the whole house tore up. I moved all the furniture out into the middle of each room to wash down my walls. I did this spring cleaning every year. But, this year it was different. Nate was retired. He hated it when I cleaned like this. It tied up my time, and house cleaning wasn't as important to him as it was to me. Spring cleaning was a vital process that I had done every year of my life. I enjoyed a clean house. It usually took me a whole week to do the entire house. I felt a real sense of accomplishment when it was clean from top to bottom. So today, I was working really hard. The sweat was rolling off of me. I wanted to hurry up and get this job done, because Nate was getting impatient with me.

While I was cleaning, Nate went downtown to a travel agency and booked us a trip to Las Vegas. He booked it for the following day. I was shocked when he came home with the airline tickets in his hand! He had made all the arrangements without my input. I wasn't a bit prepared for this. I didn't have my clothes ready. My house was an absolute mess! I didn't want to leave in the middle of my spring cleaning. Didn't Nate realize how this made me feel? I was really mad at him. I thought he was being selfish. However, to please him, I begrudgingly got our clothes ready, and we left for Las Vegas the next day.

Needless to say, I didn't enjoy this trip at all. I had a problem. I had not been eating enough lately, and I was feeling kind of ill. Nate was busy playing a slot machine. I told him I was thirsty, so he ordered me a glass of wine with 7Up in it. After I drank that, I still didn't feel right.

"I think we need to go up to our room for a little while," I suggested to Nate. "I am not feeling up to this right now. My stomach is hurting."

Nate put me off by saying, "Yeah, we will go up the room in a little while."

After a few more minutes, I told Nate again, "I am sick. I don't know what is wrong with me. But, I think we better go up to our room." I no sooner said that when I passed out cold on the Casino floor. Luckily, I didn't hit my head on anything. One of the Casino guards came to my rescue. She took me up to my room in a wheelchair and laid me onto the bed.

"Do you want me to help you take your clothes off?" the guard suggested. I had wet my pants when I passed out. I was oblivious to that fact.

"No!" I protested as I spoke to the guard. "Take my clothes off?" I was confused. Then, I was embarrassed. This was an awful feeling. I had actually lost control of my body when I passed out! I didn't know how long I had been out. It seemed like quite a while.

The female guard, Nate, and three other men were standing over me. One of the men started asking me questions.

"What kind of medicine are you on?" the guard kept firing questions at me. "What have you eaten today? Have you been drinking?" I couldn't keep up with him. Nate ended up answering all of the man's questions. I had not eaten all day, so the female guard ordered me a bowl of soup from room service. The female guard sat with me and spoon-fed me the soup. I appreciated her concern. I knew I should have eaten before now. But, I kept putting it off. Nate was too busy gambling, so I didn't want to go cat by myself. I made a mistake. After I ate the soup and appeared to be feeling better, every one left my room so I could get some rest. I fell asleep almost immediately.

The next two days, I still felt sick to my stomach. I couldn't quite put my finger on the cause of the problem. I just felt strange. I couldn't even think clear. I wanted to go home. I didn't want to be here. I was sick during the whole trip. I was so glad when it was time to fly home.

Even after I came back home, I was still sick and confused. I didn't understand what was happening to me. I sat in the living room and stared out the window. I was thinking about our trip. It baffled me to think I had lost control of my body. Also, I was mad at Nate because he didn't listen to me when I told him I didn't feel well. It made me feel bad that he didn't make me a priority. I was not only physically sick, I was emotionally upset.

After a week or so, I started eating better. I realized that I had not been eating enough to sustain my good health. I considered my body was a temple. This body was the only one I would have in my whole lifetime. I always respected my body and did whatever I could do to maintain my good health. I guess I had gone too far with my approach to lower my cholesterol. I had been on a very restrictive diet to lower my fat intake. I decided that my cholesterol would just have to get better with the medicine I was taking. I was going to eat good again. Also, I needed to stay in good shape because Nate wasn't feeling very well.

Nate was dealing with a skin cancer that refused to go away. It started out as a small pimple in the crease at the side of his nose. It would not heal. Nate tried several treatments to get rid of it. First, Nate's doctor gave him a type of medicated cream. The doctor instructed Nate to apply the cream to the affected area several times a day. The cream literally ate a whole in his skin. Nate was in so much pain he quit using the cream. He didn't think this medication was helping him. So, he went back to the doctor. The doctor then cut out a small area around Nate's nose to eliminate the cancer. More time passed. Then the cancer came back.

The next step was to burn the cancer out. The doctor did this procedure with no luck at all. After a few months, Nate's infected area started to seep a clear liquid out of it. Obviously, the doctor had not gotten rid of the cancer. Nate was getting frustrated. He had endured all that pain with no remedy. Also, he had done exactly as the doctor ordered. Four years had passed with no results. The cancer was still there and apparently getting larger.

Nate and I discussed the possibility of seeing a skin cancer a specialist. Jeannie and I picked out a dermatologist in Decatur. I called and made Nate an appointment. We went to see the new doctor.

After examining Nate, the dermatologist explained why the cancer had not gone away.

"The skin cancer on your face has fingers that spreads out under the skin and has reached into a larger area of your face," the doctor tried to explain in a way that Nate would understand. "If I were to operate on your face, I would have to cut half of your face off. I would not even think about doing your surgery. I suggest that you go to a cancer center in either California or Wisconsin to have the surgery. These two hospitals specialized in skin cancers." The doctor gave us a moment to absorb the information he has given us thus far.

"I suggest you go home and think about this, and let me know what you decide," the doctor recommended. "I can set you up an appointment in either place.

Nate and I were both speechless. We thanked the doctor and went home to think about what we were going to do next.

Nate decided to go to the hospital that was closest to us. The hospital was in Madison, Wisconsin. We made the appointment.

"Plan to stay here at the hospital for several days," the nurse said as she prepared us for what was next. "The doctor will surgically remove the cancer cell by cell until there is no cancer cells left. It is called microsurgery. The doctor will remove a slice at a time until no cancer cells are present under a microscope. This is a guaranteed method of removing the cancer."

Nate and I were apprehensive, yet we had no other choice but to do the procedure that the hospital recommended. After all, they gave us a guarantee.

We packed enough clothes to stay for a few days and drove to Springfield, Illinois. Then, we flew to Madison, Wisconsin. We stayed in a hotel three blocks from the hospital. The hotel was prearranged by the hospital staff. We were scheduled to stay for two days while the surgery was being done.

The next morning the doctor started Nate's surgery. For the first two mornings, I carried my suitcase to and from the hospital thinking we would be leaving soon. I was getting tired of carrying that suitcase back and forth. On the third day, we were still there. I finally talked to someone at the hospital who could arrange for us to stay at the hotel until we were completely finished with the multiple surgeries. I was relieved to be able to leave my suitcase at the hotel. Obviously, Nate's surgery was taking much longer than the doctor had anticipated. I was getting more and more worried as each day passed.

We really weren't prepared to stay as long as we did. And, the weather was a lot colder up north than what we were used to. We did not bring our coats with us. Also, we ran out of clean clothes to wear. We ended up wearing the cleanest of the dirtiest clothes we had already worn. My nerves were shot, and Nate's patience was wearing thin. We wanted to go home.

Into the fourth day of procedures, I asked the nurse if I could talk to Nate's surgeon. I had questions that needed to be answered. She notified the surgeon and he came to the waiting room to see me and to update me on Nate's progress.

"I understand that you needed to ask me some questions?" asked the surgeon.

"Yes, I do, "I answered. Then, I moved on to my next question. "Has the cancer made its way into Nate's facial bone?" Nate had been having more surgeries than I expected. I assumed the cancer had to be deeper in Nate's face than I initially thought.

"Yes," the surgeon said as he explained further. "The cancer had gotten to his facial bone. However, I was able to scrape it off of the bone. None of the bones needed to be removed."

I was a bit relieved to hear this news. The surgeon continued to explain what he had removed from Nate's face in the last few days.

"Up until now, I found it necessary to removed half of Nate's nose," he explained as I listened intently. "The cancer had reached almost up into Nate's eye area and all the way down to his upper lip."

I tried to picture this in my mind, but I couldn't. I didn't want to think about it. I tried to concentrate on what the surgeon was saying.

"Nate now has a permanent whole in his face that is covered with a compression bandage. The removal of the cancer is now complete," the doctor said. He went on to give me instructions on Nate's post surgery care.

"Watch over him tonight and make sure he has no excess bleeding. If you see any sign of blood, get him back to the hospital at once," the doctor cautioned me, then proceeded. "I want Nate back in my office tomorrow morning."

Nate and I left to catch the shuttle back to our hotel room. Just as we were walking to the shuttle, I saw blood coming from Nate's bandage! We turned right around, and went back into the hospital. The doctor found it necessary to apply a thicker bandage on Nate's face. After a while, the bleeding stopped. Nate was in tremendous pain by now, so the doctor gave him pain pills to ease his discomfort.

Neither Nate nor I slept that night. We were too worried and stressed out. Nate tried to sleep in an upright position to keep the bleeding to a minimum. He was too uncomfortable to get any sleep. I couldn't sleep because I felt helpless and concerned about more bleeding. We were both totally exhausted. The emotional stress was taking its toll on us. We wanted this nightmarish experience to be over. Only one thought gave me some comfort. The doctor said if everything went well tonight, we would go home tomorrow.

On the fifth morning, we went back to the hospital. All the results were in. All the cancer was gone! What a relief. The doctor put fresh bandages on Nate's face before we headed home. He instructed Nate to see his doctor in Decatur after he returned home.

We took the shuttle to the airport to catch our flight back home. We didn't have to wait very long. Our departure flight was ready to leave, and so were we.

We flew back to Springfield, Illinois. After departing the plane, we found that our suitcase didn't arrive with us. Our patience had been strained to the max, so we couldn't take any more setbacks. The airport personnel agreed to bring our suitcases to our house once they arrived. I was happy to hear that we didn't have to wait on them. I was sick of waiting. I got in the car and started to drive home.

I somehow managed to turn on the wrong road. We were lost. As if I didn't have enough stress already, Nate started yelling at me and pissed off! I struggled to find my way. In the end, we made it home. Thank God!

The next week we went to Decatur to see the dermatologist. Nate was healing well. The doctor viewed this as a good sign.

"After you have completely healed, reconstructive surgery is an option," the doctor recommended as he explained the harvesting process. "New tissue would be taken from different areas of your body and placed your face. You will need several surgeries to replace all the lost tissue. "

Nate had not seen his face since he had the four surgeries. The doctor took the compression bandage off. When Nate looked in the mirror, he was shocked at the amount of tissue that had been taken away. He didn't know what to say. There was a large hole in his face that almost reached into his eye and lip area. Half of his nose was completely gone.

The doctor placed a large bandage that looked like an eye patch over the whole in Nate's face. This covered the open area. The doctor was finished.

"I am going to give the reconstructive surgery some thought," Nate told the doctor. "I am not sure what I want to do right now. I need time to think about this."

I felt overwhelmed with the ordeal we had just been through, and Nate didn't make it any easier on me. He dug in his claws like I was his lifeline. I felt strangled and smothered both at the same time. Nate didn't want me out of his sight. I think in the back of his mind he remembered the threat I always made about leaving him when all the kids left home. He would not do one thing without my company. I felt like I needed some space away from him, but it didn't happen. My only solution was to adjust to having him around all the time.

Nate started coughing constantly. He began to spit up what looked like blood clots. I suspected that his cancer was back. I was sure that his cigarette smoking was a contributing factor. He smoked two packs of cigarettes a day for many years. His brand was the non-filtered Pall Mall's. And now, Nate was over seventy years old. He rejected my idea that cigarette smoking caused his cough. He continued to smoke his two packs a day. As a result, his cough seemed to be getting worse. I was worried about him. So, I prodded him to see a doctor.

I sensed that Nate was really sick. I thought his cancer was back. I felt bad for him. He had been through so much in the last year; I somehow wanted to make up for it.

"What would be your last wish if you could have one?" I asked Nate one day.

"I would go to Las Vegas!" Nate told me without hesitation. He loved to gamble in Las Vegas.

I told him, "Let's go!" I wanted to make him happy. In my mind, I felt like this was a dying man's last wish. I wanted to fulfill his dream.

Nate was shocked to hear me agree to go to Las Vegas. In the past, I always resisted the idea.

"I didn't think I would ever hear you say that!" Nate told me. "Great, let's go."

I knew we had enough money in the bank to take care of the trip, so I wasn't worried about that. All we needed to do was book the trip. This was my gift to him.

"Why don't we make this our gift for our 50th wedding anniversary present?" I asked Nate.

"Yeah, that's a great idea," Nate agreed.

We went to the travel agency and booked our trip. This was going to be our fourth and last trip to Las Vegas. We left that week with the idea that we were going to have fun.

While we were in Las Vegas, Nate wasn't well at all. He couldn't seem to eat anything because he couldn't swallow very easily. Also, he was restless. He wasn't able to sleep very well during the whole trip. He tried to overlook the distress and enjoy his gambling. But, all too soon, the trip was over, and it was time to go home.

When we returned home, my kids had planned a 50th wedding anniversary party. I didn't know at the time, Jeannie had called Nate in advance to clue him in on the details. Jeannie and Robin had gotten together and planned a big celebration with live entertainment. The kids wanted the party to be a special surprise for me. I didn't have the vaguest idea the party was the week we returned from Las Vegas. It was definitely a surprise!

The anniversary party was held in the local VFW hall. All kinds of food were served. For dessert, we had a three tier wedding cake. It was grand. The party was a huge success. All my kids and their families were present. And, our nephews brought their families all the way from

Arkansas to celebrate this monumental occasion with us. In addition to that, many of my lifelong friends were present. My nephew Terry provided the entertainment for the party. We had so much fun. The entertainment group involved everyone in song and dance. We laughed until we cried. I was really enjoying this excitement.

Nate, on the other hand, was worn out early into the night. He was struggling to stay at the party. He was not feeling well. At nine o'clock that night he wanted to go home. Earlier, I had a hard time getting him to the party. But, he wanted to please me, so he went. He didn't want to ruin the party for me. Also, he understood how much it meant to me to celebrate this occasion. So, he told me to stay and enjoy the party while one of the kids took him home to rest. I was worried about him, but I didn't want to just walk out on everyone who had tried so hard to make this event special for me.

I stayed at the party a little while longer because I didn't want to abruptly leave. I thanked everyone for coming and said goodbye to all my kids. They understood that I was very worried about Nate. Now, I was ready to go home to see if Nate was still feeling bad.

I wanted Nate to make an appointment see his doctor. He refused to go to his old family doctor. After the ordeal with his skin cancer, he had lost faith in him. He called him a quack. Therefore, he searched for a new doctor. He found one right away. His new doctor's name was Roy. Roy's wife was also a doctor in the same office. Nate made his first appointment and went to see his new doctor.

Nate would not allow me to go to the doctor's office with him. He wanted me to either wait in the car or sit in the waiting room while he saw the doctor.

"You ask too many questions," Nate complained. "And, you talked too much. I want to get in and out of that office as fast as I can."

Nate had high blood pressure. He felt like he was being forced to see the doctor to get his blood pressure medicine. He couldn't have his prescription filled over the phone. Also, he had a problem with his ears. They needed to be cleaned out.

The doctor checked Nate's blood pressure and issued him a new prescription. Then, he cleaned Nate's ears with a solution. Only a few minutes passed when Nate returned.

When I asked him, "How did everything come out?"

He just said, "Everything is fine." He never discussed what the doctor did while he was in his office. He acted like I didn't need to know.

Nate's doctor Roy seemed pretty lenient compared to his wife. Roy didn't rant and rave about Nate's smoking, but his wife did. Nate was forced to see her on one occasion when Roy had hurt his back. She really blasted Nate for smoking.

"You are going to have to quit smoking, because you know it is killing you," she complained to Nate.

This statement really pissed Nate off! He didn't like a woman telling him what to do.

"Women should not be doctors!" he fumed at me one day as we left the doctor's office. "She doesn't know anything." Unfortunately, he was stuck with her until Roy could return to his practice.

Finally, Roy came back to work. Nate was really happy to see him in the office on his next visit. Now, Roy was the one who checked Nate's blood pressure. He changed the blood pressure medicine several times.

When I asked Nate what the doctor said during his visit, he never give me much information. He didn't want to talk about his visit.

On one visit in to Roy office, Nate complained about an abscess on his stomach area. Nate's belt buckle had rubbed the abscess until it was raw. Roy cut the abscess out and treated the infection with antibiotics.

"What caused the abscess?" I asked Nate when he shared the problem with me.

"It was just a simple cyst," Nate said as he cut the conversation short. "You don't have to worry about it."

I was suspicious. I didn't know whether to believe Nate or not. He kept me out in the cold most of the time. He never explained his numerous visits to the doctor. And, he never wanted me to go into the office with him.

"You are not coming into the doctor's office with me," Nate threatened. "If you try to go in, I am going home!"

I didn't know where this animosity was coming from. I didn't want to get in another argument, so I kept my mouth shut and waited patiently. I could only hope that everything turned out alright.

It took a while before the doctor finally got Nate's blood pressure under control. Nate remained faithful about taking his medicine. Every morning he took a blood pressure tablet and a potassium tablet. He took them with either coffee or beer. I complained about that.

"You are not supposed to take that medicine with beer or coffee," I complained as Nate downed his medicine with a can of beer.

"It goes down better that way," Nate laughingly told me. That was the end of the conversation. He was so stubborn. I finally gave up and didn't saying anything more about the subject.

I started getting worried when Nate got more and more sluggish. He couldn't seem to get enough air to accomplish a simple job. Because he couldn't breathe so well, he quit riding his bicycle. If he walked with me, he turned back towards home after a short walk. Even riding the lawn mower exhausted him. I could tell that he was progressively getting worse. In addition to that, his feet were swelling all the time.

I had a physician's book that diagnosed medical problems. Whenever Nate or I had any kind of a symptom, I looked it up in my book. Many times during the last five years, I looked up Nate's nagging symptoms which included, coughing, spitting, tiredness, swelling feet, and breathlessness. The results of my search indicated lung cancer might be a possible cause of these symptoms. Therefore, I had inkling that Nate had lung cancer. I tried not to think about that possibility because it scared me to think that he might be that sick.

I was scared about losing Nate, and I was mad. I had been married to Nate for almost fifty years. I was going to do everything I could to help him. I knew how to take care of him. I had been doing this all my life. But, I was also mad at him. I think he knew that he had cancer, and he didn't want to tell me. I was hurt that he didn't share his problem with me. If I had known for sure that Nate was going to die, I would have been better able to plan for my future. I thought that he should have cared about leaving me unprepared. He should have taken better care of me than this. I had to let this go, because my suspicions had not been confirmed. I knew I had to stop thinking about this so much and just get on with our lives.

We had a little routine established. Every morning I walked my five miles. Then, I came home, cleaned up, and Nate and I would go to his favorite bar. The bar was called The Skyscraper. For some reason, Nate felt the need to be there by nine o'clock in the morning. When I had cleaning to do, Nate pouted until I was ready to go.

He went out and sat on the steps and yelled in to me, "Hurry up! Hurry up!" He hated for me to clean. He was always pushing me to hurry.

I was getting tired of being rushed, so; I encouraged him to go on alone by saying, "Why don't you just go on, and I will stay here and get my work done?"

But, Nate wouldn't hear of it. He told me, "No, I am not going to do it. You are going with me!"

I gave in, got dressed, and went with Nate. I realized I was getting stressed out because of the pressure I put on myself. I needed to lighten up. The cleaning would get done eventually.

I was still trying to lower my cholesterol and lose some weight. I had been on medicine to reduce my cholesterol, but it didn't seem to be working well. Again I tried to change my diet by eliminating the fat. However, my dieting methods were still too extreme. I had cut down on the calorie and fat intake so much that I was passing out. I was living on low fat yogurt and salads. And, I made sure the fat content was the lowest I could find. The doctor had told me to lose weight, but I wasn't eating enough food to sustain me.

I passed out cold several times. It started to scare Nate. He was worried that I would get sick. He started getting mad at me.

"I don't like you passing out like that! I want you to start eating," he demanded.

I knew he was right. I had gone too far. So, I started eating more food. I didn't pass out any more after that. I had given the diet a good effort, and I hoped it had reduced my cholesterol enough to make a difference.

After we got home from the bar every day, Nate was ready for a nap. He climbed into the recliner, turned on the television, and went to sleep. He did this every afternoon. While he was asleep, I went into my extra bedroom and watched my favorite soap opera. When Nate woke up from his nap, I would get busy doing whatever he wanted to do. And, it was usually time to fix supper.

Every day we fell into our usual routine. We always got up at 4:30 am. For thirty years, that was our usual time to get up. Now that we were retired, we still got up at that time. Then, we drank two cups of coffee apiece. I fried up a pound of bacon for Nate to munch on during the day because he was a finicky eater. I knew he would eat the bacon. He ate four pieces for breakfast, and nibbled on the rest of it the rest of the day. We were fairly comfortable with our routine. We enjoyed our peaceful time together. However, that peace was about to be interrupted.

Early one morning, Nate had a real problem. He had gotten up early and made our morning coffee. He sat down at the kitchen table and waited for me to wake up. He got impatient. He started hitting his spoon on the side of his cup creating a ringing sound. The sound woke me up. It irritated me to wake up this way. I was testy as I got out of bed to see what was going on.

"I am really in trouble," Nate stated without much emotion. I could tell by the look on his face, he had a serious problem.

I looked at him and said, "What do you mean, you are in trouble?"

"Look at my feet," Nate said as he looked down at his feet.

I naturally looked down to his feet. I was shocked! His feet were so swollen that the skin on them was literally splitting apart. It looked like someone had taken a knife and slit his feet open in several places. Also, a clear liquid was seeping out of his feet. It looked like water was pouring out of them. The rug in the front of Nate's recliner was sopping wet where he had sat that morning. I had never seen anything like this before. This seemed to happen overnight.

I called Nate's doctor right away. He was on vacation. The nurse in his office told me to call another doctor who was taking Roy's calls. This new doctor's name was Dr. Williams. I called Dr. William's office and talked to the nurse. I told her about the swelling in Nate's feet. She insisted that I bring him into the office right away. We went into the office together. Nate was scared and, for the first time, he needed my support.

Dr. Williams examined Nate's feet, and told him he needed to check into the hospital for further tests. "I need the test to determine why your feet are swelling," Dr. Williams explained. "This is the only way I can diagnose your problem. I need more tests."

Nate rejected this idea. He did not want to go to the hospital.

"I smoke," Nate told the doctor. "I can't smoke in the hospital. Would you put a nicotine patch on me to help me resist the urge to smoke?"

"Yes," Dr. Williams agreed. "I'll do that right away."

Nate checked into the hospital with the intention of staying no longer than three days. I stayed there with him day and night. Robin happened to be visiting at this time, so she was able to keep us company while we waited for the test results. Robin understood that Nate and I were both worried. We all anxiously waited for the tests results.

In the meantime, Nate started to get grumpy. He wasn't a good patient at all. He baulked at everything. He could breathe well lying in a prone position. At home, he was able to sleep in his recliner. He wanted to get this whole thing over with. And, of course, he was edgy because he couldn't smoke.

When Dr. Williams visited Nate's hospital room, Nate asked him questions.

"Are you going to call in a specialist?" Nate asked.

"No, I am not going to do that at this time," Dr. Williams said as he explained his next step. First, I am going to do a CAT scan of your entire body.

Nate's patience was getting thin. The thought of having a CAT scan terrified him. He had claustrophobia, and he didn't think he could do this test.

"I can't do that!" Nate said s he further explained. "I am claustrophobic. You would have to put me completely under to do that test on me."

Dr. Williams eased Nate's tension by saying, "No. This test isn't the one you have in mind. This test is just like a tire tube that we slide you through and then back out. It isn't enclosed. The test will over in no time at all."

Nate listened to the doctor and said, "Oh, well, would you give me a valium to calm me down?"

"Yes, I will give you a light sedative to calm you before the test," Dr. Williams agreed.

The CAT scan was scheduled for the second day Nate was in the hospital. Nate stayed fairly calm that day because he was somewhat drugged.

After the tests were completed, Nate asked the doctor again if he was going to call in a specialist.

Dr. Williams said, "No, no. I don't think so. You may go home tomorrow, but I want you to come into my office on Monday morning to get the results of your tests."

Nate was happy to be going home. Robin had to go back home that evening, so I promised to call her as soon as we knew anything about the test results. I remained at the hospital until the next morning when Nate was released to go home.

On the way home, Nate said, "Stop at the tavern, I want a beer."

We stopped at a local tavern downtown. Nate stood at the bar and ordered a beer. He reached for the beer, took a drink, and down went his pants! I was standing right next to him when his pants hit the floor. I casually reached down and pulled his pants back up as if the incident never happened. I held them up while he drank his beer. His pants were loose, because he had lost so much weight. Nate acted like he didn't notice his pants had fallen down. He drank one beer and was ready to go home. It was Friday. Nate always looked forward to having a few beers on Friday. But today, one beer was enough. After Nate drank the beer, we left and went home to rest. We were both exhausted physically and emotionally.

Over the weekend, Nate feet continued to seep water. I put a throw rug in front of his recliner to put his feet on. In no time at all, the rug was soaked and needed to be changed. We both knew this was a serious problem. We were beside ourselves with worry, but Nate rested like the doctor ordered. I, on the other hand, had some work to do.

The yard needed to be mowed. Nate usually did this job, but right now, he couldn't even think about it. I fired up the mower and started mowing the yard. It hurt Nate to see me have to do this job. However, it needed to be done. He came out of the house and sat on the back steps to watch me as I mowed with the riding lawnmower. He decided to make arrangements to pay someone to come every week and mow for us. After I finished mowing, Nate told me his plan. This took some pressure off of both of us. Now, we could rest. It had been a really stressful week. Sunday we rested all day long.

On Monday, we went to see Dr. Williams. Nate sat in a wheelchair in his office. I was standing behind him. We knew the news couldn't be good. The doctor didn't delay.

"I am sorry to tell you this, Nate, you have lung cancer," the doctor informed him. "The type of cancer you have is the worst kind. This cancer has tentacles that reach out to all the organs of your body. I want you to get into the Hospice Program right away."

Nate and I were both quiet as we listened to the bad news. We were devastated.

Dr. Williams continued to explain further, "The trachea is where you get air from your lungs, and the esophagus is used as a passage to your stomach. The cancer has wrapped itself around these two parts of your body. There isn't anything anyone can do to fix this."

I finally found my voice when the doctor paused and waited for the information to sink in. I asked Dr. Williams, "Why are Nate's feet swelling?"

"The cancer has reached all the way down into that area. That is why his feet are swelling." Dr. Williams patiently explained.

I was in a state of shock! This was too much for me. This was a confirmation of my worst fear. Nate had cancer and it was all over his body. He was going to die. There was no more to be said.

Nate and I left the doctor's office in a daze. We had paperwork in our hands, but we didn't understand what this information meant.

The doctor gave us all kinds of paperwork to sign. I was mad and confused. First of all, I didn't even know what Hospice was. Second, I never signed anything that I wasn't sure of. So, I did the only thing I knew to do. I called Jeannie. She came to the house right away and explained what the papers were about. She explained what I was about to sign and said it was alright to sign it.

"Mom, Hospice is a service that is offered to terminal patience so they don't have to come to the hospital every time they need medication to control their pain," Jeannie explained. "It is OK to sign this paperwork and get the service started. You need to sign right here at the bottom of the page." Jeannie tried to explain more about the Hospice Program, but I really didn't want to hear it. I needed more time to adjust. However, I signed the papers, took them back to the doctor's office, and the Hospice Program was set up for us.

To be honest, I still didn't understand what was going on. I didn't realize that they called Hospice in when you had less than six months to live. I just did what I was told to do and was learning as I went along. This was all new to me. I didn't want to believe that Nate was going to die and leave me. What's more, it was going to be sooner than I expected. I didn't want to think about this!

That same week, the Hospice nurse came to our house. She introduced herself. Then, she took Nate's blood pressure and gave him medication to manage his pain. She wanted to bring a hospital bed into the house for Nate to sleep on. He resisted that idea.

"No way!" he told the nurse. "I am going to sleep on that new couch right over there." Nate had made up his mind and there was no talking him out of it. I had just paid that couch off, and I was proud of it. I was worried that sleeping on it would ruin it. So, I put padding on the couch to protect it and make it more comfortable for Nate to sleep on. There really wasn't much else we could do. The nurse could only manage his pain and keep him as comfortable as possible. The nurse told us she would come to see Nate once a week. I didn't really understand why we needed her. I could take care of Nate myself. I did everything for him.

I took real good care of Nate. I fed him. I bathed him. And, I comforted him in any way I could. I rubbed his back to ease his pain. Also, I fix him any kind food that he asked for. I was trying to make him feel better. I guess, I thought, I could fix him. I could make him well again.

Nate had not been sleeping well for a long time. At first, I thought it was because the bed was too small, and he didn't have enough room to move around. To solve that problem, I purchased a queen size bed. The bigger bed didn't help him. Many nights, Nate ended up going back to the living room and sleeping in his recliner. Then he went to sleep on the couch for a little while. He laid on his side in a fetal position. This seemed to give him the most relief.

Before long, the Hospice nurse was coming every other day. She gave Nate morphine tablets for his pain. Nate never complained about the pain, but he took the tablets every day. I assumed the nurse knew what she was doing. But, I had to admit, I had second thoughts when she doubled the morphine.

After a month of this treatment, Nate began to sleep more and more. And now, he was on the couch more than his recliner. I waited until he was asleep. Then, I would run to the grocery store. I bought him some cookies and milk for when he woke up. He seemed to crave cookies, so I always kept them on hand.

I worried every time I got in the car. I was afraid it would die on me. We were having problems with the battery. When I went to the grocery store, I had to keep the car running while I was inside. Finally, I called a battery specialist to take care of this problem. Nate had always taken care of our car before he got so sick. He hated it that I had to take care of it now. He told me, "When I get well, I am going to buy us a brand new Buick." He kept telling me that. He gave me hope that he might get well. I wanted to believe him. But deep inside, I knew it was his time to go, although I knew I would never be ready for that day.

Another clue that Nate was getting closer to death came from the Hospice nurse. She told me that Nate had a clicking sound inside his heart. She noticed the click when she was taking his vital signs. This worried me, so I asked Nate's doctor about the click in Nate's heart.

The doctor told me, "His heart is getting weaker." I understood what he was alluding to. I went home and tried not to think about it.

Nate had other signs that his time was near. His feet started turning a darker color. They looked like they were bruised. And, they continued to seep. I saw all the signs that Nate's life cycle was coming to an end. Yet, I held on to the belief that death might not come. I had been with Nate for fifty years. I couldn't imagine my life without him. I really thought he had at least two more weeks to live. I guessed that I would never be ready for him to leave me.

Nate ate less and less. Most of the time, he only drank water. He couldn't get enough of that. His throat was always dry, so the water soothed it. I was sure the morphine contributed to this problem. The hospice nurse recommended I get Nate a liquid supplemental drink called Insure. This would give him some much needed nutrients. So, I bought a few cans in different flavors. However, after a half of a can, Nate gave it back to me to put in the refrigerator for later. Sometimes, he drank it and sometimes he didn't. Nate's throat was slowly closing up on him. So, many times, he only took a few sips of any kind of liquid. He didn't have any desire want to eat.

The cancer around Nate esophagus was a real problem in several ways. First, he couldn't swallow very well. Second, his appetite was almost nonexistent. I tried every trick I could think of to get him to eat more. He was getting weaker all the time. He barely left his recliner. So, I brought his food to him on a TV tray.

I indulged Nate's every whim. He had always smoked cigarettes and drank beer. Several times, he asked me to give him a beer. I knew he wanted it out of habit, but I gave him one anyway. I kept it in a small refrigerator in the basement. I retrieved one and popped it open for him. He took only a few sips, and he was finished. I ended up pouring the rest down the sink. Also, Nate asked me to get him a cigarette. I kept them in the kitchen cabinet. I didn't want them to be too near Nate. I was afraid he would fall asleep with one in his hand and catch the house on fire. Usually, after I gave him a cigarette, he took a few puffs. That seemed to satisfy his urge. I knew that neither one of these vices was good for him, but it was too late for that now. I couldn't deny him anything he asked for.

I went the extra mile to get Nate whatever food he asked for. For some reason, he decided one day that he wanted some scrambled eggs. But, he didn't want regular eggs. He wanted the ones called Egg Beaters. He had seen them advertised on television. Since I didn't have these in the house, I had to go to the grocery store to get them. When I returned home, I fixed the eggs for Nate right away. I brought them to him on his tray.

He sat there looking at them for a minute. Then, he pushed the whole tray onto the floor. He was mad because he couldn't eat them.

"I thought you wanted those eggs?" I commented.

"No, I don't," Nate said after his angry fit.

I didn't know what more I could do for him. I felt helpless as Nate continued to get weaker.

Not long after that episode, Nate started to hallucinate. He sat in the recliner one day and started brushing something off his blanket that was wrapped around him. He appeared to be agitated.

"What are you doing?" I curiously asked Nate.

"I dropped a piece of cake, and I can't find it," Nate said. "Where did I drop it?"

"Nate, you didn't have any cake."

Nate told me, "Yes, I did. I was eating a piece of cake and dropped it."

I couldn't convince him otherwise, so I gave up and went about reading my book.

Later on, Nate said, "Oh, I seen a rat run across the room!"

"There is no rat in here," I told him.

Nate accepted my answer. But, that same day, he asked me, "Who is that sitting over there in that chair?"

I quickly told him, "There isn't anyone sitting in that chair. You are sitting there, and I am sitting here. There is no one sitting in that chair."

Nate just looked at me and calmly said, "Oh, yes, there is."

"There isn't anyone sitting in that chair," I told him again. "You just think there is." That ended the conversation. I was familiar with this erratic behavior. I had experienced this same thing years ago when Mable was dying of uterine cancer. I had learned the best way to deal with the hallucinations was to just ignore them.

As the next month progressed, Nate was unable to do anything for himself. He had no energy to even bath himself. I slowly walked him to the bathroom to accomplish this task. He put his arm around me and walked with some of his weight on me. I placed a chair in the middle of the bathtub and helped him onto it. Then, I lathered him up with lots of soap bubbles. I tried to make it a fun thing. After the soap sat on him a few minutes, I rinsed him off with fresh water. Next, I toweled him dry and helped him out of the tub. I sat him on the stool while I finished drying him. It took so much energy for him to take his bath. By the time he was finished, he was ready to go back to the couch and rest.

Because Nate was either lying down or sitting in the recliner, he developed sores on his body. I padded his chair as much as I could, but it didn't seem to help. The biggest sore was right on his butt. I asked the Hospice nurse to give me some medicine to heal the sore. Nate complained when I used the salve. He said, "Oh that hurts so badly when you put that stuff on me." I felt bad about that, but I knew it was the only way to heal that sore.

Nate tried to show me he loved me until the very end. He was so sick. But, he reached over and patted my leg. This was his way. After fifty years, I knew this was his way of showing affection. I got it. I knew he loved me. This small gesture meant so much to me. I knew how much he appreciated me.

Before long, Nate lost control over his bowels. He didn't seem to be aware that he messed in his pants. I told him, "You stink." Then, I took him to the bathroom and cleaned him up. Because of this problem, I found myself doing laundry two or three times a week. The padding on his chair and the sheets on the couch were often a mess. I was beside myself. I didn't know how to handle this. Jeannie came to visit us and recommended I use Depends to keep the mess under control. The Depends were like disposable diapers for adults. I bought them that day and started using them daily. This helped me tremendously. Now, I could change him while he lay on the couch. I continued to use these adult diapers until the very end.

The end was near. I felt it. One night after I went to bed, I heard Nate say, "Come on, come on, come on." I got out of bed and went to the living room.

"Is there something that you want?" I asked Nate. He didn't answer me.

He just kept on saying, "Come on, and come on."

I sat in the living room chair for a few minutes and watched him. I didn't understand why he kept saying the same thing over and over. I felt anxious. A small voice inside prompted me to take my shower and get dressed. I needed to be ready. Ready for what; I wasn't sure. It was ten o'clock at night. After Nate went back to sleep, I went to the basement and took my shower. Then, I got dressed. I went back to the living room, sat in my chair, and fell asleep.

At daylight Nate woke me up by saying, "Come on, and come on."

I walked over to him. He smelled so bad that I had to wake him up. I told him, "Oh man, you've really messed. You smell so bad. Do you think you can walk to the bathroom with me?"

Nate replied, "Sure, I can walk to the bathroom with you." He was so weak that I wasn't sure he could make it all the way there. I walked behind him with my arms around him. We slowly made our way down the hallway into the bathroom. I washed him the same way I did every day. Then, I put his medication on his sore. I had just finished and was pulling up his pajama bottoms when he told me, "You have got to get me out of here right now!"

"OK, we are going right now," I assured him. "Let me get you pants pulled up." I held him by the pant as we started walking back to the couch.

As I walked behind him, Nate said, "You know, my feet feel like I have on lead shoes." I can't seem to pick my feet up to walk."

I encouraged him forward by saying, "Oh Yeah, you can do it. One more step. We are getting closer." We made it down the hallway, and entered the living room. I encouraged Nate further by saying, "One more step, and we will be on the couch.

Without any advanced warning, Nate slumped to the floor face down. I tried to catch him as he fell, but instead, I went to the floor with him. He let out his last breath. I heard it come forward. It sounded like a release. I felt that his spirit had left his body even before I realized this fact. I got up and turned Nate onto his back. I put my face down by his mouth to see if I could feel any breath at all. I felt for a pulse in several areas. I couldn't find one. I was starting to panic.

"Nate, Nate talk to me!" I called to him. "Come on, open your eyes. Come on, talk to me." I ran and got a pillow and placed it under his head. Again I said, "Nate, talk to me! Come on, open your eyes and look at me."

It was too late. I finally realized that he was gone. I sat there in a state of shock. I didn't know what to do.

After a time, I decided to call the Hospice nurse. I remembered she had told me to call her in case of an emergency. When I dialed the number, an answering machine took my call. I don't remember what I said in my message. But, of course, the voice on the machine said we will get back with you as soon as possible. That was no help at all!

My mind was going so fast I didn't know what to do next. I was scared. For some reason, I thought there was a chance Nate might be still alive. I knew that I needed to do something. I wanted to get him off the floor and onto the couch. I managed to do that. Then I called 911. They responded to my call within minutes.

The rescue squad, an ambulance, and the police came to my house all at one time. I opened the door and let them in. They immediately the EMT asked me, "Do you want us to revive him?"

"No, no, no, he wouldn't want that," I told him.

Then they asked, "Do you have a form that says Do Not Resuscitate?"

I told them, "Yes, it is in my purse." I ran to my purse and retrieved it.

The hospice nurse arrived right at this time. She came into the living room and grabbed me by the arm. She seemed kind of pushy.

"Honey, you might want to take a shower," she said.

I cried, "No! I don't want to take a shower."

Then the nurse said, "You might want to get dressed."

"I am dress!" I told her. I was getting mad. I wanted her to just leave me alone. I didn't know what to do. I was frantic in my own mind. Then, the nurse wanted me to go into the bedroom and get away from the activities in the living room. I resisted her.

"No! I don't want to go in there. I want to stay in here with Nate," I told her.

The nursed lowered her voice and said, "No, honey, you can't stay in here." She ignored my protest, grabbed me, and pulled me into the kitchen.

Again, I told her, "No, I don't want to be in here! I want to be in there." I wanted to see what they were doing to Nate. One of the rescue workers came to my side. He said, "We can't do anything." I understood. It was over. Nate was gone.

Someone called Sutton's Funeral Home to come and collect the body. Nate and I had already preplanned the funeral arrangements with them. Nate wanted to be cremated when he died. Mr. Sutton had told me to call him immediately after Nate's death. I wasn't to waste any time. That was important. Less time after death was crucial in their cremation process. Within a few minutes, the hearse arrived.

When Sutton's came to take the body away, I couldn't pull my eyes away from the shock of it all. They were putting Nate into a black plastic bag. Nate's eyes had popped wide open. They had an eerie unreal look to them. He looked like he was alert in a real intense way. They didn't try to close his eyes. They just zipped him into the bag like that. This picture stayed in my mind. It horrified me! I couldn't quit thinking about that look in his eyes. I knew everyone was trying to save me from this sight, but I couldn't look away. I just cried and cried. My grief was unbearable.

When my long time neighbors across the street saw the hearse pull away, they knew what had happened. My friend came rushing over.

"Where are your kid's phone numbers?"

My mind was a complete blank. I was still in shock. I couldn't think straight. All of this was happening too fast. But, I finally told her, "Robin works at Wal-Mart in Washington, Missouri." For some reason, I didn't think I had everyone's phone numbers. I just couldn't think. My neighbor called Robin in Missouri. Then, she found the rest of the kid's phone numbers and called each one. I needed my kids there. I waited for them to come.

Mac was the first one to arrive. Nate was already gone by now. The first thing Mac asked me was, "Where's dad?" I told him the funeral home had taken him away. They told me to say goodbye to him, because the next time I saw him he would be cremated in a small box. I did what they had told me to do. I didn't hesitate to wait for the kids. I just took care of business. I thought I was doing the right thing.

The funeral was pretty much a blur to me. I was lost. I just went through the motions and got it over with as soon as possible. In two days, it was over. I was so glad we had made the arrangements in advance. I had very little decisions to make at this overwhelming time.

I wasn't ready for Nate to go. No matter how sick he was, I didn't want him to leave me. I felt lost without him. I often went to the graveyard and sat by his grave. I talked to him. And, I cried for the loss of his company. I missed him. The only since of relief I had was that he didn't have to suffer anymore.

Chapter Fifteen
WHO AM I?

After the funeral was over, I really felt lost. I didn't know what to do with myself. I didn't know who I was anymore. I had always been Nate's wife. For fifty years, I had been Mrs. Nate Gentry. I now questioned myself, I said, "Who am I? Who am I now that Nate is gone? Then I would answer the question, "Dottie Gentry. You are Dottie Gentry. This is a new life for you." I had to think about that.

I couldn't stand to be home alone with my thoughts. So, I went outside every morning and walked and walked. I walked all over town. I tried to sort out my troubled thoughts. I figured this would kill two birds with one stone. I could think better outside. And, the exercise wore me out enough so I could sleep at night.

I went out to eat. I didn't want to eat alone. The truth was, I didn't really want to eat. When I tried to eat enough to stay healthy, I couldn't swallow the food. It seemed to get stuck in my throat. Usually, I left the restaurant with most of the food uneaten. I took the leftovers home for later. I knew I had to eat so I wouldn't get physically ill, so I ate only a little bit at a time. I continued to do this for five months.

I reviewed the chapters of my life. The first chapter was raising my kids. Of course, that was the longest chapter. Six kids were a handful. The second chapter of my life was enjoying Nate's company. It was just the two of us. Nate and I truly enjoyed our one on one time. Each day had been a gift. Now, the third chapter was living alone. This wasn't going to be easy for me. I had to keep busy.

I worked at keeping myself busy. I wanted to wear myself out so I could sleep at night. I didn't want to lay awake and think hurtful thoughts. So, I found things to keep me busy. I worked in the yard. I cleaned my house. And, I walked every day.

I felt sick inside, and I didn't know what to do with myself. I had been married to Nate for fifty years of my life. He dominated my life. He told me every move to make. And, I obeyed his wishes. Now, I was the only one left. I had to keep telling myself, "I am Dottie Gentry. I am not Nate's wife anymore." I had to think about what I wanted to do with the rest of my life.

Jeannie always came to visit and talk with me about anything and everything. I told her that I didn't know what to do with myself. She suggested that I do the things that I always wanted to do.

She said, "Mom, you have always wanted to go to church regularly. Now, is the time for you to pick a church that you want to attend?"

"Yes that is something I always wanted to do. I want to belong to a church and get closer to God." I liked that idea.

I had to push everything into the back of my mind. I didn't want to think about the fifty years I had been with Nate. I couldn't just sit in the house and be depressed all the time. And, I didn't want to dwell on being lonely. I needed to create a new life for myself, and I knew it was unproductive to live in the past. It was time to get on with it!

On Sunday morning, I got up and dressed for church. I wasn't sure where I was going, but I was ready. Then, at the last minute I back out. I couldn't make myself walk out the door. One time, I made it to the church door, but I couldn't go inside. I kept trying until one day I finally made it inside the church.

I picked the Nazarene Church. My kids had gone their most of their lives. I was familiar with it. I didn't go regularly when my kids were little. On the days I did go to church, a fight broke out between me and Nate.

"Yeah, you go to church, and you'll find a boyfriend," Nate had told me. "You don't need to go to church!" He argued with me so much that it wasn't worth the fight. It was easier to just stay home. But, I made sure my kids were there every Sunday. I gave in and went to church to see their Christmas and Easter Programs when they sang in the choir. It was not only their special time, but it was mine, too. I had always enjoyed going to this church. So naturally, I made my decision to attend this particular church.

As I neared the front door of the church, I took a big breath. I pulled the door open. It was locked. So, I walked to the side of the church where the fellowship hall was located. Everyone seemed to be in there. I slowly opened the door and saw the entire congregation. I panicked. As I stood there, I wondered what I was doing here. Happily, someone spoke up and said, "Come over here, Honey, and sit down beside me." It was the pastor's wife. She must have seen the apprehension on my face when I walked into the room. She eased my tension and made me feel welcomed, so I sat down beside her. The service started, so I sat there and listened. Afterwards, I felt better. I was glad that I went.

The next day, the Pastor came to my house. He explained, "I am calling on people today, and I wanted to talk to you. Maybe you could tell me a little bit about yourself. "

I felt comfortable talking with him. I told him about my six kids. Also, I told him I had just lost my husband of fifty years. He seemed to relate to everything I told him. I liked him and teasingly called him a hillbilly like myself. I enjoyed our conversation. I felt better after he left.

Two days later, the Pastor came back to my house. He wanted to invite me to dinner at his house. I had never in my life had anyone ask me to do this. I was a bit shocked! The Pastor assured me that other guests would be attending the dinner. He and his wife often invited members of the church to dine with them. Suddenly, I felt better about the invitation. I accepted. The Pastor gave me his address. He lived in a house near the church.

When I went to dinner at the Pastor's house, three other ladies were also there. We greeted each other, and proceeded to have a very nice dinner. The Pastor's wife had made cherry pie for dessert. After I finished my dessert, I rose out of my chair to take my plate to the kitchen sink. I was going to help with the clean up. But, the Pastor insisted I go into the living room and visit with the other ladies.

"This is my job," he explained. "My wife does the cooking, and I do the cleanup."

This was really a nice change for me. I enjoyed dinner and didn't have to clean up. I felt like a queen! I thanked the Pastor and his wife for a lovely dinner. Later, when I left their house, I had a warm feeling inside. This was a beginning.

I started going to church every Sunday, Sunday night, and Wednesday night. I became very involved with the church activities. I started to feel special like I had something to contribute to others. I developed a relationship with other church members. And, I reconnected with some friends that I had hadn't seen for a long time. My dear friend Mattie Larks attended this church. Mattie and I often went to lunch together when the church service was over. This church felt like my second home to me.

The Pastor continued to do things that gave my life new meaning. He came to my door one day and brought me a new Bible. "I bought you a new Bible," he said as he handed it to me. "It has large letters, and I thought you would enjoy this feature." I thanked him for his thoughtfulness. It had been hard to read the small print of my regular Bible. The Pastor and his wife were really kind people. I still thought they were hillbillies, but I really liked them. They had helped me adopt and new lifestyle; I was eternally grateful for their kindness.

My church went through many changes over time. The Pastor's come and went. When a Pastor decided to leave; I missed them. However, I welcomed the new ones. Some were old and some were young. I understood why they had to move on. Our congregation was small older congregation. We were a poor church. But, even as the church changed, I continued to take part in the activities. I enjoyed every minute of it.

I taught Sunday school for a while. I studied for my Sunday lesson, and I tried to make it interesting for the kids. Most of the time, the kids enjoyed the class. Unfortunately, a few of them were uncontrollable. I couldn't seem to make them mind. They started getting on my nerves. The kids got to be a little too much for me. So, I decided to let the young people teach the class. I gave up teaching the Sunday school class and moved on to other things.

The church had a variety of activities that kept me busy. I helped with weddings and baby showers. I helped with the dinners that we held after funerals. Also, I cleaned and painted inside the church. And, I attended revivals. No matter how tired I was, I loved it all.

I was always trying to recruit new church members. We needed young people. So, I talked Harris into coming to church with me. One of the ladies in the church gave him a new suit. He surprised me one Sunday when he walked in the door with his new suit on. It made me feel proud. Then Mac and his wife Deb started coming to church, too. I really enjoyed having my kids there with me. This was special.

After going to church for a while, I talked to a man that soon became a good friend. His name was Vern Friar. I had met him many years ago. His wife, named Jan, used to tend bar at a tavern Nate and I frequented. Mr. Friar and his wife were both alcoholics at that time. I talked with them quite often over the years. They also visited us when we lived in Stonington. They had two kids of their own who enjoyed playing with my kids. Since that time, Mr. Friar's life had changed. His wife had passed away. And, he had given up drinking. He was now an upstanding member of the Nazarene Church. Every Sunday, Mr. Friar greeted everyone as they walked into the church. That included me.

One Sunday when Mr. Friar greeted me at the church door, he asked me, "Could I ask you to have dinner with me? You wouldn't feel bad about that would you?"

"Well, we have got to eat," I told him. "Sure, I will go with you." So, when the church service ended, we went out for a bite to eat. I drove my car, and Mr. Friar paid the bill. After that time, this became a regular habit.

I would describe Mr. Friar as a distinguished looking older gentleman. He was very tall and thin. But most of all, he was a perfect gentleman. Also, he was legally blind. He could just see enough to get around by himself. But, of course, he could no longer see to drive a car. He either rode the bus, or caught a ride to church with someone from the church.

After our first lunch date, Mr. Friar and I often went to dinner together. I refused to call him Vernon. I wanted to call him Mr. Friar. This was going to be a friendship kind of relationship, and I intended to keep it that way. This made me feel more comfortable with our time together. And, I did enjoy the company.

Mr. Friar and I had many topics of conversation. We relived experiences from our pasts. Since we both lived in this area all our lives, we remembered the old businesses that used to be here. Some of the landmarks had been torn down; like the old hotel that used to be downtown. We talked about the Ritz Movie Theater I went to as a kid. And, we reminisced about many changes that happened in our pasts. It seemed that we had a lot in common.

Mr. Friar was a refreshing. He was very social and enjoyed other people. If someone approached our dinner table, he introduced me as his church friend. I liked that. One day Mr. Friar asked me, "Did you ever think we would be going places together years ago when we were both married?"

"No, I never thought about that way back then," I replied honestly. But right now, I was enjoying his company. Often as we were riding in the car, he would break out in song.

Mr. Friar asked me to go to the Senior Center where he ate lunch almost every day. My first reaction was, "I don't want to go eat with those old people!" After I said that, I realized we were both that old.

Mr. Friar ignored my first reaction and said, "Oh, you will like it after you go a few times." He convinced me to there for lunch the next day. The Center was located across the street from our church. Mr. Friar was right. I did enjoy it! I started going there every day for lunch. It only cost me two dollars and twenty-five cents a day. Not only was it cheap, it was good food. At this time, I didn't realize the Senior Center would become such a big part of my life. But, it did.

Eventually, I went to the Senior Center at ten o'clock in the morning and stayed for four hours. I volunteered to do various jobs. I sat the places at the table for several people who were on walkers. One of the ladies was one-hundred years old, and the other, was blind. Before lunch, we all said the Pledge of Allegiance to the flag. Then, we said our prayer. Next, I helped to serve up the food, ate my meal, and did the dishes when we were finished. Mr. Friar dried them. After the dishes were done, I took cards around for everyone to sign. These cards were for people who couldn't make it to the Center for various reasons. Usually, they were ill. This gave me a purpose. Many of the people at the Center were no strangers to me. I had known some of them for years. I really enjoyed socializing with them. I met a lot of people that were older than me who needed my help. I felt needed. I was making a difference in their lives. Also, I began to deliver meals to shut-ins who couldn't get to the Center.

The Center gave me food to take home for my dinner. I didn't cook much anymore, so this offering was good for me. I ate my largest meal at lunch, so I didn't need much for supper. Usually, I kept my favorite fruit or dessert for later. The staff at the Center would rather give the leftover food away rather than throw it out.

Once a month, the Senior Center offered a Mystery Tour. The senior van was filled with ten to fifteen people each trip. This tour was merely a get-a-way that lasted all day long. No one knew where we were going until the day we left. We went a variety of places including, Arthur, Springfield, Tuscola, Decatur, and other towns surrounding our area. Once, we rode on a ferry across the Mississippi river. We ate at a restaurant that had a large aquarium that held fish and turtles. We watched them while we ate our lunch. This was a peaceful experience. The total cost of the trip was six dollars per person. That covered the cost of the gas for the van. Other than that, we had to pay for our own lunch and souvenirs. I went every month.

I wasn't frivolous with my money. I only indulged myself in a few luxuries. The Mystery Tour was one of them. I never spent much money on these trips, but I enjoyed them very much. I especially enjoyed going to Arthur. I liked to buy the homemade products that the Amish made. Other than that, I had my hair washed and set in the beauty salon once a week. And, I had a permanent put in my hair three times a year. Looking well groomed was a priority to me, and I was always ready to go.

The Center had many continuous activities. They usually had a puzzle set up on one of the tables. When I was not busy, I sat down a looked for pieces that fit. I participated in the exercise classes that were offered. Some days, I was asked to teach the class. It was fun. We selected our music from an old jukebox in the corner of the room, and then, we would go for it. We used a pedometer to measure our steps and give us incentive to do more. Earlier, we had calculated that one mile equaled twenty-one laps around the interior of the Center.

In addition to our regular activities, we did a variety show for the hospital every year that was fund raiser for the hospital. The seniors were the entertainment. We practice our routines and learned dances like the funky chicken, the electric slide, and the hokey pokey. We were all having a great time. While we were doing the show, we encouraged the audience to participate.

I also signed up to deliver Meals on Wheels for St. Vincent's Hospital. I delivered the meals to the hospital rooms. I walked up to the patients door with the food, and said, "Meals on Wheels, hello." Then, I walked in the room, set the food on the hospital tray table, and said, "God Bless You." This was heartfelt. I felt really special like I was giving something back. I did this job once a month. Also, I used my car to deliver meals to shut-ins.

Mr. Friar got sick enough that he couldn't leave his house. His age was catching up with him. I took meals to his house, too. He was always happy to see me, and I sat and talked with him a while. Then, I went back to the Center for a few hours.

Eventually, I had to give up this job. My car was getting older. It had quite a few miles on it, and I was worried that it would break down on me. Also, I was the only one paying for the gas; it got expensive. Along with that, I was giving up quite a bit of my time. It took about three hours to deliver all the meals. I had done this job long enough. It was time for someone else to take over. I was tired.

When I returned home, I was so tired that I was ready for a nap. But usually, I read for a while or watched TV until nine o'clock at night. Then, I was ready for bed. I slept like a rock until four-thirty in the morning. That was my usual wake up time.

I am a very habitual person. Every day I did the same things. I woke up early and turned on the television. I listened to the news while I put on a pot of coffee. I drank my usual two cups. Then, I ran my sweeper and cleaned my house for a few hours. This made me hungry, so I ate a bowl of oatmeal. This may sound like a boring routine to someone else, but I felt good doing the same things every day.

Outside of my other activities, I had work at home. I mowed the yard and kept my house spotless. My yard was an acre lot. It took a long time to mow it and keep it trimmed. I was constantly pulling weeds. The inside of the house was a lot of care, too. Even though I was the only one in the house, I worked constantly to maintain a perfectly clean house. The basement was as large as the whole house. When it rained, it really gave me some grief.

On Mother's Day it rained so hard that there was a foot of water in the basement. I expected that. I fretted and worried every time it rained. Once before it rained so much that I had five feet of water down there. It ruined my furnace, hot water heater, and my dryer. My fear was grounded in reality. I never wanted that to happen again. But today, the water was coming in fast. I started to panic! I was scared, and I was alone. I had to get help, and it must be fast. I was never one to ask for help, but this problem was more than I could handle by myself. I decided to ask for help.

Harry Hill was a man that I knew for years and a member of our church. Harry and his wife were in my Sunday school class. I thought Harry might know how to help me with this water problem. It was five o'clock in the morning. Harry and his wife were eating breakfast when I knocked on their door. They gladly invited me in.

"The water is pouring into my basement, and I don't know what to do."

Without a moments delay, Harry told me, "I will be right over to help you."

I thanked him and went back home. Harry came right away with a small sump pump. He hoped this would pump the water out. Unfortunately, the water was coming back in as fast as it was being pumped out. So, Harry went home and brought back a larger sump pump. Thank God that worked.

After that episode, I worried every time it rained. My basement continued to get flooded three more times that same year. I told my neighbor, "All it takes is one more time of being flooded, and I am out of here! I am going to move even if I have to live in an apartment." I had worried too much about that basement. I was upset constantly. I had lived in this house thirty-three years. Maybe it was time to move. I had been thinking about this for a while.

My house had been paid off for years. Now, I only had to pay my taxes every year. I was worried about my finances, because I was on a fixed income. But, after I thought about it, I figured I could sell my house and use that money to buy a new one. I decided to start looking.

Chapter Sixteen
MY FINAL CHAPTER

I looked and looked for a new house. At first, the houses I looked at were a mess. Each one needed to much work to make them livable. I was discouraged.

Jeannie patiently searched for a house with me and suggested that I go up in price range. We looked at houses for months. Then one day, my realtor called and said he had a really nice house for me to look at. This house had not been placed on the market, yet. He warned me that this house was going to sell fast because it was very nice and maintenance free. I would need to make a decision fast. The realtor's sign was going to be put in the yard that day. Jeannie and I went to look at the house right away. We both agreed that this house was the best one we had looked at so far. The house was very well kept and in a good location. Nevertheless, I still had a problem making the final decision to buy it.

The house was more money than I expected to pay. I was scared. Actually, it was more money than I had ever paid for any house. It was hard for me to make a decision. Jeannie coaxed me to go ahead and just do it. She knew we couldn't find a nicer house at this price.

While we were looking at the house, another lady came to see it. That put more pressure on me. In the end, I decided to go for it even though I had some doubts in my mind.

My move into the new house went pretty smooth. I had new carpet installed in my three bedrooms before I moved in. Then, I called a moving company to move everything to the new house. It all went like clockwork. I guess it was meant to happen. But, I was still unsure.

I thought of all the reasons I shouldn't have moved. I had lived in the same neighborhood for many years. I knew I would miss my close neighbors. One of my neighbors walked with me every morning. Now, I didn't know anyone. I really felt alone for the first time in years. Also, I was used to everything being just right. I had put a lot of sweat into my old house getting it just the way I wanted it. Now, as I looked around my new house, I only saw things that needed to be changed in order to get it up to my standard.

I focused on the fact that many changes needed to be made in order for me to feel comfortable with my new home. The windows were painted over, and I couldn't get them open. I needed new windows. And, the screens in the back porch needed to be replaced. They looked old to me. Also, I needed to replace the back door. There was too much cold air coming in during the winter. In addition to that, the bathroom stool obviously had run over several times during the past years. The wood under the carpet appeared to be damp. Not to mention the holes in the back yard where trees had been taken out. The holes needed new dirt. All of this was overwhelming to me! I was depressed just thinking about it. I asked myself, "What have I done?" But it was too late. I bought this house, and I needed to face the facts.

I started on the yard first. I hired some men to chop up the whole back yard, put more dirt in it, smooth it down, and put in new grass seed. I also had them replace some of the concrete outside the screened in porch. Next, they took out the overgrown bushes. Termites were in the roots, so I had to spray the entire house. After all of that was done, I had to admit, the yard looked really nice.

Within a short time, I had an unexpected experience. I had to put in a new garage door opener. It actually fell off onto the top of my car. This was an unpleasant surprise. I was really kind of mad about that. I knew it was going to cost me some money to replace it. But, I had no choice. I needed to have the opener to feel safe.

Over time, I got the house fixed up just like I wanted it. I replaced all the windows. My trusted contractor put in the kind that could be washed from the inside of the house. I loved that. I knew they would cost a little more, but I bit the bullet and paid for them. It was worth it to me. I always wanted that kind of windows.

My last project waited another year to be completed. I replaced the floors in my bathroom and laundry room. Then, I had the bathroom redone. I had a new bathtub, shower, and carpet put in the bathroom. I was getting more and more comfortable all the time.

After six years in my new home, I am pretty happy with it. As I remember that old house on England Street, I am so grateful to be out from under the stress. Now, I don't have a basement to worry about, and I don't want one. I have no water problems now. Also, I live on a dead in street. It is quiet and peaceful. I feel safe here by myself. That is really important to me. Now, I only want time to enjoy the fruits of my labor. I am at peace. I love my home, and I am content in my life.

My mechanic lives just down the street from me. I always used to worry about having problems with my car. My car is getting older, and it has a lot of miles on it. It was used when I bought it twelve years ago. Nate used to take care of that for me. But now, I call up Herb, my mechanic, and he tells me to bring my car down to the end of the cul-de-sac. He does my regular maintenance like oil changes. And, he makes me feel comfortable to call at any time I have a question concerning the car. But most of all, he doesn't overcharge me. This is quite a relief to me. My car allows me the freedom to do what I want to do.

I really enjoy spending time with my three best friends, Jill Dublin, Mattie Larks, and Mr. Friar. Since I am the only one who drove a car, I pick everyone up when we want to go somewhere. We often ate together, went to revivals, enjoyed the Mystery Tour at the Senior Center, and attended to church together. Mattie always sat in the front with me. Jill and Mr. Friar sat in the back seat. I often teased them by saying, "Alright you guys, I can look in this mirror and see you. I don't want any hanky panky going on back there." Then, everyone would laugh and laugh. We were having a good time.

Mr. Friar tried to be a back seat driver. Even though he was legally blind, he still told me how to get to different restaurants. One day as I was driving, I ran a stop sign. Mr. Friar quickly told me, "You ran that stop sign back there!"

"That's OK, I stop twice when I come back," I laughingly told him as I drove on. I thought it was funny. Mr. Friar was almost blind, but he knew I had run a stop sign.

Mr. Friar always surprised me. When I walked into the church on Sunday, Mr. Friar often said, "You've got a pretty dress on today." I appreciated the compliment. He was always so nice.

"Thank you," I said, and then asked. "Can you see this dress?"

Mr. Friar laughed as he honestly said, "I can see the color." I could depend on him always being sincere.

My other friend, Jill Dublin had been a long time friend of mine. Jill was from England. I met her years ago when I was looking for a babysitter. Jill was recommended to me. I got her address and went to her house. She was working outside in the yard. She was a very gracious lady. She invited me into her house for a cup of tea. I accepted her invitation. I noted that her house was a small shack, but it was spotless. I was impressed with that. After talking a while, Jill agreed to babysit for me. This was the start of a very long friendship.

Mattie Larks and I were also long time friends. Mattie was a country girl from Alabama who never met a stranger. She had a kind loving disposition. And, she had a quick laugh. I became friends with her when Nate and I rented a house from her many years ago. We often sat and drank coffee together and talked. Also, I cleaned house for her for years. To this day, we are still good friends.

Outside of my friends, I took care of my brother Tom. He was two year younger than me. He used to live in Palmer, Illinois. But now, he is in a nursing home. He has bad lungs. They call it COPD. Chronic Obstructive Pulmonary Disease is the official name for his illness. Because Tom can no longer take care of his business, I was elected to be his power of attorney. So, I had to make the decisions concerning Tom's health care. No one wanted the job, so I took it.

My brother Tom resided in Meadow Manner Nursing Home for only a short while when his health issues became a problem. The nursing home called Tom's son to get his permission to administer medical care at the hospital. Tom's son wouldn't respond. So, the nursing home called Tom's ex-wife. She and Tom had been divorced for years. She passed the message on to me.

She called me and said, "Dottie, you better get to the emergency room at the hospital. Someone needs to sign the papers for them to take Tom to the Springfield hospital. "Obviously, they needed a family member to sign the papers for Tom's medical treatment.

No one stepped forward, so I went to the hospital and signed my name on the paperwork. I put sister beside my name. The hospital wanted me to ride the ambulance with Tom to keep him calm. He was being taken to Springfield Memorial Hospital. I agreed to accompany him. I rode in the front seat of the ambulance. I didn't want Tom to be alone at a time like this. I ended up making this trip several times during the next year.

The nursing home asked me to be Tom's power of attorney. Someone had to make decisions concerning his health. I was the only one who cared enough to take on the job. Neither of his kids wanted the responsibility. So, I took it. It overwhelmed me at times when the nursing home called me in the middle of the night to ask my permission to medically treat Tom. Also, when he needed to go to the hospital; I got up, dressed, and went to the hospital to be with him, so he wouldn't have to be alone. Many times, they just needed me there to calm him down.

Also, I took care of Tom's little bit of spending money. He never asked for much. Usually, he wanted food and my company. I took supper to him several times a week. And I visited him at the nursing home at least three times a week. The visits gave Tom something to look forward to.

After we ate, I put him in a wheelchair and pushed him all around the nursing home. Meadow Manner was constructed like a big square. The hallways went all around the exterior of the building. I pushed Tom around the square three or four times every time I came to see him. I wanted him to get out of bed and socialize with other people. I insisted that he carry on a conversation with others, and I tried to make it fun for him. Tom resisted; he didn't even want to eat in the lunch room with the other residence. He refused to eat there, so the nurses brought his food to his room. Only while I was there visiting, did Tom try to talk to other people. I felt good about that. And, I knew Tom appreciated everything I did for him.

On Tuesdays, Tom asked me to bring Kentucky Fried Chicken for his dinner. I ordered the chicken, picked it up, and took it to the nursing home. We ate it in the TV room. The nurses supplied us with something to drink. After we ate, I pushed him around the hallways a couple of times. Then, we went to the dining room to listen to a sermon put on by the Pentecostal Church. When the sermon was over, we were served donuts. That was our dessert. Tom really enjoyed this evening, and so did I.

I was really committed to the Senior Center. I went in at ten o'clock and worked until one. Then I returned home and rested until three o'clock. Next, I went to the nursing home to see Tom. That was my regular pattern. It kept me busy, and I liked that. I felt useful and needed.

On Wednesday of the next week, my car broke down. I called my daughter-in-law and asked her to take me to the nursing home to see Tom. He wasn't feeling well, so I didn't want to miss seeing him today. And besides, he had asked me to bring him some candy bars. I thought they might make him feel better.

As soon as I gave Tom the candy bars, and he gobbled them up as fast as he could. "Tom, don't eat so fast," I cautioned.

"I'm hungry!" he exclaimed.

We visited with him a short while longer. When I was ready to leave, I promised Tom I would get my car fixed and be back to see him on Sunday. That was my plan.

On Sunday, I went to church as usual. When I got home, the nursing home had called and left a message for me to call. I called the home right away and found that Tom had passed away. I was so sad that I cried for a long time. I was going to miss him. We had spent so much time together in the last few years that we had formed a close bond.

I went to the nursing home and cleaned out Tom's meager personal belongings. I called Tom's son and let him know I had Tom's belongings, and I needed him to come and pick them up. I gave him Tom's TV, wheelchair, and other miscellaneous items. I was happy to give everything to Tom's kids. I felt a deep sorrow as I let go of the past.

I missed going to see Tom. When I got home from the Senior Center, I always felt like I was supposed to go somewhere. I was used to the habitual trips I had made to the nursing home. Now, I felt lost. It took me a long time before I truly adjusted to the loss. My consolation was that Tom wasn't in pain anymore. Getting older can be a tough process.

When people talk about the golden years, I am not so sure why they call it that. I always said, "I don't know what is so golden about getting older." Many of the people at the Senior Center are in their eighty's and ninety's. Some are ill, hurt, and dying. I have seen a many people come and go in the seven years I attended. One day, a regular just doesn't show up for lunch. One lady passed away and was found on the floor in her house. Three days passed before anyone found her. Everyone at the Center felt sad when they heard she had died alone. After that, we all made a pact with each other. When someone doesn't show up for lunch, we call them to see if they needed our help. We looked after each other in that way.

I feel that life is about people. I think it is necessary to treat people the way you want to be treated. That is the way God intended us to live. This is the Christian way. Therefore, I treat everyone kindly and give them a helping hand when they needed it. I try to be there for all my friends and family in their time of need.

All of my close friends were getting old and passing away. It was hard on me to see this happen to them. I watched them deteriorate right before my eyes. My heart went out to them in their time of suffering. I made a point to be there for them whenever I could.

Mr. Friar eventually had to be put in the nursing home because wasn't able to take care of himself. He had to have a feeding tube placed in his stomach to receive nourishment. Otherwise the food went into his lungs. I felt very sad to see him go downhill so fast. I visited him often. He was only at the nursing home two months when he passed away. I lost a really good friend, and I missed him for a long time after that.

I often wished that I could have another relationship with a man like Mr. Friar. I was open to that idea. Unfortunately, so far, that hasn't happened yet. I figure if it happens again, that's great. If it doesn't happen, that's OK, too. I don't mind being alone anymore. I have gotten used to it.

My friend Jill also got sick and had to go to the hospital. I wasn't sure what kind of problem she was having. I went to the hospital to see her. After a few days, she seemed to get better, so the doctor sent her home. Not long after that, she got out of bed one morning and just fell backwards onto the floor of her bedroom. She was gone. She was eighty-four years old at that time. I assumed that she had a heart attack. I went to her funeral in a state of shock. Her death came too fast for me. I had no idea that she was going to die. She always was the healthy one. Now, I lost two close friends in a short amount of time.

My best friend Mattie was about the same age as Jill. Mattie was getting feebler all the time because she had dementia. It was hard to carry on a regular conversation with her. She couldn't remember anything after a few minutes. And, she no longer knew who I was. This was so frustrating for me that I finally gave up trying to talk to her. And, I felt guilty for feeling the way I did. I hated to see my friend go through such drastic changes. I blamed Mattie's doctor for her demise. The medication he gave her took away her ambition to do anything. She even stopped coming to church and the Senior Center. She merely stayed at home all the time and slept in her chair. I felt so sad for her. Eventually, she wasn't able to live by herself anymore. It was too dangerous. So, Mattie's daughters came to live with her. I felt like I lost her friendship, although she was still here. I grieved for her loss.

I have to face up to the fact that my own mortality is at risk, too. My physically body is slowly breaking down. That happens with age. Also, I have suffered with osteoarthritis all my life. Pain has forced me to have many surgeries during my lifetime. My index finger had to be whittled down because the arthritis caused it to be practically deformed. Eventually, all my fingers became permanently bent causing me to struggle to get the small things done like buttoning my blouse. And, I've had shoulder surgery, a hip replacement, a hysterectomy, cysts removed, gallbladder removal, carpal tunnel surgery in both my wrists; and bunions removed from both my feet. In addition to that, I have had numerous cortisone shots in my spine. Now, at the age of seventy-eight, I am facing a total shoulder replacement. Again, the pain is too much for me to bear. I hope my body holds up. It is a little scary. Sometimes, my body fails me. But overall, I am pretty healthy, and I expect to live to be one-hundred years old.

Although I have endured many painful moments in my life, I remain positive in my mind. I am happier right now than I have ever been in my whole life. I am comfortable with my lifestyle. I get up every morning and do exactly what I want to do. My life is so much easier than it has ever been. Now, I feel free. I can think for myself. I can do for myself. I do exactly what I want to do when I want to do it. I don't have to ask anyone for anything, because I don't have to. This type of freedom is something I always searched for, and now, I have it. God and I are the only ones I have to answer to. And, I am closer to God than I have ever been before. I feel at peace.

I am thankful that I have a nice home, and it is clean. It stays clean because I am able to keep it that way. Once a month I clean real well. Other than that, I do the surface cleaning. I hate to dust, but I do it anyway. Sometimes I talk my daughter-in law into doing it for me. And, once a year, I still do my spring cleaning. Keeping my house nice is important to me. It always will be.

Another thing that is important to me is forgiving those who have wronged me. I don't want any direct contact with them, but I forgive them. I forgave Mable for her terrible treatment during the time I stayed with her. It took me a really long time, but I finally let it go. And, I forgive old Slimy Slim. I knew that it took two people to have that affair. The blame wasn't all hers. Time has a way of healing old wounds. Most of all, I forgive Nate. I know that he loved me in his own way. I knew it was necessary to forgive everyone. Otherwise, the anger would have festered inside me like a cancer. I didn't want that to happen. In addition to that, I didn't want to give my power to them. I took my power back in order to use it for the good things in my life.

My biggest accomplishment in life was raising my six kids. It took a lot of blood, sweat, and tears, but I did it. I raised them to have pride and dignity. And, I they all turned out to be great kids. I always knew that God blessed me with each and every one of them. I am thankful for those gifts.

My life right now is about living alone and keeping busy. I don't want to sit around and feel sorry for myself. Each day is a gift, and I don't want to waste a moment on nonsense. I have many things in my mind that I still want to do. But, I take one day at a time. I live in the moment.

One of my best pastimes is reading. It always has been. When I was younger, I read True Stories. This was a magazine that had love stories in it. I used this for recreational reading. But now, my true passion is reading the Bible. I thirst for God's word. Although I have always read the Bible, it wasn't until later in my life that I opened my eyes and understood more. When I used to read, it didn't mean anything to me. But now, every word I read registers with me. It means something. For some reason, I am seeing it in a different light. My mind is like a sponge. I just can't get enough of it.

As I reflect back on my life, I think about the good memories that gave me joy. Once when Nate and I went to Las Vegas, I encountered a real thrill. Nate had won quite a bit of money, so the hotel we were staying at made us VIP's. We were given first class treatment the whole time we stayed at the hotel. The hotel staff served us a five course meal that was fit for a king. The waiters brought us a tray of desserts that were so pretty they didn't look real. We had to pick one. Wow! I felt like royalty. Now this was a good time! I felt like I was living like rich people. This was the first time I ever really enjoyed going to Las Vegas.

My other precious moments are spent with the people I love. Nothing makes me feel better than to spend time with my kids. When I know they are coming for a visit, I drop everything to devote my time to just them. This gives me great joy.

And, I like helping other people. This gives me a purpose in life. And, it makes me feel needed. Because, people are what life is all about.

In closing, I have several pieces of advice that I would like to leave behind for anyone who wants to listen. First, have faith in God. He is always with us, and He wants what is always best for us. Work with Him.

Trust in Him. Along with that, never give up hope. Hope will always drive you forward. Lastly, live with love in your heart for yourself and others. God Bless You All

THE END